Martial Law in India

Historical, Comparative and Constitutional Perspective

Martial Law in India

Historical, Comparative and Constitutional Perspective

by

Dr. K. Ratnabali

&

Dr. U. C. Jha

Vij Books India Pvt Ltd

New Delhi (India)

First Published in 2020

Published by

Vij Books India Pvt Ltd
(Publishers, Distributors & Importers)
2/19, Ansari Road
Delhi – 110 002
Phones: 91-11-43596460, 91-11-47340674
Mob: 98110 94883
e-mail: contact@vijpublishing.com
web : www.vijbooks.com

ISBN: 978-93-89620-69-6 (PB)

ISBN: 978-93-89620-70-2 (ebook)

Contents

Preface

In India, the military are bound to aid the civil authority in maintaining law and order when lawfully called upon to do so. However, in a disturbed area, conditions of extreme disorder may arise when the civil authorities, even with the help of the armed forces, are unable to bring the situation under control. In such a scenario, the government may authorize the military commander to bring normalcy in the disturbed area by issuing an enabling proclamation declaring a state of national emergency on account of violence in the affected area. Such authorization to the military leads to imposition of martial law.

Terms such as 'state of emergency', 'state of alarm', 'state of exception' and 'state of siege' have been used in other countries to refer to the crisis situation that calls for imposition of such special legal order. Imposition of martial law amounts to predominance of the military authority over the civil authority for the sole purpose of restoring normal conditions as expeditiously as possible to enable the civil authority to resume charge.

Over the course of history, martial law has been imposed in many parts of the world, as and when there is breakdown of civil government, due to rebellion or internal disorder, and is not limited to any one geographic or ethnic domain. In undivided India, martial law was proclaimed on many occasions during the British rule. Post independence, it has never been invoked in India but a number of times in Pakistan and on a few occasions in Bangladesh.

Martial law must not be confused with military law, which is a statute for the preservation of discipline in the armed forces. Martial law is the answer of common law to situations of grave disorder and rests on the legal maxim *salus populi suprema est lex* (safety of the people is the supreme law). It is based on the premise that when the civil power in an area becomes incapable of maintaining law and order, it is lawful for all loyal citizens, including the military, to use necessary force for the restoration of order.

When martial law is imposed, a military commander assumes the position of martial law administrator (MLA) and takes control of the affected area. The MLA issues a proclamation to inform the inhabitants of the area that martial law has been declared. The military commander also issues martial law regulations (MLR), specifying therein the martial law offences and punishments for such offences. The MLA constitutes military courts to deal with all offences, including breaches of MLR. A civilian member having judicial experience may be appointed to a military court. The functions of all civil tribunals may be suspended temporarily except in so far as the military commander might require their assistance. The authority to appoint martial law courts and approve their sentences rests only with the MLA. The rules of procedure and of evidence of martial law tribunals may not be of international standard.

This book investigates the proclamation of martial law in India during British rule and examines the feasibility of imposing martial law in the present time. The first chapter of the book is introductory and deliberates on the concept of martial law, its origin, definitions, kinds, and its comparison with military law. It also examines a few provisions of martial law in the Indian Military Manual. The second chapter examines instances of the imposition of martial law in British India.

When law and order is restored and the civil authority resumes charge, civil courts may inquire into the legality of the acts of military authorities while martial law was in force. Thus, it is necessary to protect persons administering martial law from actions and prosecutions by civil authorities. This is done by an Act of Indemnity passed by Parliament to prevent enquiry into the justification for acts committed in executing martial law. Chapter three examines Article 34 of the Constitution under which an Act of Indemnity may be passed by Parliament.

Whenever martial law was declared in British India, military authorities had the power to arrest and detain any person engaged in activities prohibited under MLR. There were very few instances of petitions being filed on behalf of detained persons for the issue of the writ of *habeas corpus*. The arrest and detention of an offender under a martial law regime and the possibility of recourse to the rights to *habeas corpus* are discussed in the fourth Chapter.

The Armed Forces (Special Powers) Act or AFSPA, which has been in force in parts of the northeastern states and Kashmir, grants special powers to the armed forces. Under the AFSPA, a designated member of the armed forces can use lethal force, enter and search premises, and arrest any person acting in contravention of the law. Various human rights organizations in the country and abroad and foreign and local media have alleged that areas where the AFSPA is applicable are under de facto martial law. In the fifth Chapter, a comparison of the provisions of the AFSPA and martial law has been undertaken to understand the true nature of these laws.

There may be an apprehension in the minds of members of the civil society that military men are anxious to exercise martial law powers over the civil community. With few exceptions, military authorities prefer to support civil authorities rather than act independently of them in civil affairs. The last Chapter critically analyses whether the proclamation of martial law is feasible in India in the future.

In an age where the idea of nation-state fails to evoke the ethos that had united peoples by an abstract thread of commonality, and the divisive forces are on the rise, it does not need the foresight of an oracle to predict the gradual breakup of the current nation states. This will necessitate the use of state's authority and forces to stop the tectonic forces at work and hence the resurgence of martial law that shall leave its imprint as part of birth pangs of new states or stillborn.

K. Ratnabali

U. C. Jha

Chapter I

Martial Law: An Introduction

Martial Law, as it is understood today, is a common law concept. It is not clearly defined but relates to the use of the armed forces to counter certain emergent situations like insurrections or rebellion in a country. Martial law is the will of the military general who commands the army. It overrides and suppresses all existing civil laws and civil authorities. In the past, the term martial law was loosely used to mean any one of the three systems of authority: (i) law for the governance of the armed forces which we call military law; (ii) law enforced by the armed forces in time of war, both in conquered territory and in disaffected regions at home; and (iii) law enforced by the armed forces authorities in time of peace when troops are used for the suppression of internal disorder. The first one i.e. military law, is statutory law and may be reviewed by the civilian tribunals. It has very little concern to the public at large. The second form of law belongs to the realm of public law, and has been said to be necessarily the will of military commander subject to customs of war. The third form of martial law is very significant and relates to employing military forces for the protection of life and property during insurrections and rebellion. Martial law in the third form cannot be said to operate when the soldiers act in subordination to the civil authorities, doing nothing more than what the civil authorities themselves could do under the police power. It exists only when the military supplants the civil power and transcends the constitutional limitations, with respect to the invasion of life, liberty and property, placed up on the civil power.

The discretion of the government in declaring martial law is not subject to review by the civil courts. However, there are two views as to the powers of the military authorities in such exigencies. The doctrine prevailing in England has been that the troops act merely for the suppression of violence, and that they have no power to promulgate and enforce regulations or to try civilians by court-martial for any offences whatsoever. The opposite view that a proclamation of martial law by the proper authorities places all persons in the affected region under the jurisdiction of military courts or commissions, and clothes the troops, acting under the orders of military commander, with authority even outside the zone of martial law, to suppress sedition and arrest and detain persons suspected of fomenting disorder. This form of martial law, involving a suspension of constitutional guarantees, was expressly authorized under the name of State of Siege by the Constitutions of France from time to time. Such provisions do not appear in most of Constitutions around the world.[1]

The fourth kind of martial law which could be added to the above list is the one which have been enforced in Bangladesh,[2] Pakistan[3] and many other countries, where it comes into existence after a senior military officer or a group of military officers (sometimes in partnership with some politicians) overthrow a legitimate civilian regime by means of a *coup*. Martial law in such states has been proclaimed not for the purpose of restoring law and order and for establishing peace and security, but

1 Martial Law, Notes, *Columbia Law Review*, Vol. 15, No. 2, February 1915, pp. 177-179.

2 The declaration of martial law in Bangladesh in 1975 is to be seen as an extra-constitutional act since throughout the text of the 1972 Bangladesh Constitution no reference has been made to martial law. As the Constitution is the supreme law of the land and does not contain the term martial law, it seems that it excludes the common law rule as a basis for martial law for the purpose of restoring law and order. Bari M. Ershadul, The Imposition of Martial Law in Bangladesh, 1975: A Legal Study, *The Dhaka University Studies*, Part –F, Vol. 1(1), p. 73.

3 Military dictatorship has been a common phenomenon in post-colonial states of Africa and Asia. In the short history of Pakistan, martial law has been proclaimed on five occasions: October 1958, March 1969, July 1977, October 1999 and November 2007. During the last proclamation, General Musharraf imposed martial law on 3 November 2007. He suspended the constitution, sacked the chief justice of the Supreme Court and removed other judges of that court who declared his act illegal. Police arrested lawyers, politicians and human rights activists. Independent television channels were taken off the air and reporting restrictions imposed. Replacing dissenting judges with hand-picked appointees, and ruling by decree, Musharraf's objective was to retain personal power by gaining judicial approval for martial law, followed by the creation of a democratic facade through rigged elections. The general's proclamation was made in his capacity as army chief, not as president. This was unconstitutional. In response to this, the US, the UK and the European Union (EU) expressed disappointment, but signalled they wish to continue cooperation with President Musharraf and his government. Winding Back Martial Law in Pakistan, Policy Briefing, International Crisis Group, Asia Briefing No. 70, Islamabad/Brussels, 12 November 2007.

to obviate any public opposition to their extra-constitutional acts.[4] The martial law imposed after a military coup is not within the purview of this book.

Origin of Martial Law

The term martial law (originally spelt marshal law) owes its origin to the legal system of England. Various systems of law, namely the common law and equity, the canon law, admiralty, and martial law coexisted in medieval England. Each of these rival jurisdictions had its own court or courts. The Court of the Constable and Marshal could deal with almost every crime in the time of war and could award punishment.[5] Its jurisdiction was both civil and criminal, and fell under several heads.[6] In other words, the Court

4 In 1963 the East Pakistan High Court in *Lt. Col. G.L. Bhattacharya v The State* [PLD 1963 Dhaka, 377], held, with reference to the imposition of Martial Law in Pakistan in 1958, that the declaration of Martial Law after a revolution constituted a new departure and had little to do with 'Constitutional Martial Law'. He observed that there is a "Kind of Martial Law brought about by a successful revolution which had abrogated an 'existing Constitution' thereby bringing about a total new dispensation. ... (this) kind of Martial Law, that is, one brought by a revolution or a *coup d'etat* ... is outside the scope of constitutional law... What had happened on 7 October 1958, was in fact, a revolution and *coup d'etat* which imposed a Martial Law on the entire country. This kind of revolution or imposition of Martial Law constitutes a class apart and has nothing to do with 'Constitutional Martial Law'. For more details see: Bari M. Ershadul, The Imposition of Martial Law in Bangladesh, 1975: A Legal Study, *The Dhaka University Studies*, Part –F, Vol. 1(1), pp. 59-73.

5 The Court of the Constable and the Marshal was a part of the *Curia Regis*, or the Supreme Court established in England by William, the Conqueror. Under the British King, the Constable and Marshal had a double Power: (i) A Ministerial Power, as they were two great ordinary Officers; anciently, in the King's Army the Constable or *Comes Stabuli* was the commander-in-chief of the King's army and as such governed all persons and exercised jurisdiction over all offences committed in the army especially when it was on service overseas, and the Marshal was employed in marshalling the King's Army, and keeping the List of the Officers and Soldiers therein. (ii) The Constable and Marshal had also a Judicial Power, or a Court wherein several matters were determinable: (a) Appeals of Death or Murder committed beyond the Sea, according to the Course of the Civil Law; (b) The Rights of prisoners taken in War; (c) The Offences and Miscarriages of Soldiers contrary to the Laws and Rules of the Army. During the preparation for actual war, the Kings of this Realm, by Advice of the Constable, (and Marshal) were used to compose a Book of Rules and Orders for due order and discipline of their officers and soldiers, together with certain penalties on the offenders; and this was called, Martial Law.

6 The civil jurisdiction of the Court of Constable and Marshal was exercised by the Court of Chivalry which was a court of honour, and consisted in redressing injuries of honour, and correcting encroachments on coat armour, precedence and other distinctions of families. In the exercise of its criminal jurisdiction the Court of Constable and Marshal

of the Constable and Marshal had jurisdiction in the crimes committed abroad, violations of the articles of war by the soldiers, violations of contractual obligations relating to war beyond the realm, and the matters relating to war within the realm.[7]

Martial law was recognized by statute in England as early as the reign of Richard II, nearly the end of the fourteenth century. During this period, the Parliament demanded that restraints be placed upon the Court of the Constable and Marshal. During the next fifty years or so, various limitations were placed over the jurisdiction of the Court of the Constable and Marshal. For instance, during the reign of Henry VI in 1439, the punishment of desertion from the King's army was entrusted to the courts of common law. Martial law was invoked only once in the reign of Henry VIII, during the suppression of the Pilgrimage of Grace in 1536 and 1537. Elizabeth I was compelled to invoke martial law for its traditional purpose viz, in the suppression of the Northern Rebellion of 1569. Between the accession of Edward VI and the death of Elizabeth, martial law had been transformed. By 1603, the jurisdiction of martial law was no longer limited to those situations in which the common law courts could not function and the power to exercise martial law could be granted by Royal Commission. Commissions of martial law were issued by James I in 1617, 1620, 1624, and 1625, and in 1626 and 1627 by Charles I. These Commissions were concerned with the maintenance of order in the areas where armies were billeted and in ports where the fleet lay at anchor, mainly on the south coast. The authority to execute martial law was awarded to a number of military and civil officers, including Royal Commissioners and the Chief Officials of the towns in which the troops were stationed. Both soldiers and civilians were subject to martial law.[8] In 1628, Charles I was made to

---

was empowered to punish murder and other civil crimes committed by Englishmen abroad. In time of war it took cognizance of the offences and miscarriages of soldiers contrary to the law and rules of the army. British Manual of Military Law (1958), Section I, p. 4.

7 Fairman Charles, 1930, *The Law of Martial Rule*, Chicago: Callaghan and Company, p.3.

8 A typical commission of 1625 provided: "[Z is hereby granted] full power and authority... to proceed according to the justice of martial law against such soldiers, or other dissolute persons joining with them ... who shall commit any robberies, felonies, mutinies or other outrages or misdemeanors which by martial law should be punished with death, and by such summary course and order as in time of wars, to proceed to the trial and condemnation of such delinquents and offenders and them to cause to be executed and put to death as an example of terror to others and to keep the rest in due awe and obedience.

renounce the use of Commissions of martial law in the Petition of Right. In 1640, the Marshal's court was severely criticized in Parliament and its use gradually diminished.[9] A few writings suggest the last case tried before the Marshal Court was in 1737 and it died of atrophy.[10]

Defining Martial Law

Few attempts have been made to define the term "Martial Law". According to the US Supreme Court, martial law is: "the law of military necessity in the actual presence of war. It is administered by the General of the Army, and is in fact his will. Of necessity it is arbitrary, but it must be obeyed."[11] In another case, the Court said: "All respectable writers and publicists agree in the definition of martial law that it is nothing more or less than the will of the general who commands the army. It overrides and suppresses all existing civil laws, civil officers and civil authorities, by the arbitrary exercise of military power. ... Martial law is regulated by no known or established system or code of laws, as it is over and above all of them."[12]

Martial law was defined by the Duke of Wellington as nothing more or less than the will of the general who commands the army and therefore it is no law at all. This concept or definition of the martial law has been found favour in the military because it makes entire civil law system subordinate to them. According to Wiener (1940), martial law is the public law of necessity. Necessity calls it forth, necessity justifies its exercise, and necessity measures the extent and degree to which it may be employed. That necessity is no formal, artificial, legalistic concept but an actual and factual one: it is the necessity of taking action to safeguard the state against insurrection, riot, disorder, or public calamity. What constitutes necessity is a question of fact in each case.[13]

---

9 Following the Petition of Right, questions arose over what exactly had been prohibited. Undoubtedly martial law as employed in the later sixteenth century against civilians was the target of the prohibition, and the debates in the Commons seem to suggest that the framers of the Petition did not intend to prohibit the use of martial law in the army when it was actually in the field. During the Civil War, the parliamentary army and navy were subject to martial law. The problem of military discipline was eventually solved by the passage of the Mutiny Acts following the Glorious Revolution. But martial law as a peacetime law-enforcement measure remained proscribed.

10 Fairman Charles, 1930, *The Law of Martial Rule*, Chicago: Callaghan and Company, p. 6.

11 *United States v. Diekelman*, 92 US 520 (1876), 526.

12 In the case of *In re Egan*, 8 Fed.Cas. No. 4303 (1866).

13 Frederick B. Wiener, A Practical Manual of Martial Law (1940), p. 16.

Black's Law Dictionary defines the term martial law as, "The law by which during wartime the army, instead of civil authority, governs the country because of a perceived need for military security or public safety. The military assumes control purportedly until civil authority can be restored." Further, "A body of firm, strictly enforced rules that are imposed because of a perception by the country's rulers that civil government has failed to function. Martial law is usually imposed when the rulers foresee an invasion, insurrection, economic collapse, or other breakdown of the rulers' desired social order."[14]

According to Winthrop (1920), Martial law is military rule exercised by a State over its own citizens (not being enemies), in an emergency justifying it.[15] Martial law could be compared to the state of siege in France,[16] a condition of domestic military rule imposed in besieged towns, as also in cities or districts during foreign or civil war, or at periods of grave public disorder, especially those succeeding upon a state of war. The English authorities have differed as to the proper nature of martial law and the extent of the military control which it justifies. Thus, some have considered that it simply permits the application to the citizen of the code of the soldier; others opined that it places in the hands of the military commander a discretionary power to be exerted so far as the necessities of the exigency may require.

Martial law is a resort to the military authority in cases where the civil authority is not sufficient for the maintenance of the laws, and it gives to legally appointed military officers summary power, for the purpose of restoring tranquility and sustaining the State. ... They are to judge the degree of force which the necessity of the exigency demands; and there is no limit to their exercise of the power conferred upon them by the martial, except the nature and character of the exigency.[17]

---

14 Garner Bryan A, Black's Law Dictionary, Tenth Edition, Thomson Reuters, 2014, p. 1122.

15 Winthrop William, 1920, *Military Law and Precedents*, Washington: Government Printing Office, p. 817.

16 The state of siege in France corresponds to martial law in England and the United States. There is, however, an important distinction: what lawfully may be done under a state of siege is fixed by statute, while martial law—subject to individual responsibility for its enforcement, is a rule unto itself.

17 Judge Joseph Story, the Circuit Justice while delivering judgment in New Orleans case. Quote in: Stephen I. Vladeck, The Field Theory: martial Law, the Suspension Power, and the Insurrection Act, Washington College of Law Research Paper No. 2008-01, pp. 57.

Martial law is thus that rule which comes into play when civil authority in that area is made subordinate to military, either for repelling invasion or suppressing rebellion or to secure the primary objectives of a government when the ordinary administration fails to do so. It is at once both a domestic and ordinarily an unwritten law. It is exercised over districts of that country where its military authorities runs the administration in such exigencies, and the limits prescribed for that exercise are not often the subject of statutory regulation.[18]

> To some, the term martial law is misleading, since it is not law at all in the ordinary sense and carries no precise meaning. This view appears incorrect. When a military commander controls the persons or property of citizens who are beyond the sphere of his actual operations in the field, when he makes laws to govern their conduct, he becomes a legislator. Those laws may be made actually operative; obedience to them may be enforced by military power; their purpose and effect may be solely to support or recruit his armies, or to weaken the power of the enemy with whom he is contending. But he is a legislator still; and whether his edicts are clothed in the form of proclamations, or of military orders, by whatever names they may be called, they are laws.[19] According to Carbaugh, "It is the will of the commander, limited by the customs of warfare as recognized by civilized nations, and sometimes restrained by the orders of his military superior or the sovereign authority under which he operates."[20] The officer executing martial law is at the same time supreme legislator, supreme judge, and supreme executive. As necessity makes his will the law, he only can define and declare it and whether or not it is infringed, and of the extent of their fraction, he alone can judge; and his sole order punishes or acquits the alleged

18 When martial law is invoked in face of invasion or rebellion that rises to proportions of belligerency, it is a simple war power. When established as incident to the governor proclaiming a part of the State to be in insurrection or rebellion, it carries many military features growing out of the fact that the condition of affairs in the community is greatly assimilated to that of war. When martial law is proclaimed because of lawlessness and violence which has paralyzed the civil administration in a country, it may be regarded as an extension and development of the police power. Its characteristics at any one time may be a combination of these. Birkhimer, William E., 1914, *Military Government and Martial Law*, Missouri: Franklin Hudson Publishing Company, p. 371-372.

19 Birkhimer, William E., 1914, *Military Government and Martial Law*, Missouri: Franklin Hudson Publishing Company, p. 377.

20 Carbaugh, H. C., Martial Law, *Illinois Law Review*, Vol. VII, March 1913, p. 495.

offender.[21] From these definitions it may be concluded that martial law is the law of necessity, and that, in the last resort, it is nothing more or less than the will of the authorities to whom has been given the power of instituting martial law.[22]

The concept of martial law has been included in the Constitutions or other legislations in a few States. For instance, Article 1 of the Ukraine's law on the 'Legal Regime of Martial Law' defines the term martial law as a special legal regime that is introduced in the country in case of an armed aggression or a threat of an attack, a threat to state sovereignty and territorial indivisibility of the country. This rule involves granting the relevant State Executive, Local Self Government organs, the Military Command and military administrations, necessary powers to prevent threats, repel armed aggression and to guarantee national security, remove the threat of danger to national security of Ukraine and its territorial integrity. It also involves temporary (threat determined) restrictions of human constitutional rights and freedoms as well as the rights and legitimate interests of all legal persons with an indication of the period of effectiveness for these restrictions.[23]

Martial Law or Martial Rule

Fairman (1930) in *The Law of Martial Rule*, argues, "martial law is not a law, but something indulged, rather than allowed, as law. It is not built upon settled principles, but is entirely arbitrary in its decisions; it is nothing more nor less than the will of the general; and it is not a fixed, but a transitory law, variable by the general." He further clarifies that the term "martial Law" has several meanings. Fairman concludes that the expression martial law is a misnomer and it could be more accurately described as "martial rule", during which the military authority carries on some of the functions of the government. Martial rule is a will of the military commander, subject to few regulations. He clarifies that 'martial rule' is different from the 'use of troops in the aid of civil authorities'. When so employed the troops

21 Rossiter Clinton L., 1948, *Constitutional Dictatorship: Crisis Government in the Modern Democracies*, Princeton University Press, p. 9.

22 Rankin Rober S., 1935, *When Civil Law Fails: Martial Law and its Legal Basis in the United States*, Duke University Press, p. 174.

23 Article 1, Law of Ukraine "On the Legal Regime of Martial Law."

are merely supporting the civil authority and the commander looks for directions to the magistrate, who has summoned him for a specific task.[24]

Martial Law and Military Law

For many years, the terms "martial law" and "military law" were considered synonymous and were used indiscriminately by some authors to express the same meaning.[25] Until 1689, when in the First Mutiny Act permanent articles of war[26] were provided for the newly-established standing army, martial law was understood to encompass what is now referred to as military law.[27] Thus the system of military justice gradually became divorced from the offices of constable and marshal. Until around the 1830s martial law was equated with military law – the rules governing armed forces during war. In its original meaning, the term thus refers to jurisdiction over soldiers of the Crown and alien enemies. In 1842, a rebellion took place in Rhode Island in the United States which resulted in proclamation of martial law. The most interesting aspect of this regime of martial law was that it gave rise to the case of *Luther v. Borden*, the first case in which the US Supreme Court laid down rule concerning its use. The Court held that the martial law is the suspension of the common law, for the purpose of giving summary power to the military. Further, the insurrection constituted "a state of war" and, "a State may use its military power to put down an armed insurrection;" and the state was itself the final arbiter in such a decision. The court thus held that the declaration of martial law to subdue the Rhode Island insurrection was acceptable, adding that such governmental actions should not be questioned in a court of law. Two books published during this period tried to distinguish martial law from military law and argued that the Constitution in fact sanctioned martial law as the only means of defence when civil institutions were closed or suppressed by emergency conditions.[28] This altered the understanding of martial law in the United States and elsewhere.

24 Fairman Charles, 1930, *The Law of Martial Rule*, Chicago: Callaghan and Company, p. 29-39.

25 Clode Charles M., 1872, *The Administration of Justice under Military and Martial Law*, London: John Murray, Albemarle Street, p. 20.

26 The articles of war (the rules promulgated for the government of the troops to be raised in time of war) were a code framed by the King and authorized the military commander to punish the violators.

27 Capua J.V., The Early History of Martial Law in England from the Fourteenth Century to the Petition of Right, *Cambridge Law Journal*, Vol. 36 (1), April 1977, p. 153.

28 John Paul Jones O'Brien, 1846, A Treatise on American Military Laws and the

Military law is a body of special laws passed by the Parliament and includes subordinate rules and regulations governing the members of Army, the Navy and the Air Force; for example the Army Act, 1950, the Air Force Act 1950 and the Navy Act, 1957. The examples of subordinate legislations are the Army Rules, 1954 and the Regulations for the Army, etc. These laws are applicable to the members of the armed forces, in peace as well as in war. Certain civilians who are associated with the armed forces can also be subject to these laws under specific condition. For example, the civilians who accompany the army on move during active service or war, become subject to the Army Act. Military tribunals or courts martial are constituted to try those military persons who violate military law. The tribunals by which military law is enforced are not a part of the judicial system. Their judgments are subject to review by the Armed Forces Tribunal and by the Supreme Court in India. Under specific conditions military person can be tried by civilian courts also. A person subject to military law, who commits certain serious offences against civilians, is to be tried by civil court, unless he commits the said offences on active service, at any place outside India, or at a specified frontier post.

Lieber Code and Martial Law

In 1862, the US President, Abraham Lincoln, asked Columbia University professor, Francis Lieber, to formulate rules of conduct in war for use by the Union army during the American Civil war. Professor Lieber formulated "Instructions for the Government of Armies of the United States in the Field", known as the Lieber Instructions or the Lieber Code. The Code was promulgated as General Order No. 100 by President Lincoln in 1863.[29] These instructions explicitly cover the case of domestic imposition of martial law. The "Instructions" specified:

Practice of Court Martial, Philadelphia: Lea and Blanchard; William C. DeHart, 1859, *Observations on Military Law*, New York: Wiley & Halstead, pp. 433.

29 Though the Lieber Code was not a treaty, it represented a codification of the current usages and customs of war in North America and Europe. The Lieber Code strongly influenced the further codification of the laws and customs of war and the adoption of similar regulations by other States. The Lieber Code consisted of 157 articles and provided detailed rules on the entire range of land warfare, from the conduct of hostilities and the treatment of the civilians to the treatment of specific groups of persons such as prisoners of war, the wounded and so on. Some of the problems addressed by the Lieber Code are still relevant to the situations of contemporary armed conflicts such as guerrilla warfare, the status of rebels, the applicability of IHL in non-international armed conflicts and the penal sanctions for violations of laws of war. Yves Sandoz, The History of the Grave Breaches Regime, *Journal of International Criminal Justice*, Vol. 7, No. 1, 2009, p. 659.

Article 1: A place, district, or country occupied by an enemy stands, in consequence of the occupation, under the Martial Law of the invading or occupying army, whether any proclamation declaring Martial Law, or any public warning to the inhabitants, has been issued or not. Martial Law is the immediate and direct effect and consequence of occupation or conquest. The presence of a hostile army proclaims its Martial Law.

Article 2: Martial Law does not cease during the hostile occupation, except by special proclamation, ordered by the commander in chief; or by special mention in the treaty of peace concluding the war, when the occupation of a place or territory continues beyond the conclusion of peace as one of the conditions of the same.

Article 3: Martial Law in a hostile country consists in the suspension, by the occupying military authority, of the criminal and civil law, and of the domestic administration and government in the occupied place or territory, and in the substitution of military rule and force for the same, as well as in the dictation of general laws, as far as military necessity requires this suspension, substitution, or dictation. The commander of the forces may proclaim that the administration of all civil and penal law shall continue either wholly or in part, as in times of peace, unless otherwise ordered by the military authority.

Article 4: Martial Law is simply military authority exercised in accordance with the laws and usages of war. Military oppression is not Martial Law: it is the abuse of the power which that law confers. As Martial Law is executed by military force, it is incumbent upon those who administer it to be strictly guided by the principles of justice, honor, and humanity - virtues adorning a soldier even more than other men, for the very reason that he possesses the power of his arms against the unarmed.

Article 5: Martial Law should be less stringent in places and countries fully occupied and fairly conquered. Much greater severity may be exercised in places or regions where actual hostilities exist, or are expected and must be prepared for. Its most complete sway is allowed - even in the commander's own country - when face to face with the enemy, because of the absolute necessities of the case, and of the paramount duty to defend the country against invasion. To save the country is paramount to all other considerations.

Article 6: All civil and penal law shall continue to take its usual course in the enemy's places and territories under Martial Law, unless interrupted or stopped by order of the occupying military power; but all the functions of the hostile government - legislative executive, or administrative - whether of a general, provincial, or local character, cease under Martial Law, or continue only with the sanction, or, if deemed necessary, the participation of the occupier or invader.

Article 7: Martial Law extends to property, and to persons, whether they are subjects of the enemy or aliens to that government.

Article 12: Whenever feasible, Martial Law is carried out in cases of individual offenders by Military Courts; but sentences of death shall be executed only with the approval of the chief executive, provided the urgency of the case does not require a speedier execution, and then only with the approval of the chief commander.

Several aspects of the "instructions" are of relevance. These "instructions" specify that military commanders could permit the continued administration of civil laws. They differentiate between the kind of martial law that should be applied in "places and countries fully occupied and fairly conquered" and that appropriate for "places or regions where actual hostilities exist." They likewise distinguish martial law not only from military law but also from military or martial rule, writing that whereas martial law covers a country's own citizens and subjects, martial rule pertains to foreign enemies or occupations.[30]

Martial Law in the Indian Military Manual

The Manual of Military Law contains certain provisions relating to martial law in India. According to the Manual, "Martial Law" means the suppression of the civil authority, by military authority, whose sole object is to restore conditions, as expeditiously as possible, to enable the civil authority to resume charge. The Manual provides that conditions of extreme disorder may sometimes arise when the civil authorities, even with the help of the armed forces, are unable to bring the situation under control. In such cases Martial Law may be imposed in the disturbed area by a military commander. Martial Law may also be imposed by a military commander when there is a complete breakdown of civil administration

30 Meyler Bernadette, Originalism and Forgotten Conflict Over Martial Law, *North Western University Law Review*, Vol. 113, 2019, pp. 1335-1370.

e.g., during an insurrection against the Government. Martial Law is thus, the exercise of the right of private defence by repelling force by force.[31]

The Manual provides that a military commander by imposing Martial Law assumes the appointment of Martial Law Administrator (MLA) and takes control of the affected area. He may require the civil authorities to discharge their normal functions under such conditions as may be prescribed by him. Being an extreme step, the decision to declare Martial Law has to be taken at the highest level possible. Before imposing Martial Law, as far as practicable, the military commander should obtain the approval of the Central Government. Where the situation is grave, and the circumstances are such that it is not possible to obtain the prior approval of the Central Government, the military commander may, on his own, assume supreme authority for the maintenance of law and order.[32] He should, however, inform the Central Government as soon as possible after Martial Law is proclaimed. He should also issue proclamation for the information of the inhabitants that Martial Law has been declared.[33]

Since the main object of imposition of martial Law is to restore law and order and the functioning of essential services vital to the community, the military commander should issue Martial Law Regulations, specifying therein the Martial Law offences, punishments for such offences, and constitute military courts for the trial of offenders against Martial Law.[34] Para 18 of the Manual provides that the military courts under Martial Law may be convened under the orders of the MLA. One civil member having judicial experience should, if possible, be appointed to each court.

---

31 Para 15, The Manual of Military Law (2011), Vol. I, Chapter VII.

32 The Military Manual also highlights the principles governing use of force. It states that the use of force in dispersal of unlawful assemblies is governed by the principles of necessity, minimum force, impartiality and good faith. The principle of necessity specifies that: (i) There must be justification for each separate act; (ii) Action should not be taken in one place with the object of creating effect in another place; (iii) There should be no reprisals; and (iv) Action should be preventive and not punitive. As regard the minimum force, the Manual specifies, "no more force is to be used than is necessary to achieve the immediate object. This refers to the actual amount of force used and not to the number of troops employed." Officers and other persons must be impartial in their action and should not accept gifts or show favours. Lastly, the officers and other persons must act in good faith. The Indian Penal Code, 1860 defines the term "good faith" in section 52 as, "Nothing is said to be done or believed in good faith which is done or believed without due care and attention."

33 Para 16, The Manual of Military Law (2011) , Vol. I, Chapter VII.

34 Para 17, The Manual of Military Law (2011) , Vol. I, Chapter VII.

These courts will deal with all offences including breaches of Martial Law Regulations.

When law and order has been restored, and civil authority resumes charge, civil courts may inquire into the legality of acts of military authorities while Martial Law was in force. For this reason it is necessary to protect persons who have been administering Martial Law from actions and prosecutions. This is done by an Act of Indemnity passed by the Parliament (under Article 34 of the Constitution). Such an Act would make transactions legal which were illegal when they took place; free the individuals concerned from legal liability, and make the judgments/ sentences of Military Courts valid and fully operative irrespective of whether the martial law continues to be in force or not. It is to be borne in mind that protection is afforded under an Act of Indemnity only to those where acts were bonafide and performed in the honest belief that they were part of their duty.[35]

'Absolute' and 'Qualified' Martial Law

In the United States, although the proclamation of martial law is unusual, domestic disturbances frequently require that Federal troops aid the civil authorities in maintaining law and order. The extent to which the military forces are used depends upon the necessity of the situation. In various states in the US whenever disorders have occurred, there could be three distinct situations in which the armed forces could be deployed: (i) when the military has been called out for the purpose of aiding the civil authorities, martial law has not been declared and the troops have simply acted as police officers; (ii) when qualified martial law has been declared, either the soldiers have turned offenders over to the civil courts for trial or have kept them in detention until the restoration of peace; and (iii) when punitive martial law has been declared and the military commander has been permitted to establish military courts for the trial of offenders against the rules that might be established by the orders of superior officers. The soldiers in the first scenario have had the same responsibilities and have been subject to the same limitations as have been placed on civil officers in the enforcement of civil law.[36] According to Weiner (1940; 16), the term absolute (punitive) martial law is applied to a situation where necessity requires the replacing of every civil instrumentality by a corresponding

35 Para 19, The Manual of Military Law (2011), Vol. I, Chapter VII.

36 Rankin Robert S., 1939, *When Civil Law Fails: Martial Law and its Legal Basis in the United States*, Duke University Press, p. 146.

military agency; and the term qualified martial law is used to describe a situation where the necessity requires the military only to supplement the civil authorities.[37]

Absolute (Punitive) Martial Law: According to the extreme view, absolute martial law may be proclaimed by the executive. This means that the will of the commander is law and whatever the soldiers may do, under orders, is above the law. This creates the same situation as military occupation of enemy territory in a war, and those engaged in insurrection and riots are treated as enemy. The military authorities are of the opinion that the troops are only called out when the civil authorities have failed in the exercise of their powers. Control must be gained before anarchy is supreme. Hence, the military should have the ample powers to accomplish results in the shortest possible time, and all constitutional guaranties must be suspended.

According to Finalson (1868),[38] martial law is only legal in time of rebellion which amounts to war. The declaration of martial law is only the formal acceptance and recognition of the existence of a state of war already begun. It places under absolute military power all the inhabitants of the district and subjects them to military rule, as if they were enemies in a public war. By rising in rebellion, the rebels forfeit all their constitutional rights and this applies to the entire population of the district which is in a state of rebellion. All those in the district in a state of rebellion are outlaws and rebels, whether actively employed in support of the rebellion or not. Martial law, thus, means the establishment of absolute discretionary military authority, such, as in times of war, is exercised against the enemy. The military measures to be adopted remain a matter of military discretion. The summary infliction of flogging or death, destruction of hideouts, the burning of houses and other measures would all be legal though employed against prisoners or other persons not in actual resistance. It is of the very essence of martial law that it involves a power of military punishment more speedy and severely than the proceedings of ordinary law. Since there is absolute discretionary authority to do anything which could possibly be termed necessary or expedient, there can be no legal liability as regards those who give or obey military orders. Martial law deals only with rebellion so formidable as to amount to war and to require measures of

37 Wiener Frederick Bernays, 1940, *A Practical Manual of Martial Law*, Harrisburg: Military Service Publication, para 16.

38 Finalson W.F., 1868, *A Review of the Authorities as to the Riot or Rebellion, with special reference to Criminal and Civil Liability*, London: Steven & Sons, pp. 224.

war. It is an independent power of action when riot turns into rebellion too serious for military force acting merely in aid of the civil power. Martial law allows of summary procedure and military executions. The efficiency of the military should not be impaired by court writs or orders. They should not be called upon to prove in court the precise amount of force which appeared reasonably necessary to an officer in a given emergency when menaced by rebellions. Subordinates should not be permitted to question the lawfulness of military orders at a critical time of action.[39] A more accurate and descriptive term for absolute martial law is martial rule.

Qualified Martial Law: Qualified martial law is the use of martial law in civil disturbances for preserving order, while at the same time avoiding direct and gross interference with the private rights of citizen. The use of qualified martial law could be due to the unwillingness of the executive to use punitive methods during certain situations. Qualified martial law has been used in the United States to control the riotous situations and to preserve law and order. The state governments in the US have proclaimed qualified martial law, and its use has been upheld not only in the state courts, but also by the Supreme Court. For instance, during martial law in Idaho, the federal forces were deputed under the command of military officer strictly in aid of the civil authorities. The military authorities were empowered to arrest and detain rioters, who could be then tried by the civil courts when they start functioning.

The arrested individuals claimed that they are deprived of their personal rights guaranteed by the Federal Constitution, and they therefore approached the civil courts for writs of *habeas corpus*. In order to make qualified martial law function effectively, it was necessary that the civil courts must refuse to issue any writ. The Supreme Court of Idaho held:[40]

> The action of the Governor in declaring Shoshone County to be in a state of insurrection and rebellion, and his action in calling to his aid the military forces of the United States for the purpose of restoring good order and the supremacy of the law, has the effect to put into force, to a limited extent, martial law in the said county. Such action is not in violation of the Constitution, but in harmony with it, being necessary for the preservation of the government. In such case the government may, like an individual acting in self-defence, take those steps necessary to preserve its existence.

39 Henry Winthrop Ballantine, Qualified Martial Law, a Legislative Proposal-I, *Michigan Law Review*, Vol. 14, No. 2, December 1915, pp. 106-107.

40 *In re Boyle* 6 Idaho 609-612 (1899)

The court said that, all the actions of the Governor being necessary and lawful, there should be no interference by the court in carrying out martial law. Therefore, the writ was not granted. In this way the benefits of the suspension of the writ were accomplished without any direct suspension of the writ itself. The court further said: "We are of the opinion that whenever, for the purpose of putting down insurrection or rebellion, the exigencies of the case demanded for the successful accomplishment of this end in view, it is entirely competent for the executive or for the military officer in command, if there be such, either to suspend the writ or disregard it, if issued."

A qualified martial law and the administration of justice by civil courts can proceed side by side in a community which is in a state of insurrection and riot when the courts do not perform their proper functions without military protection. In such a situation, where the courts are open but intimidated, where the mandates of the court would not have been obeyed if issued, martial law should not depend on whether the courts are open, but on whether the courts are able to function in a proper manner. Sometimes all that the courts may need is support. Sometimes the courts might have reached so degenerate a stage that they have to be reconstructed. In both cases, martial law is the remedy. The use of martial law in such situations is to restore order and to support the courts. It may be possible that without the protection and the influence of martial law, intimidation of witnesses would have rendered all prosecution impossible and that the courts would have been made useless. This kind of Martial law has been called qualified or preventive martial law.

During May 1902, in Pennsylvania riots took place in which people were killed and property destroyed. The civil authorities could not preserve order, and asked the Governor for aid. At first, the Governor called out a part of the militia as an aid to the civil authorities. Disorder, however, continued. The Governor was then forced to call out an entire division of the National Guard to keep peace and protect lives and property. The Governor also issued General Order 39, whose legality was later challenged. The Court held,

> Order 39 was as said a declaration of qualified martial law. It was qualified in the sense that it was put in force only as to the preservation of the public peace and order. It was not for the ascertainment or vindication of private rights, or the other ordinary functions of government. For these the courts and other agencies of the law were still open and no exigency required interference with their

functions. But within its necessary field and for the accomplishment of its intended purpose it was martial law with all its powers. The government has and must have this power or perish. And it must be real power, sufficient and effective for it sends, the enforcement of law, the peace and security of the community as to life and property. ... When the civil authority, though in existence and operation for some purposes, is yet unable to preserve the public order and resorts to military aid, this necessarily means the supremacy of actual force, the demonstration of the strong hand usually held in reserve and operating only by its moral influence.[41]

According to Rankin (1939; 76), the reason given by the court for this form of martial law was that it was better suited for minor insurrections than punitive martial law. Further, an executive should be more explicit in his proclamation. He should state the type of martial law that he is declaring and outline the duties and powers of the military. When the proclamation is couched in ambiguous terms, not only is the military force uncertain concerning their powers, but the courts may have difficulty in determining the exact nature of the martial law being used and the consequential extent of the military power. If it should become necessary to alter the type of martial law, subsequent proclamations could be issued.[42]

The martial law was proclaimed in Galveston in 1920. The proclamation was followed by another which suspended city officials and made provision for military authorities to enforce the law in the military zone. Not only were civil laws enforced by the military, but also certain rules that regulated the activities of the citizens of Galveston were issued under the authority of the military commander. A mass meeting in opposition to this use of martial law was called by the city fathers. The military commander refused to permit the gathering to take place, and the meeting was called off. The military was in complete control of the city, and a military court was set up for the trial of all offenses against both civil and military regulations.

William McMaster, a citizen of Galveston, was arrested by the military force for the violation of a traffic ordinance. He was tried before the provost judge and was fined, but he was committed to jail in default of payment. McMaster petitioned the Federal District Court for a writ of *habeas corpus*, claiming that his trial was illegal and that he was deprived

41 *Commonwealth v. Shortall*, 206 Pa. State Reports 165 (1903), p. 169-171.

42 Rankin Rober S., 1935, *When Civil Law Fails: Martial Law and its Legal Basis in the United States*, Duke University Press, p. 76.

of his liberty in violation of his constitutional rights. It was maintained, on the other hand, that the trial was properly conducted since the Governor had declared martial law and suspended the city officials who had "failed, refused and neglected to preserve the peace," and that the commanding officer had issued an order directing the provost marshal to take charge of the police work formerly done by the city officials. Judge Foster in this case declared that the Governor of Texas had the power to call out the militia in case of insurrection and that the question whether there had been an insurrection was one for the Governor to decide and not for the court. The Judge said: "Since had the authority to institute martial law, notwithstanding there is no statute of the state of Texas authorizing him to do so, he could do anything necessary to make his proclamation effective."[43]

Notwithstanding the distinction of absolute and qualified martial law, the primary mission of troops carrying out either military aid or martial rule is fundamentally the same, to restore order and permit the normal functioning of the civil authorities at the earliest. Federal military forces employed in aid of State or Federal civil authorities derive their authority from the President, and the commanders of such troops take their orders from the President issued through military channels. Federal troops do not take orders from civil officers, but rather after being informed of the missions desired, they render assistance according to military orders and directives.[44]

Doctrine of Necessity and Martial Law

Martial law is a consequence of circumstances where the usual functioning of civilian government has practically ceased. In such a situation, the doctrine of necessity enables those in de facto control, such as the military, to respond to and deal with a sudden and stark crisis in circumstances which had not been provided for in the written Constitution or where the emergency powers machinery in that Constitution was inadequate for the occasion. The extra-constitutional action authorized by that doctrine is essentially of a temporary character and it ceases to apply once the crisis has passed.[45] The imposition of martial law becomes essential to

43 *United States v. Wolters*, 268 Fed. 69 (1920).

44 War Powers and Military Jurisdiction, JAGS Text No. 4, The US Judge Advocate General's School, Michigan, 1943, p. 43.

45 Fiji Court of Appeal, Casey J (Presiding), Barker, Kapi, Ward and Handley JJA, in *Republic of Fiji v Prasad*,1 March 2001.

the continued existence of government and law. A more extreme view is that martial law is an instrument of state terror. It knows very few bounds and authorizes extreme measures of brutality in order to terrorize certain elements of population into submission.

According to Dicey, "The only principle on which the law of England tolerates what is called martial law is necessity;[46] its introduction can be justified only by necessity; its continuance requires precisely the same justification of necessity; and if it survives the necessity on which alone it rests for a single minute, it becomes instantly a mere exercise of lawless violence. When foreign invasion or civil war renders it impossible for courts of law to sit, or to enforce the execution of their judgments, it becomes necessary to find some rude substitute for them, and to employ for that purpose the military, which is the only remaining force in the community. While the laws are silenced by the noise of arms, the rulers of the armed force must punish, as equitably as they can, those crimes which threaten their own safety and that of society; but no longer."[47]

In the United States, proclamation of martial law is a constitutional power vested in Congress, and in cases of emergency, in the President. It is purely the doctrine of necessity as applied to the right of national self preservation; neither expressed nor included in any written law, but depending for its justification upon a question of fact---the fact of necessity. In the US, conflicting views on the subject were stated in the case of *ex parte Milligan*,[48] in which five of the justices sustained the theory of necessity, and the Chief Justice and three others contended for the constitutional theory. The majority of the court held as follows:

46 Black's Law Dictionary defines the term "necessity" as, "Something that must be done or accomplished for any one of the various reasons, ranging from the continuation of life itself to a legal requirement of some kind; context normally supplies a sense of the degree of urgency; Criminal Law: A justification defence for a person who acts in an emergency that he did not create and who commits a harm that is less severe than the harm that would have occurred but for the person's actions." Garner Bryan A, Black's Law Dictionary, Tenth Edition, Thomson Reuters, 2014, p. 1193.

47 Dicey, A. V., 1885, *Introduction to the study of the law of the Constitution,* London, p. 398-415.

48 71 US 2 (1866). In this case, Lambden P. Milligan was sentenced to death by a military commission in Indiana during the Civil War for engaging in acts of disloyalty. Milligan sought release through habeas corpus from a federal court. The Court held that trials of civilians by presidentially created military commissions are unconstitutional. Specifically, it is unconstitutional to try civilians by military tribunals unless there is no civilian court available. The military commission therefore did not have jurisdiction to try and sentence Milligan, and he was entitled to discharge.

> It follows, from what has been said on this subject, that there are occasions when martial rule can be properly applied. If, in foreign invasion or civil war, the courts are actually closed, and it is impossible to administer criminal justice according to law, then, on the theatre of active military operations, where war really prevails, there is a necessity to furnish a substitute for the civil authority, thus overthrown, to preserve the safety of the army and society; and as no power is left but the military, it is allowed to govern by martial rule until the laws can have their free course. As necessity creates the rule, so it limits its duration; for, if this government is continued after the courts are reinstated, it is a gross usurpation of power. Martial rule can never exist where the courts are open, and in the proper and unobstructed exercise of their jurisdiction. It is also confined to the locality of actual war. And so in the case of a foreign invasion, martial law may become a necessity in one State, when, in another, it would be 'mere lawless violence'.

Chief Justice Chase, in the minority opinion in *ex parte Milligan*, adopted both theories of justification---martial law as a legislative act and martial law as founded in necessity. He stated: "It is called into action by Congress, or temporarily, when the action of Congress cannot be invited, and in the case of justifying or excusing peril, by the President, in times of insurrection or invasion or of civil or foreign war, within districts or localities where ordinary law no longer adequately secures public safety and private rights."

According to Dr. Francis Lieber, "Martial law may become necessary in cases of foreign invasion, as well as in cases of domestic troubles. The military power may demolish or seize property, or may arrest persons, if indispensable for the support of the army, or the attaining of the military objects in view. This arises out of the immediate and direct physical necessity. This operation of martial law is not exclusive or exceptional. Any immediate physical danger, and paramount necessity arising from it, dispenses with the forms of law most salutary in a state of peace. The only justification of martial law is the danger to which the country is exposed, and as far as the positive danger extends, so far extends its justification."[49] It is also the reason as to why the military officer should not be held to a strict accountability under the doctrine that necessity alone will justify his

49 As stated by Dr Francis Lieber in a manuscript note to the "Instructions for the government of the armies of the United States in the field," which was found among his papers after his death. Quoted in Lieber G. Norman, What is Justification for Martial Law? *The North American Review*, Vol. 163, No. 480, November 1896, pp. 549-563.

act. The Constitution of the United States affords protection, therefore, against the danger of a declaration of martial law by the legislature of a State as well as against the danger of its declaration by Congress.[50] The principle holds true both as to the United States and the States that the only justification of martial law is necessity.[51]

The only principle, on which the law of England proclaimed martial law, was necessity. The necessity which justifies proclamation of martial law will vary with circumstances. A number of constitutional experts believe that martial law is not built upon settled principle, but is entirely arbitrary in its decisions. It is not permitted in time of peace, when the civil courts are open to perform their functions and enforce their mandates. It is therefore extremely difficult to fix upon any definite rule or event by which it could be anticipated, whether or not martial law shall be proclaimed. No court of law could determine whether exigency which gave rise to proclamation of martial law was correct or otherwise. The grounds of their judgments cannot be inquired into, nor can they be held responsible, therefore, in a civil action.[52] This protection and immunity are essential for a military commander to discharge an important public duty without any fear of consequences. It would be most unreasonable and unjust to hold a military commander liable for the lawful and honest exercise of that judgment and discretion with which the law invests him, and which he was bound to use in the discharge of his official duties.

50 "No State shall make or enforce any law which shall abridge the privileges or immunities of citizens of the United States, nor shall any State deprive any person of life, liberty, or property, without due process of law, nor deny to any person within its jurisdiction the equal protection of the laws."

51 Lieber G. Norman, What is Justification for Martial Law? *The North American Review*, Vol. 163, No. 480, November 1896, pp. 549-563.

52 The Supreme Court of Massachusetts has held, "the law vests in an officer or magistrate a right of judgment and gives him discretion to determine the facts on which such judgment is to be based, he necessarily exercises within the limits of his jurisdiction a judicial authority. So long as he acts within the fair scope of his authority he is clothed with all the rights and immunities which appertain to judicial tribunals in the discharge of their appropriate functions. Of these none is better settled than the wise and salutary rule of law by which all magistrates and officers, even when exercising a special and limited jurisdiction, are exempt from liability for their judgments, or acts done in pursuance of them, if they do not exceed their authority, although the conclusions to which they arrive are false and erroneous." Quoted in Birkhimer Willaim, 1914, *Military Government and Martial Law*, USA Franklin Hudson Publishing Company, p. 338.

The sole justification of martial law is "necessity"; and the great advantage of proclaiming martial law is that it recognizes the continuity of "necessity" and establishes unity of control. Unity of control makes the military authority the sole responsible agent for carrying out the policy of the Government. Recognition of the continuity of necessity is also an important factor in forming plans and in framing orders for the conduct of the civil community. During martial law, the troops are justified in taking the action which the immediate necessity of the situation confronting them demands. When martial law is in force the task of restoring order does not rest entirely on the Army. The machinery and forces of the civil power are then at the disposal of the military authority and to be used not only to increase its power but re-establishing civil control and respect for it at the earliest.[53]

The principle of necessity justifies a resort to all measures which are indispensable for securing the speedy submission of the 'enemy' with the least possible loss of life and damage to property. Martial law consists of such rules as are adopted, at his own discretion, by a Commander-in-Chief in the field, supplementary, or wholly or partially superseding the laws ordinarily in force in a given district. In most countries, certain laws are made applicable to a state of emergency or a state of siege or insurrection when a city or county is wholly or partially placed under military authority. In such situations, the authority is forced by necessity to suspend the ordinary legal procedure and justify itself for using exceptional power. The following principles, according to Pratt (1915), could be observed in executing martial law: (a) It is not retrospective; an offender cannot be tried under it for a crime that was committed before martial law was proclaimed; (b) It does not extend beyond the proclaimed geographical limit or district outside of which an offender cannot be either arrested or tried by the military personnel; (c) It should not be kept in force longer than necessary; (d) and the process of military law should, as far as practicable, be adhered to.[54] However, these rules are for general guidance and are amenable to varying facts and circumstances.

In the year 1900, the greater part of South Africa was under martial law. The legislatures of Natal and Cape Colony passed Acts creating special courts for the trial and punishment, without juries, of persons charged

53 Gwynn Charles W., 1939, *Imperial Policing*, London: Macmillan and Co. Limited, p.16-17.

54 Pratt Lt Col Sisson C., 1915, *Military Law: Its Procedure and Practice*, London: Kegal Paul, Trench, Trubner and Co. Ltd.

with high treason and crimes of a political character. The jurisdiction of these courts, both in regard to time and the class of offences dealt with, was limited and eventually martial law was everywhere administered by military courts acting under detailed instructions. The following principles were laid down:

- The persons subject to martial law were those within the limits of the proclaimed districts who were not subject to military law under the Army Act.
- No person was to be arrested or tried under martial law except for an offence committed within a proclaimed district, and since the date of the proclamation.
- Ordinary common law offences, except such as rendered the offender liable to trial by military courts were, if practicable, to be dealt with before a magistrate under the ordinary law.
- Minor breaches of martial law regulations were to be summarily treated by an authorized officer or magistrate, who could award a fine up to 10 shillings or imprisonment up to thirty days.
- Treason, aiding or abetting the enemy, overt acts endangering the safety of H.M. Forces, and serious breaches of martial law regulations, were to be tried by military courts.
- A military court, consisting of not less than three members, had unlimited powers, and, in addition to the punishments authorized by the Army Act, could award a fine, and order the removal of a convicted person from a proclaimed district. Sentences of death and penal servitude had to be confirmed by the General Commanding-in-Chief.
- Instructions were issued that military courts were to conform as far as possible to the Rules of Military Law as laid down for courts-martial in the Manual of Military Law. The forms of general, district, and field general courts-martial were nearly always used.
- The commandants of districts or areas were made responsible for the administration of martial law in the territory they controlled, but eventually special administrators of martial law were appointed for each area, who dealt solely with martial law regulations, and did not exercise any military command.[55]

55 Pratt Lt Col Sisson C., 1915, *Military Law. Its Procedure and Practice*, London: Kegal

Martial law, as mentioned earlier, is based upon necessity. It is a measure that is not usually used until less drastic measures have failed. Martial law may arise out of strict military necessity. Its proclamation or establishment is not expressly authorized in many Constitutions today. It can be proclaimed in a part of the territory of the state in time of war or in time of peace in which the proper civil authority is unable to exercise its proper function. Martial law in this sense is merely a necessity; and what necessity requires it justifies.

Martial law never was intended to be of a permanent or even semi-permanent nature. Its existence is bottomed upon necessity and may be called into play irrespective of any proclamation or statute authorizing its declaration. Its purpose is to afford a justification for the exercise of extraordinary powers which otherwise would render a military commander answerable in damages. Martial law has always been employed to put down civil strife, insurrection or repel invasion so that the civil authorities could be reinstated (if disrupted) to function under the law. The moment order is restored, the necessity for martial law (hence its justification) ceases to exist.[56] The International Law Commission defines necessity as existing when a state is threatened by a grave and imminent peril and its sole means of safeguarding an essential interest is to adopt conduct not in conformity with what is required of it by an international obligation.[57]

Limitations of Martial Law

The justification for martial law is necessity and its proclamation has been likened to the exercise of the right of self-defence by an individual. The execution of martial law devolves on the discretion of the commander. It is not an absolute power, but one to be exercised with such stringency only as circumstances may require. The often-quoted remark that martial law is the will of the general who commands the army, is in fact inappropriate with reference to domestic martial law. Martial law is indeed resorted to as much for the protection of the lives and property of peaceable individuals as for the repression of hostile or violent elements. It may supersede the

Paul, Trench, Trubner and Co. Ltd, p. 267-268.

56 Anthony Garner, Martial Law, Military Government and the Writ of *Habeas Corpus* in Hawaii, *California Law Review*, Vol. XXXI, No. 5, December 1943, pp. 477-524.

57 International Law Commission, Draft Articles on State Responsibility, Year Book of International Law Commission, Vol. 2, 1980; U.N. Doc.A/CN.4/SER.A/1980/Add.1 (Article. 33(1)(a) of the Draft Articles on Responsibility of States for Internationally Wrongful Acts).

existing civil institutions; but, in general, except in so far as relates to persons violating military orders or regulations, or otherwise interfering with the exercise of military authority, martial law does not in effect suspend the local law or jurisdiction or materially restrict the liberty of the citizen. It may call upon a citizen to perform special service or labour for the public defence, but otherwise usually leaves him to his ordinary avocations.

Martial law is elastic in its nature, and easily adapted to varying circumstances. It may operate to the total suspension or overthrow of the civil authority; or its touch may be light, scarcely felt or not felt at all by the mass of the people, while the courts go on in their ordinary course, and the business of the community flows in its accustomed channels. It is a principle of the exercise of martial law that even when required to be executed with exceptional stringency and for a protracted period, it shall not be permitted to serve as a pretext for license or disorder on the part of the military; and acts of undue violence and oppression committed in its name will, by the laws of war, be visited with extreme punishment. It is further a principle that, while martial law is not to be inaugurated precipitately or inconsiderately, so it is to be continued only so long as the public exigency on account of which it was declared shall prevail. It is not indeed essential to the discontinuance of such state that the original declaration of the same be formally revoked: when the emergency has ceased, or within a reasonable interval thereafter, the status may be deemed to have lapsed, and cannot lawfully be further continued or enforced.[58]

Advantages

A few advantages of martial law are that actions not normally offences can be made criminal, or the scale of punishment for crimes can be raised which can act as a deterrent. This could be applicable in the case of things done to hamper military action. Similar advantage also occurs from the fact that judicial machinery remains under the military authority and prosecution can be speeded up to ensure maximum deterrent. The establishment of martial law may also facilitate the establishment of an efficient intelligent service since the police intelligence organization may be brought under the direct control of the military. At the same time, it remains an important task of the military leadership to ensure that when martial law is applied

58 Winthrop William, 1920, *Military Law and Precedents*, Washington: Government Printing Office, pp. 820-821.

no abuse of the powers conferred by it should occur, as it is likely to lead to an increase of prejudice.[59]

There could be six different components of martial law: (i) It is invoked as an extreme measure which pressing necessity alone can justify; (ii) It refers to direct governance by the military; (iii) It may involve the displacement of the jurisdiction of the ordinary courts by special courts, typically military tribunals, which employ procedures that accord less respect to due process; (iv) It allows for more assertive use of force; (v) It allows for extended powers of search and detention, the seizure of property, the compulsion of labour, and restrictions on freedom of movement such as curfews; and (vi) It is closely linked to its purported purpose, the protection of public safety and national security.[60] Martial law should never be retrospective; only acts committed after its proclamation should be tried under its powers. Martial law is distinct from merely using force in aid to civil power to suppress internal disturbances or riots because it extends to fulfilling some functions of civilian government, even legislative and judicial functions. Martial law is, therefore, the most extreme manifestation of executive power as exercised by a military force. Constitutionally, empowering the military to assume some of the functions of the government is significant, in particular in a democracy where military remains subordinate to the civilian government. At its highest, martial law permits the military to exercise every functions of the government.[61] Sir Charles Napier, once Commander-in-Chief of the British Army in India, said: "The union of Legislative, Judicial and Executive Power in one person is the essence of Martial Law."[62]

59 Individual officers must be forbidden to invent punishments; though at times punishments, not normally recognized, may be authorized by responsible authority. In that case they are awarded and recorded in the same way as normal punishments. Torture and punishments of a nature humiliating to a community or which outrage religious susceptibilities must be prohibited during martial law. Gwynn Charles W., 1939, *Imperial Policing*, London: Macmillan and Co. Limited, p.17.

60 Roberts, Christopher N.J. , From the State of Emergency to the Rule of Law: The Evolution of Repressive Legality in the Nineteenth Century British Empire, *Chicago Journal of International Law*, Vol. 20: No. 1, 2019, pp. 1-61.

61 Moor Cameron, 2017, *Crown and Sword, Executive Power and the Use of Force by the Australian Defence Force*, Australian National University Press, p. 129-130.

62 Quoted in: Charles Clode M., 1874, *The Administration of Justice under Military and Martial Law: As Applicable to the Army, Navy, Marines and Auxiliary Forces,* John Murray, p. 184.

Chapter II

Martial Law in India

The East India Company (in short, EIC) functioning under the Charter issued by Queen Elizabeth on 31 December 1600,[1] had limited powers of legislation. Under the Charter, the Company was empowered to make reasonable laws, orders and ordinances, which were necessary and convenient for its governance and to impose such pains, punishments, and penalties by imprisonment of body or by fines as considered necessary or convenient for the observation of such laws and ordinances, in consonance with the principles of English law. The 1660 Charter empowered the Company to send ships of war, men, and arms to their factories for defence of the same, and to make peace or war with any people not Christians. By 1708, the Company established three Presidencies at Bombay, Madras and Calcutta. Each Presidency was under a separate President who was also the Commander-in-Chief of military forces.

During these initial years, the Company followed the policy of peaceful trade, and avoided all attempts for gaining territorial possessions, because it felt that it could prove ruinous to the English interests in India. However, towards the close of the eighteenth century a paradigm shift took place in the policy of the English. Taking advantage of the downward trend in law and order situation in India, they began entertaining political ambitions and gradually adopted the policy of territorial acquisition

1 A Charter was issued by the Queen on 31 December 1600 which granted the merchants' newly formed organization: "The Governor and Company of Merchants of London, trading to the East-Indies" to purchase lands, and to dispose thereof, and to have a common seal, to ratify and make public their acts. A second Charter was granted to the original Company on 31 May, 1609; a third, 3 April, 1661; a fourth, 5 October, 1677; a fifth, 9 August, 1683; a sixth, 12 April, 1686; a seventh, 7 October, 1693; and an eighth, 13 April, 1698. In addition to these Charters, the Company obtained a grant, dated 27 March, 1669, of the Island of Bombay, and another, 16 December, 1674, of the Island of St. Helena.

through various means. The British faced hostile powers like Marathas, threatening the safety and public order. The Company authorities were also under continuous threat from natives who could rise in rebellion owing to grievances. Once the East India Company established itself as a territorial power, the British Parliament passed statutes to regulate the Company's governance of the Indian territories. In order to give a statutory basis to the administration of martial law in India, the Bengal State Offences Regulation was passed in 1804, commonly referred to as the martial law regulation.[2]

Martial Law under East India Company Rule

Regulation X of 1804 appears to have been based on a general recognition and acceptance of the doctrine of immediate necessity regarding martial law.[3] The Preamble to the Regulation stated:

> Whereas, during wars in which the British Government has been engaged against certain of the Native Powers of India, certain persons owing allegiance to the British Government have borne arms, in open hostility to the authority of the same, and have abetted and aided the enemy, and have committed acts of violence and outrage against the lives and properties of the subjects of the said Government;
>
> And whereas, it may be expedient that, during the existence of any war in which the British Government in India may be engaged with any power whatever, as well as during the existence of open rebellion against the authority of the Government, in any part of the British territories, subject to the Government of the Presidency of Fort William, the Governor General in Council should declare and establish martial law, within any part of the territories aforesaid, for the safety of the British possessions, and for the security of the lives and property of the inhabitants thereof, by the immediate punishment

2 Regulation (X of 1804), declaring the powers of the Governor General in Council to provide for the immediate punishment of certain offences against the State by the sentence of courts martial. A copy of the Regulations is placed at Appendix A in the book. Similar Regulations were issued for Madras (The Madras Regulation XX of 1802) and Bombay (The Bombay Regulation XIV of 1827).

3 This Regulation as declared was to apply to the whole of the Lower Provinces of Bengal and of the North-Western Provinces, except as regards the Scheduled Districts, by the Laws Local Extent Act, 1874 (XV of 1874), s. 6. It was in force in Oudh by virtue of s. 3 (e) of the Oudh Laws Act 1876 (XVIII of 1876). It was in force in the Punjab vide the Punjab Laws Act 1872 (IV of 1872), s. 3, and Sch. I.) It was extended to Arakan vide Regulation IX of 1874.

> of persons owing allegiance to the British Government, who may be taken in arms, in open hostility to the said Government, or in the actual commission of any overt act of rebellion against the authority of the same, or in the act of openly aiding and abetting the enemies of the British Government, within any part of the territories above specified.

The main provisions of the Regulations were that, during the existence of any war in which the government might be engaged as well as during the existence of open rebellion against the authority of the government, the Governor-General in Council might suspend the functions of the ordinary courts and establish martial law and direct the immediate trial by court martial of all persons owing allegiance to the British government in India, who should be taken in arms in open hostility to the government or in the act of opposing its authority by force of arms, or in the actual commission of any overt act of rebellion against the State, or in the act of openly aiding and abetting the enemies of the British government. Section 3 prescribed the punishment of immediate death and forfeiture of all property as the only punishment to be awarded on conviction. The legislature thus carefully limited the jurisdiction of the court martial to cases clearly and indisputably of the highest criminality and of easiest proof. This regulation was supplemented, for reasons of public security, by Bengal Regulation III of 1818 which provided for preventive detention of individuals against whom there might not be "sufficient ground to institute any judicial proceeding" or when such proceeding might be "unadvisable or improper."[4] Similarly, the Madras Regulation VIII was enacted in 1808, which corresponds with the Bengal State Offences Regulation, 1804. It was declared to be in force in the whole of the Madras Presidency baring few scheduled districts.

During the period 1817 to 1844, there were many instances of imposition of martial law in India. Martial law was proclaimed in Cuttack (1817-18), Vizagapatanam and Palkonda (1832), Kimedi (1833),

---

4 The preamble of the Bengal Regulation III of 1818 recited reasons of state, embracing the due maintenance of the alliances formed by the British government with foreign powers, the preservation of tranquility in the territories of native princes entitled to its protection and the security of the British dominions from foreign hostility and from internal commotion as the ground for such detention, "without any immediate view to ulterior proceedings of a judicial nature," by means of a warrant of commitment under the authority of the Governor-General. Minattur Joseph, 1962, *Martial Law in India, Pakistan and Ceylon*, The Hague: Martinus Nijhoff, p. 16.

Gumsuror Goomsur (1835)[5] and in Savantawadi (1844).[6] During this period an interesting case came up which highlighted the relevancy of martial law in relation to a state of war. The case originated in the capture of a Peshwa's treasurer during the Third Maratha War in 1817. Elphinstone was the Commissioner of territory in British India. He proclaimed martial law in the said territory and appointed Captain Robertson as the military commander of the area. Narroba Outia, the treasurer, was in charge of the fort at Raigarh when it was besieged by British troops. Narroba agreed to the terms of capitulation and surrendered the fort; the treasure was seized by Captain Robertson (the collector, judge and magistrate of Poona). However, Capt. Robertson suspected that Narroba hid some of the treasure in his house at Poona. Robertson searched Narroba's house and found a large sum of gold. Robertson seized it as booty of war. Narroba claimed it was his private property, demanded compensation and started to complain about the harsh treatment he received from Robertson. Narroba sent petitions to the Deccan Commissioner, William Chaplin, who made an inquiry and rejected Narroba's claim. Narroba filed a suit in the Recorder's Court in 1822 but died soon afterward and the case was not heard. His trustee, Ameerchund Bedreechund, a banker and merchant, sued the EIC in the Supreme Court of Bombay in 1826.

The case of *Amerchund Bedreechund v. Elphinstone, Robertson and EIC* was decided in favour of the plaintiff by the Supreme Court of Bombay. On 28 November 1826, the Court held that the government's seizure of Narroba and his property occurred after the end of the war; therefore, Narroba had ceased to be an alien enemy when he was captured, and thus he should have been under the protection of the government as a King's subject. Further, the seizure was not based on *jure belli*, since Naroba was under the protection of the conqueror, and rejected the government's claim that the seizure was done *bona fide* as booty. The court ordered the defendants to pay Rs 1750,000 with costs of Rs 16,000.

5 In 1835-36, a serious insurrection occurred in the Goomsur district (Madras) and the Government of Madras issued a proclamation delegating extraordinary powers to a special commissioner. Under his orders rebels were tried summarily by a court composed of military officers, sentenced to death and were forthwith executed by the orders of the special commissioner. Bhatia H.S., 'Martial Law: Its Meaning, Legality and Scope', in Bhatia H.S. (ed.), 1979, *Martial Law: Theory and Practice*, New Delhi: Deep & Deep, p. 26.

6 The Special Laws Repeal Act, 1922 (Act IV of 1922) had repealed Regulation X of 1804.

Reversing the decision of the Supreme Court of Bombay, the Privy Council allowed the appeal of Elphinstone with regard to a seizure of treasure from Poona. Lord Tenterton observed, "We think that the proper character of the transaction was that of hostile seizure made, regard being had both to the time, the place and the person, and consequently that the municipal court had no jurisdiction to adjudge upon the subject" further that "if anything was done amiss, recourse could only be had to the Government for redress".[7] The fact remained that, in India, the Government could seize private property without compensation in cases of emergency, unrestrained by the judiciary.[8] Although often treated as an act of state decision, in legal terms this opinion is best treated as authority for a rule that actions carried out in the course of hostilities in a foreign country were subject to the exclusive jurisdiction of military and not civilian courts.

Martial Law was proclaimed at various other places in 1857 following the First war of Independence. During the mutiny, for a considerable time and over a large extent of territory, all civil courts were suspended and the military authorities were empowered to constitute court martial for the trial of mutineers. On 9 June 1857, martial law was proclaimed in the Divisions of Varanasi and Allahabad. While the forces were engaged in fighting, everyone who appeared to be a rebel or to be siding with the rebels was dealt with as an enemy. The State Offences Act, 1857, (XI of 1857) empowered the Executive to proclaim any district which was, or had been, in a state of rebellion and to issue a commission for the trial of the rebels for any offence against the State or for murder, arson, robbery or any other serious crime against person or property. The proceedings were to be summary and without appeal; but no sentence was to be passed except such as was authorized by law for the offence. The Act XI of 1857 provided:

> I. All persons owing allegiance to the British Government who, after the passing of this Act shall rebel, or wage war against the Queen or the Government of the East India Company, or shall attempt to wage such war, or shall instigate or abet any such rebellion or the waging of such war, or shall conspire so to rebel or wage war, shall be liable,

7 The Privy Council decision in *Elphinstone* v. *Bedreechund* 1830 Knapp P.C. 316. In this case, the Privy Council reversed a judgment of the Supreme Court of Bombay which had awarded to the estate of Narroba Outia, and costs for the seizure of his treasure by an agent of the East India Company.

8 Inagaki, H., Law, agency and emergency in British imperial politics: Conflict between the government and the King's Court in Bombay in the 1820s, *East Asian Journal of British History*, Vol. 5, 2016, pp. 207-224.

> upon conviction, to the punishment of death, or to the punishment of transportation for life, or of imprisonment with hard labor for any term not exceeding fourteen years; and shall also forfeit all their property and effects of every description.
>
> II. All persons who shall knowingly harbour or conceal any person who shall have been guilty of any of the offences mentioned in the preceding Section shall be liable to imprisonment, with or without hard labour, for any term not exceeding seven years, and shall also be liable to fine.

On 13 June 1857, an Act (Act No. XVI. of 1857) was passed to make temporary provision for the trial and punishment of heinous offences in certain districts where martial law had been proclaimed. It provided that persons who shall commit or attempt to commit any "heinous offence"[9] in any district or place in which Martial Law has been or shall be established, shall be liable, on conviction, to the punishment of death, or to the punishment of transportation for life, or of imprisonment with hard labour for any term not exceeding 14 years; and shall also forfeit all his property. A person accused of heinous offence was to be tried either by Court Martial appointed under Act XIV of 1857,or by a Commissioner or Commissioners authorized by a Commission issued under the said Act, or by the ordinary Courts of Judicature.

Martial Law under the British Rule

After the Government of India Act, 1858, was passed and the British Crown assumed direct responsibility for the Government of India, the Indian Councils Act, 1861 authorised the Governor-General to promulgate ordinances having the force of law in cases of emergency. Section 23 of the Act provided:

> Notwithstanding anything in this Act contained, it shall be lawful for the Governor-General, in cases of emergency, to make and promulgate, from time to time, ordinances for the peace and good government of the said territories or of any part thereof, subject,

9 Section II of the Act XVI of 1857. The words "heinous offence" deemed to include an attempt to murder, rape, maiming, dacoity, robbery, burglary, knowingly receiving property obtained by dacoity, robbery, or burglary, breaking and entering a dwelling-house and stealing therein, intentionally setting fire to a village, house, or any public building, stealing or destroying any property provided for the conveyance or subsistence of Troops, and all crimes against person or property attended with great personal violence, and all crimes committed with, the intention of assisting those who are waging war against the State or forwarding their designs.

however, to the restrictions contained in the last preceding section, and every such ordinance shall have like force of law with a law or regulation made by the Governor-General in Council, as by this Act provided, for the space of not more than six months from its promulgation, unless the disallowance of such ordinance by Her Majesty shall be earlier signified to the Governor General by the Secretary of State for India in Council, or unless such ordinance shall be controlled or superseded by some law or regulation made by the Governor-General in Council at a meeting for the purpose of making laws and regulations as by this Act provided.

The ordinance making power was continued by the various Acts. Under the ordinance-making power, martial law was proclaimed in the Punjab (1919), Malabar (1921), Sholapur (1930) and Peshawar (1930). The Martial Law Ordinances modified the common law concept of martial law by authorizing punishment of offenders by commissions or special tribunals.[10]

Of the above instances, martial law proclamation in Malabar, Sholapur, Peshawar and Sindh is covered in this Chapter, while the 1919 Martial Law proclaimed in Punjab is discussed in greater detail in the next Chapter.

Martial Law in Malabar (Madras Residency)

In August 1921, Moplahs (Muslim peasants) from Malabar in the Madras Presidency rose up in revolt against their imperial rulers, resulting in one of the bloodiest and most horrific risings in India after the 1857 Mutiny.[11] The Moplahs started a tenancy movement in 1919 as a result of the increase in rent and the eviction of from their holdings by Hindu (Nambudurior Nair) landlords.[12] When the movement was in its height, the Khilafat movement

10 Minattur Joseph, 1962, *Martial Law in India, Pakistan and Ceylon*, The Hague: Martinus Nijhoff, p. 15-25.

11 The Malabar rebellion extended over the whole of the Ernad taluk and to parts of neighbouring Walluvanad, Ponnani and Calicut taluks, an area of over 2000 square miles, about two-fifths of the district of Malabar. The rebels adopted insurgent tactics, melting away into the jungle and using their superior mobility to conduct 'hit and run' attacks, as well as terrorizing the local Hindu population.

12 During the successive invasions by Hyder Ali and Tipu Sultan in the late eighteenth century, Malabar was thrown into social turmoil. Many Hindus fled in fear of death or forced conversion before the advancing army and the even more terrifying bands of marauding Moplahs (Muslim peasants) who in the areas of Ernad and Walluvanad had become a law unto themselves. The defeat of Tipu and the subsequent British land

came into existence. A Khilafat Committee, consisting of both Muslims and Hindus, had been formed in Malabar in June 1919. To win over the Moplah peasants who formed more than three quarters of the population of Malabar, the Khilafat movement in the district lent its support to the tenancy movement.[13] When peasant unions were formed and tenancy meetings held, section 144 of the Criminal Procedure Code was enforced and meetings were forcibly dispersed by the police.[14] In retaliation, Moplah prepared for an armed rising and a religious leader proclaimed himself the head of an independent state. On 21 August 1919, a mosque was besieged and forcibly entered, under orders of the District Magistrate by the police and the military to arrest a few leaders of the tenancy movement. A fight between the government forces and the peasants who had assembled near the mosque ensued. The next day martial law was declared in four Taluks

settlement policies in Malabar, leading to the restoration of the social and economic position of the dominant castes, severely affected the position of the Mappillas in South Malabar. Reduced to insecure tenancy, vulnerable to rack renting and eviction at the hands of Hindu landlords sustained by British courts, the Mappillas responded in a series of outbreaks. Each one was a jihad in a social context. The ideology of jihad had become an heroic ideal, leaving the Mappillas with a belief in the virtues and rewards of martyrdom and a disposition to justify and sanctify disputes with non-Muslims in terms of jihad. Hardgrave Robert L., The Mappilla Rebellion 1921: Peasant Revolt in Malabar, *Modern Asian Studies*, Vol. II, No. I, 1977, pp. 57-99.

13 The Khilafat-Non-Co-operation movements were started by the Indian National Congress under the leadership of Mahatma Gandhi seeking the immediate redressal of Punjab atrocities and the ill-treatment meted out to the Khalif of Turkey in the post World War I period by the Allied powers. This was in response of the national leadership of the Indian freedom struggle who lost faith in the words of the British administrators of India who offered to consider the Indian issues positively after the victory of the Allied powers in the World War I. Instead the government proceeded with repressive measures that led to the Jalianwala Bagh Tragedy. These developments led to the launching of the Khilafat-Non-Co-operation movements throughout India by the Indian National Congress.

14 Section 144 of the Code of Criminal Procedure, 1898, was enacted to provide experienced Magistrates with summary powers to meet local emergencies. It provided that, whenever it appeared to a District Magistrate, Sub-divisional Magistrate, or other Magistrate specially empowered under the section that immediate prevention or abatement of a public nuisance or speedy action to prevent an apprehended danger to the public was desirable, he could issue a written order setting forth the material facts of the case and served as a summons, directing any person to abstain from a certain act or to take specified order with certain property in his possession or under his management. Such a direction could be given to prevent obstruction, annoyance or injury to any person lawfully employed, danger to human life, health or safety, disturbance of the public tranquility, or riot or affray. It could either be directed to a person individually or to the public generally when present in a particular place.

in the Malabar district (Walavanad, Ponnai, Ernad and Calicut) of the Madras Residency and contingents of army were sent to Malabar.[15]

The Martial Law Ordinance, 1921, issued on 26 August 1921, provided for the proclamation of Martial Law to empower military authorities to make regulations and issue order to provide for the public, safety and the maintenance and restoration of order, to authorize the trial of certain offences by special courts constituted under the ordinance.[16] The military authority could authorize a Magistrate or a military officer of seven years' service to make and issue martial law orders. They were not required to frame a formal charge or to record more than a memorandum of evidence. No offence which was punishable with imprisonment for more than five years could be tried by a summary court. Though an accused before a summary court was given the right to be defended by a legal practitioner, the court might not grant an adjournment if it thought that an adjournment would cause unreasonable delay in the disposal of the case. There was to be no appeal from an order or sentence of a summary court and no court had jurisdiction of any kind in respect of any proceedings in such a court. Ordinary criminal courts were empowered to try any offence in respect of which the military commander made such a direction to the court as also any offence against a regulation or martial law order which was not triable by a summary court.

Martial Law (Supplementary) Ordinance III of 1921 was issued on 05 September 1921, which made provision for the constitution of Special Tribunals of three persons, a president and two members, for the trial of offences under the martial law.[17] In case of a sentence of death,

15 The issue of martial law was a point of great sensitivity for the Government of India in 1921. The British military headquarter at Simla was loathe to repeat what it regarded as the mistakes of the past, most notably the much-maligned employment of martial law in the Punjab in April 1919, which had caused a scandal of grave proportions across the empire. The wraith of the Jallianwala Bagh, the findings of Lord Hunter's committee of inquiry, and the continual agitation over the 'Punjab wrongs', haunted the officials responsible for dealing with the unrest in Malabar and influenced their actions. For the Viceroy the lesson of 1919 was that the government must proceed slowly and surely. There must be no military 'outrages', the army must be kept on a tight leash and martial law had to be tightly controlled by civilians. Lloyd Nick, The Indian Army and the Malabar rebellion 1921-22, BCMH Summer Conference 2012 – Indian Armies, pp. 10.

16 A copy of the Ordinance No II dated 26 August 1921 is placed at Appendix B of the book.

17 The special Tribunal shall consist of three persons who are to be appointed by the Local Government. The President of the Tribunal shall be a person who has acted or is acting as Judge of a High Court, established under the Indian High Courts Act, 1861, or the

transportation for life or for imprisonment for ten years or more, an appeal would lie to the High Court. The Martial Law (Military Courts) Ordinance, 1921, passed on 15 October 1921 enabled the military commander and any officer whom he authorized in this behalf to convene a Military Court in order to try certain offences specified in the Ordinance. A Military Court was to follow the procedure as a Summary General Court Martial (SGCM) convened under the Indian Army Act, 1911, except that a Magistrate of the First Class or a Sessions Judge could be appointed as a member of the SGCM. The finding and sentence of a Military Court were to be confirmed by the convening officer, and a sentence of death was required to be reserved for confirmation by the General Officer Commanding. The Martial Law (Special Magistrates) Ordinance V was passed on 11 November 1921 to provide for the trial by special magistrate of certain offences committed in the area where martial law was in force. The Special Magistrate was to follow the procedure laid down for the trial of cases by a Special Tribunal. A sentence of transportation or of imprisonment for more than two years passed by a Special Magistrate was subject to appeal to a Special Tribunal.[18]

Although the government sanctioned martial law, it was to be kept firmly under control and only used sparingly. Stronger measures, principally military court martial with powers to punish offenders were not available. The Government of India stressed that punishment should be done primarily by civilians. From military point of view, one of the greatest handicaps they had to deal with was 'the inadequacy of the Martial Law Ordinance'. It was a mere shadow of martial law and under it, a commander, who was nominated to administer Martial Law in Malabar, had practically no powers except to make regulations. Furthermore, all powers of punishment were in the hands of the special Civil Courts. The only way of dealing with the rebels were open to the troops; they could either kill them if they encountered them in armed opposition, or they could hand them over when arrested or captured to the civil authorities. This meant endless delay in every case; it also meant that notorious leaders

---

Government of India Act [24 & 24 Vict., c. 104], and the other two members shall be persons who have acted for a period of at least two years in the exercise of the powers of a Sessions Judge under the Code of criminal Procedure, 1898. See: Section 3 of the Martial Law (Supplementary) Ordinance III of 1921.

18 Nair Diwan Bahadur C. Gopalan, 1923, *The Moplah Rebellion, 1921*, Calicut: The Norman Printing Bureau, p. 61-62.

lingered on in confinement, unpunished, almost indefinitely as they had successive rights of appeal.[19]

Malabar (Restoration of order) Ordinance No. I of 1922 provided for speedy trial of certain offences committed during the period while Martial Law was in force, or arising out of the circumstances which necessitated the enforcement or continuance of Martial Law, and also to enable the local Government to take certain steps for the protection of law-abiding citizens and for the restoration and maintenance of order in those areas, was passed on the 25 February 1922.

Martial Law was withdrawn from 25 February 1922 and the Ordinances No. II, III, IV, and V of 1921 were repealed. Malabar (Completion of Trials) Ordinance No III of 1922 was issued on 19 August 1922 to provide for the trial of certain persons whose trials had commenced before or who were awaiting trial by the courts constituted under the Malabar Restoration of Order Ordinance 1922 and for the disposal of appeals pending under that Ordinance. On 4 January 1923, Act I of 1923 (Madras), The Malabar (completion of trials) Act, 1922 was issued to provide for speedy trial of certain classes of offenders.

Special Commissioner for Malabar affairs issued a proclamation on 20 March 1922 providing for the suspension of sentences in certain cases passed under the above Ordinances. The proclamation desired that the people resume their ordinary avocations and live in amity with their neighbours. It further stated, "Whenever therefore it appears that an offender now realizes and regrets the crime which he has committed and is prepared by his future conduct to show his repentance, the Government propose to give him an opportunity of escaping the term of imprisonment, which may have been imposed upon him. Persons selected for this leniency will have their sentence of imprisonment suspended so long as they remain of good behaviour, and pay punctually the fine which the court has ordered. Such fines will be recovered in installments."

Cases: In the case of re *Kochunni Elaya Nair,* an application for issuance of writ of *Habeas Corpus* was moved before the High Court for determining the legality of his detention.[20] It was stated that Kochunni Elaya Nair was arrested on 3 September when he had just arrived at his own residence

19 Lloyd Nick, The Indian Army and the Malabar Rebellion 1921-22, BCMH Summer Conference 2012 – Indian Armies, p. 5.

20 In *Re: Kochunni Elaya Nair* AIR 1922 Madras 215: (1921) 41 MLJ 441, decided by Madras High Court on 19 September 1921.

situated within the limits of the Palghat Municipality and no warrant of arrest was shown to him and that he was not told anything about the offence with which he was charged. His application for bail was rejected by the Sub-Divisional Magistrate of Palghat.[21] It is added that the Taluk of Palghat, and the town of Palghat within which the petitioner's residence and the Sub-Jail are situated, were outside the Martial Law area. Justice K. Sastri, observed, ".... a summary court appointed under the Martial Law Ordinance could not try offences committed outside the martial law area or hold court outside such area. The High Court had power, apart from Section 491 of the Criminal Procedure Code, to issue a writ of *habeas corpus,* and Section 16 of Ordinance No. II of 1921, which excluded the interference of other courts, did not refer to such general jurisdiction and the High Court could issue such writ if the summary court acted without jurisdiction.[22] The accused could apply for bail to the Tribunal as it has all the powers of a Court of Session having original jurisdiction and as appeals from the Tribunal lie to the High Court. He can move this Court if bail is wrongly refused. He has therefore an adequate remedy. The petition for the issue of a writ of *certiorari* was dismissed."

In *E. P. Govindan Nayar and* v. *Emperor,*[23] case which arose from the Martial Law Ordinance, 1921, a petition for a writ of *habeas corpus* was made by two persons undergoing a sentence of 18 months for alleged participation in the Moplah rebellion. They were charged with rioting under Section 147, Indian Penal Code, an offence cognizable by the ordinary courts. It was alleged that they had assisted the rebels in destroying a

21 The petitioner was charged with having committed offences under Sections 121, 395, 431, 436, and 380 of the Indian Penal Code alleged to have been committed by him within the area proclaimed to be under Martial Law. He was arrested by the police while he was in Palghat a place outside the area and was remanded to Jail by Mr. Batty, who was the Sub Divisional Magistrate of the Palghat Division and also a Magistrate invested with summary powers of trial under the Martial Law Ordinance.

22 Section 16 of the Ordinance provided: (1)Notwithstanding the provisions of the Code of Criminal Procedure 1898, or of any other for the time being in force, or of anything having the force of law by whatsoever authority made or done, there shall be no appeal from any order or sentence of a Summary Court, and no Court shall have authority to revise such order or sentence, or to transfer any case from a Summary Court, or to make any order under section 491 of the Code of Criminal Procedure, 1898, or have any jurisdiction of any kind in respect of any proceedings of a Summary Court. (2) The power of the Governor General in Council or the Local Government to make orders under section 401 or section 402 of the Code of Criminal Procedure, 1898, shall apply in respect of persons sentenced by Summary Courts.

23 *Eradu Padinharedil Govindan Nair v. Emperor,* AIR 1922 Madras 499, Criminal Misc P. No. 31 of 1922 decided by Madras High Court on 4 May 1922.

bridge. This they admitted, but stated that they were compelled to do so under threat of death. They alleged, that they were tried outside the martial law area by a Summary Court constituted under the Ordinance. Further, owing to the trial being summary and taking place away from the scene of action and far from their homes, they were not in a position to substantiate this defence by evidence which they could have called, if the trial had taken place under the ordinary law and in its proper place. From the decision of such Summary Courts there was no appeal, and further by Section 16 of the Ordinance, all powers of interference with such decision by writ of *Habeas Corpus* or otherwise was prohibited. The Madras High Court held that there was no right at all to hold a summary court except in the martial law area and the jurisdiction of such a court was local. Outside the area, the ordinary rules of law would prevail and there was nothing in the Ordinance to prevent the High Court from interfering with the decision of any court outside that area purporting to exercise a criminal jurisdiction which it did not possess. The Court has the power to issue this writ and thus the writ was issued.

Malabar rebellion was a major revolt against the British in India. During the campaign, 2,339 rebels were killed, over 1,500 wounded and almost 6,000 captured. In this rebellion, 43 army soldiers, including five British officers were killed and 132 others were wounded. The Malabar rebellion was notorious for the vicious communal violence that took place, with forcible conversions of Hindus, looting, arson and other outrages, as well as anti-government violence. It was also accompanied by extensive communal unrest, including the killing and mass rape of Hindus and the destruction of temples. At least 10,000 Hindus were murdered and at least 1,000 more were forcibly converted. The disorders were the work of four distinct classes of men: (a) An oppressed tenancy, (b) Some Musalmans who felt the Khilafat wrong and never believed or understood non-violence or the theory of suffering, (c) Men who were ready for an opportunity to loot or rob, and (d) Religious fanaticism.[24] The British Government put down the rebellion with an iron fist; British and Gurkha regiments were sent to the area where martial law was imposed. One of the most noteworthy events during the suppression, later came to be known as the "Wagon Tragedy", in which 67 out of a total of 90 Moplah prisoners destined for the Central Prison in Podanur suffocated to death in a closed railway goods wagon. The British strategy for restoration of law and order was entirely different from the policy which they had adopted in each case. The entire south Malabar which was under martial law was treated

24 C. Rajagopalachari, The Riots and After, *The Hindu*, Madras, 4 October, 1921.

as enemy territory and military strategy was adopted for recapture. Special courts were set up to deal with enormous number of criminal cases. Court martial were employed mainly in case of rebel leaders. Martial Law Regulations and summary courts were, however, but sparingly used. For a number of offenders, a scheme of suspended sentence and instalment fines was devised.

Martial Law in Sholapur

The Civil Disobedience movement (1930-34), the second mass movement launched by the Indian National Congress under the leadership of Mahatma Gandhi, was mainly aimed at seeking complete independence. The Government used the coercive methods to suppress the movement and many leaders were arrested. Riots took place at Sholapur on 8 May following the arrest of Mahatma Gandhi on 5 May 1930.[25] Gandhi's arrest sparked a wave of protests in the big textile city of Sholapur. The textile workers went on strike from 7 May and burnt down liquor shops and attacked all symbols associated with the Government such as railway station, law courts, police stations and municipal buildings. When some persons were arrested in connection with the riots, the mob obstructed the movement of police vehicles and threw stones at the police. In the police firing, few persons were wounded. The riotous crowd then attacked a police station and killed two police constables and an Excise Inspector. They drew the police force out of the town and burnt the court buildings.

On 8 May, a company of soldiers arrived and additional military enforcement reached four days later. In the evening of 12 May, the military took charge of the town from the civil authorities and proclaimed martial law. The next day certain martial law regulations were issued. On 15 May, the Sholapur Martial Law Ordinance, 1930 (IV of 1930) was issued for proclamation of martial law in the town of Sholapur and its vicinity in the Bombay Presidency. Sholapur remained under martial law for about seven weeks and Ordinance was withdrawn on 30 June 1930.

25 When the British Government in India enhanced the land revenue and salt tax, the Congress got a good cause for resisting the Government. The Congress Working Committee vested Mahatma Gandhi with full power to launch Civil Disobedience Movement. Gandhiji decided that he would first defy the salt laws. On 12 March 1930, Gandhiji set out on a march, collected salt from the sea and appealed to the people of India to celebrate the week from 6 April to 13 April 1930 as the national week and follow the programme of the Civil disobedience Movement during the week. The people responded enthusiastically to his call. Gandhiji was arrested on 5 May 1930 to forestall *hartal*. Gandhiji arrest was followed by spontaneous demonstrations through the country.

Under the Ordinance, the area in which Martial Law was in force, the Commander-in-Chief in India or the General Officer Commanding-in-Chief was empowered to appoint one or more military officer (not below the rank of Lieutenant Colonel) as Military Commander to administer Martial Law and make regulations for the public safety and the restoration and maintenance of order. The power to make regulations was subject to the following conditions:

(i) In making any regulation the Military Commander shall interfere with the ordinary avocations of life as little as may be consonant with the exigencies of the measures which he deems to be required to be taken for the purposes of Martial Law;

(ii) Before making any regulation the Military Commander shall, if possible, consult the senior civil officer in direct charge of the administration area in which he exercises power, but shall not be bound to follow his advice; and

(iii) The penalty, if any, for the contravention of a regulation shall be specified therein.[26]

The Military Commander could empower any Magistrate or any military officer of seven years service (rank of captain or above), to issue Martial Law Orders (MLO) for supplementing the regulations. Such orders were required to be published and forwarded to the military commander, who had the power to add to, modify or rescind any such MLOs.

Under section 6 of the Ordinance, the following offences were created: (a) Communication with the enemy;[27] (b) With the intention of communicating it to the enemy, collecting, publishing or attempting to elicit, any information with respect to the movements, numbers, description, condition or disposition of any of His Majesty's forces or any police force engaged in administering Martial Law or in restoring or maintaining order, or with respect to the plans or conduct or supposed plans or conduct of any military operations by any such forces, or with respect to any works or measures undertaken for, or connected with or intended for, the defence of any place; (c) Committing any act, which is calculated to mislead or hamper the movements or imperil the success of any operations of His

26 The Sholapur Martial Law Ordinance, 1930 (IV of 1930), section 4(3).

27 For the purposes of section 6 of the Ordinance, the expression "enemy" meant any mutineers, rebels or rioters against whom operations were being carried out by His Majesty's force or the police for the purpose of restoring or maintaining order in any area in which martial law is in force.

Majesty's force or any police force engaged in administering Martial Law, or in restoring or maintaining order; or (d) voluntarily assisting or relieving with money, victuals or ammunition, or knowingly harbouring, protecting, or concealing any enemy. The punishment for the above offences was imprisonment for 10 years. The Courts were prohibited in awarding sentence of whipping, for any offence against a regulation or Martial Law Order except where the offender has, in the commission of the offence, used criminal force within the meaning of the India Penal Code, 1860. Ordinary criminal courts could deal with offences punishable under the Ordinance and civil courts could also continue to function in the administration area provided they, in the exercise of their jurisdiction, did not interfere with the regulations and martial law orders issued under the Ordinance.

The Ordinance under section 11, gave *ex post facto* validity to regulations, orders and sentences passed, before the proclamation of the Ordinance, on or after 12 May 1930 by any officer in the exercise of military control. Section 12, by way of indemnity, protected from legal proceedings any person who acted under the Ordinance or in the exercise of military control on or after 12 May 1930, for the purpose of providing for the public safety or the restoration or maintenance of order. The proviso to the section stated that proceedings could be instituted against any person in respect of any matter where such person has not acted in good faith or a reasonable belief that his action was necessary for the purposes of the Martial Law Ordinance.

On 13 May 1930, two Regulations were issued. Regulation No VIII provided that no person shall: (a) Disobey or neglect to obey any order duly made in accordance with Martial Law Ordinance 1930 (hereinafter called the Ordinance); (b) Obstruct, impede or interfere in any manner with any officer or other person who is carrying out the orders of any authority administering Martial Law, or who is otherwise acting in the execution of his duty under Martial Law; or (c) Make any false statement which he knows to be false in order to obtain a pass issued under Martial Law. The maximum punishment for violation of this Regulation was five years' rigorous imprisonment and fine. Regulation No XI provided that no person shall display the Congress or so-called national flag or similar emblem, commit any act or be guilty of any omission: (a) Which is to the prejudice of good order or of the public safety; (b) Which is calculated to mislead, or hamper the movement or imperil the success of His Majesty's Forces; or (c) Which is likely to be interpreted as meaning as that person is performing or pretending to perform any duty or duties normally performed by persons appointed by constituted authority, himself not being appointed for the performance of that duty. The maximum punishment for the violation of this Regulation was ten years' rigorous imprisonment and fine.

Case: The relatives of 17 persons who were under detention in the Bijapur Jail, after having been convicted and sentenced by the military authorities at Sholapur, had filed petition[28] in the nature of *habeas corpus* under Section 491, Criminal Procedure Code, and the common law jurisdiction of the Court. The features common to all these cases were that each petitioner was charged and convicted at Sholapur, between 08:30 pm on 12 May and 03:45 pm on 18 May, of offences against Martial Law Regulations and each petitioner was sentenced by Military Court or Tribunal acting under those Regulations.

The Court considered the law applicable to the case. According to English constitutional law, where state of war or insurrection amounting to war, exists it is competent for the Crown, in the exercise of its prerogative, to place the country affected under Martial Law. Martial Law in that sense, as has often been said is no law at all: the ordinary Courts ex-hypothesi are not functioning except under military protection, and the effect of Martial Law is to substitute the ordinary law of the land with the will of the Military Commander. The liberty, property and even the lives of the persons in the affected area are placed at the mercy of the military. But as per the law of England, which applies in India also, the Crown is not above the law. The Crown can only declare Martial Law in cases of absolute necessity, and when the necessity ends, normal legal conditions are automatically restored.[29]

Section 11 of the Martial Law Ordinance IV of 1930 had validated all sentences passed by any officer acting in the exercise of military control between the 12 and 18 May, as if they were sentences passed under the Ordinance. Therefore, the question whether martial law was properly proclaimed on the 12 May did not arise in deciding the petition in *habeas corpus,* because all that the courts could do was to give effect to the Ordinance which, under law, had the same force and effect as an Act of the Indian legislature.

---

28 *Chanappa Shantirappa v. Emperor* AIR 1931 Bombay 57, decided by Bombay High Court Special Bench on 1 September 1930.

29 Para 4 of the judgment in *Chanappa Shantirappa v. Emperor* AIR 1931 Bombay 57.

According to Beaumont, C. J., it was not necessary to determine whether the declaration of martial law on 12 May was justified, for on 15 May the Governor-General at Simla issued an Ordinance reciting that an emergency had arisen in Sholapur which made it necessary to provide for the proclamation of martial law in the town of Sholapur and its vicinity. The Ordinance seemed to have introduced a modified form of martial law; the trial of offences was not left to the will of the Military Commander, but was to be held by the ordinary criminal courts. The state of martial law was not to determine the necessity for it, but was to continue until brought to an end by a notification in the Gazette of India. Where martial law has been declared, it is competent for the courts - and is indeed the duty of the courts if called upon – after the restoration of normal conditions to decide whether and to what extent martial law was justified. ... I think all that the courts can do is to inquire whether there is evidence upon which the Governor-General may reasonably conclude that an emergency exists. If that question be answered in the affirmative, there is an end of the matter.

Madgavkar, J., referred to a number of cases [*Phillips v. Eyre* (1870) 6 Q.B. 1: *Marais Ex parte* (1902) A.C. 109: and *Tilonko v. Attorney-General of Natal* (1907) A.C. 93] which arose out of the administration of martial law in the British Commonwealth, and pointed out the weakness which lay in deciding important issues like the promulgation of a martial law ordinance on the report of the man on the spot. Martial law was declared by the local authorities at Sholapur and the military took charge before the Ordinance was passed. It was therefore the District Magistrate and not the Governor General,who decided whether there was an emergency. The details are stated in the affidavit of the District Magistrate are: "A toddy shop was wrecked, toddy trees were cut down, and when persons were arrested the Police lorries were obstructed on the road and stones thrown. The Police fired, some persons were wounded, and the crowd thereupon revenged itself by attacking an unarmed Police station and murdered an Excise Inspector and two Police Constables. The unarmed Police were disorganised. The Court buildings were burnt."

Madgavkar, J., referred the case of *D.F. Marais, Ex parte* [(1902) A.C. 109: where Lord Halsbury, in delivering the judgment of the Privy Council, observed:

> The truth is that no doubt has ever existed that where war actually prevails the ordinary Courts have no jurisdiction over the action of the military authorities.

> Doubtless cases of difficulty arise when the fact of a state of rebellion or insurrection is not clearly established.
>
> It may often be a question whether a mere riot, or disturbance neither so serious nor so extensive as really to amount to a war at all, has not been treated with an excessive severity, and whether the intervention of the military force was necessary; but once let the fact of actual war be established, and there is a universal consensus of opinion that the Civil Courts have no jurisdiction to call in question the propriety of the action of military authorities.

The law, however, does not invest the man on the spot with superhuman attributes. Being a man, he may be weak or incapable. He may be out of touch with the people. He may be nervous or even vindictive. He may exaggerate a riot with sticks into an armed insurrection, and disobedience of his own orders into a rebellion. The Crown has the right to put down breaches of the peace. Every subject, whether a civilian or a soldier, whether what is called a 'servant of the Government' such for example as a Policeman, or a person in no way connected with the administration not, only has the right, but is, as a matter of legal duty, bound to assist in putting down breaches of the peace. No doubt, Policemen or soldiers are the persons who, as being specially employed in the maintenance of order, are most generally called upon to suppress a riot, but it is clear that all loyal subjects are bound to take their part in the suppression of riots. This duty is not limited by the terms of Sections 127 to 132, Criminal Procedure Code, in regard to unlawful assemblies but extends far beyond. In the opinion of Madgavkar, J., … the Ordinance came into effect not from the date of its publication but from the date of the proclamation on the 18 May, so that, as all the sentences in question are after the 12 May and before 3-30 PM on the 18 May, they are all validated by the Ordinance and are not subject to our revision. Therefore, the present applications fail and must be dismissed.

According to Blackwell, J., the sentences which were passed by Military Tribunals are not by Section 11 to be deemed to be sentences passed by the ordinary Civil Courts. They are sentences which are to be deemed to be as valid as if they had been passed by the ordinary Civil Courts. They still remain sentences passed by Military Tribunals since they were validated by the Ordinance.

Martial Law in Peshawar

In 1930, martial law was proclaimed in Peshawar and this was the last occasion when legislative provision for the administration of martial law was made in India. In the spring of 1930, after years of ignoring the growing nationalist movement in the North-West Frontier Province (NWFP), the local British administration was suddenly confronted with a massive rebellion. In the NWPF, the civil disobedience movement of 1930-34 crystallized around the leadership of Abdul Gaffar Khan.[30] Earlier in 1929, the Lahore Congress was attended by a large contingent of Pathans headed by Abdul Gaffar Khan. The Pathans delegation was inspired by the pledge and its leader enlisted *Khudai Khidmatgars* or the servants of God almost in every village. The volunteers' uniforms were dyed in cheap brick-red colour, thus acquired the name, "Red Shirt Movement". The *Khudai Khidmatgars* constituted a highly disciplined and politicized body of dedicated men who emphasized liberal religion, social service and non-violence. The Viceroy in a letter to the Secretary of the Sate had explained "The name-Red Shirt" was purposely introduced by the North West Frontier Province administration as a popular substitute for the name *Khudai Khidmatgars*. [31]

Beginning with a nationalist demonstration and subsequent shooting of Indian civilians by British troops in Peshawar on 23 April, unrest quickly spread throughout the province. Within days the British had evacuated Peshawar city and most of the NWFP was beyond their control. At the beginning of June, the British position was further weakened by an onslaught of Afridi tribesmen who descended upon the Vale of Peshawar to fight the Government's forces. Following the British withdrawal from Peshawar on the evening of 24 April 1930, the city fell into nationalist

30 Ghaffar Khan, who is also known as Badshah Khan and the "Frontier Gandhi," formed the world's first non-violent army, a force of about 100,000 Pathans who took a solemn oath in joining the "Servants of God" movement, with each stating that "since God needs no service… I promise to serve humanity in the name of God. I promise to refrain from violence and from taking revenge. I promise to forgive those who oppress me or treat me with cruelty. I promise to devote at least two hours a day to social work". Initially they set to work organizing village projects and opening schools, but soon they became part of the broader Indian Independence movement, accepting without retaliation some of the most fierce British repression—mass firings on unarmed crowds, torture, personal humiliation, setting homes and fields on fire, and even the destruction of entire villages. Lester Kurtz, The Khudai Khidmatgar Movement (1933-37), International Centre for Nonviolent Movement, July 2009.

31 S. R. Bakshi S.R., Role of Pathans in Civil Disobedience Movement 1930-34, *Proceedings of the Indian History Congress,* Vol. 42, 1981, pp. 473-481.

hands. The police locked themselves in their stations and Congress volunteers took up the fundamental responsibility of the government: maintaining law and order.[32]

The violent repression of rebellion began in May 1930 with the introduction of military units throughout the settled districts and the indiscriminate aerial bombing of any tribesmen thought to be menacing the Peshawar District. Although most areas were under control by early June, the influx of Afridi tribesmen claiming to be "liberators" at that time led to major military operations taking place throughout the settled districts. The ordinary administration of the province once again came to a standstill and all low level officials in the police and revenue departments fled to Peshawar. The Red Shirts began demonstrating once more in the Charsadda subdivision and the picketing of liquor shops recommenced. There were massive arrests and on 16 August the administration declared martial law.[33]

After martial law was declared, the Province was cut off from the rest of the subcontinent. Visits to and from the province were not allowed and all sorts of communication were strictly censored. Frequent firing and lathi charge foray into the unarmed, non-violent *Khudai Khidmatgar* became a routine. The *Khudai Khidmatgars* were stripped and flogged and forced to walk naked through the cordons of soldiers who prodded them with rifles and bayonets as they passed. They were physically humiliated publicly and all kind of inhumane treatment was inflicted upon them. The *Khudai Khidmatgars* faithfully followed Ghaffar Khan and offered no resistance to the government. Before 23 April 1930, the *Khudai Khidmatgars* were about twelve hundred, but, after the government repression, their number exceeded 25,000 within a couple of months.[34]

The police encircled villages and seized suspected "agitators" and firearms. In the police firing in Bannu District, over 70 peoples were killed. By the beginning of autumn, the British Indian Army and Royal Air Force drove the Afridi and other tribal back into the hills. Martial law continued, but the civil administration remained confined in the large

32 Marsh Brandon., 2015, *Ramparts of Empire: British Imperialism and India's Afghan Frontier, 1918-1948*, London: Palgrave Macmillan, Top of Form Bottom of Form p. 115-116.

33 The Martial Law Ordinance, 1930, of 15 August 1930, extended to the district of Peshawar in the North-West Frontier Province.

34 Shah Sayed Wiqar Ali, Abdul Ghaffar Khan, the Khudai Khidmatgars, Congress and the Partition of India, *Pakistan Vision*, Vol. 8, No. 2, pp. 86-115.

towns. Throughout this period, the Red Shirt volunteers remained non-violent. In February 1931, two attempts were made on life of Captain Barnes, the Assistant Commissioner for Charsadda. The accused was tried under the "Murderous Outrages Regulation," and sentenced to death. After execution of the accused, situation further deteriorated.[35]

No special courts were set up but martial law was in force for five months until it was abrogated on 24 January 1931. During these five months, 21 men were convicted under martial law regulations, but the maximum punishment awarded was rigorous imprisonment for three months. This was interpreted by the government as indicating their moderation and by their opponents as proof that there had been no need for the declaration of martial law. The news of the proclamation of martial law acted as an effective deterrent and tended to prevent the Afridis from making further incursions, so that the necessity for a strict administration of martial law did not arise. The fact that martial law remained in force for about five months, in spite of the absence of serious disturbances, may have been due to the Chief Commissioner's apprehension of renewed incursions of the tribesmen.

The Martial Law Ordinance, 1930, (VIII of 1930) was issued by the Governor General under the power conferred by section 72 of the Government of India Act. The Ordinance, which consisted of 43 Sections, was divided into two parts, the first dealing with the proclamation and enforcement of martial law and the second with the Special Courts created by it. The General Officer Commanding, Northern Command, was appointed as the chief administering authority of martial law under the Ordinance, and he could delegate his powers to anyone he could select for the public safety and the restoration of peace and order. He could make regulations for the whole martial law area, and the Administrators under him could make regulations for the administration areas to which they were appointed. An Administrator could empower any Magistrate or military officer of seven years service (rank of Captain or above), to make martial law orders in any part of the administration area for the purpose of supplementing the regulations.[36]

35 Marsh Brandon Douglas, Ramparts of Empire: India's North-West Frontier and British Imperialism 1919-1947, Unpublished Ph D Dissertation, The University of Texas at Austin, May 2009.

36 Section 4, the Peshawar Martial Law Ordinance, 1930.

The Ordinance prohibited certain activities and provided punishment for their violations. These provisions[37] were similar to one made under the Sholapur Ordinance.[38] The Ordinance created five classes of Special Courts: (i) Special Tribunals, (ii) Special Judges, (iii) Special Magistrates, (iv) Summary Courts, and (v) Military Courts.[39] The Special Tribunals were to consist of three persons, one of whom should have acted or was acting as a High Court Judge and the other two should have acted as Sessions Judges for at least two years. They should in general follow the procedure prescribed for the trial of warrant cases by Magistrates, but should make a memorandum of the evidence of the witnesses and were not bound to adjourn the trial for any purpose, unless such adjournment was considered by them to be necessary in the interests of justice. A Special Tribunal was to have all the powers conferred by the Code on a Court of Session exercising original jurisdiction. In the event of any difference of opinion among the members of a Special Tribunal, the opinion of the majority was to prevail. Special Tribunals could pass any sentence authorized by law or regulated under the Ordinance. When an accused was sentenced to death by the Special Tribunal, the President was to inform the accused the period within which an appeal should be preferred.[40] Section 21 of the Ordinance provided that in the case of any sentence of death, or transportation or imprisonment for a term of ten years or more awarded by the Special Tribunal, an appeal could be filed under the provisions of the Criminal Procedure Code and the Indian Limitation Act, 1908.

Special Judges could be appointed by the Provincial Government from among persons who had been Sessions Judges for at least two years. They should follow the same procedure as the Special Tribunals. Any Magistrate of the First Class who had exercised powers in that capacity for two years could be appointed as a Special Magistrate. Special Magistrates could be empowered to try any offence not punishable with death. They could follow the same procedure as prescribed for the Special Tribunals. They could pass any sentence which a Magistrate specially empowered under Section 30 of the Criminal Procedure Code was enabled to pass. If they passed a sentence of transportation or imprisonment for more than two years, appeal lay to the Special Tribunal. The Court of a Magistrate could pass any sentence authorized by law except a sentence of death or

37 Section 7, the Peshawar Martial Law Ordinance, 1930.

38 Section 6, the Sholapur Martial Law Ordinance, 1930.

39 Section 15, the Sholapur Martial Law Ordinance, 1930.

40 Section 17-20, the Sholapur Martial Law Ordinance, 1930.

of transportation for a term exceeding seven years or imprisonment for a term exceeding seven years.[41]

An Administrator could empower any Magistrate to exercise the powers of a Summary Court which could try offences other than those punishable with imprisonment for more than five years, but could not pass a sentence of imprisonment for a term exceeding two years or fine exceeding one thousand rupees.[42] It should follow the procedure laid down for the trial of warrant cases but was not required to record more than a memorandum of evidence, or to frame a formal charge. If the offence was one punishable with imprisonment for a term not exceeding one year, it could follow the procedure for summary trial of cases in which an appeal lay.

The Administrator or any officer, not below the rank of a Field Officer authorized by him in this behalf could direct that certain offences should be tried by a Military Court convened by him, if the exigencies of the situation, in his opinion, required the adoption of such a course for restoring and maintaining order. A military court was to be constituted in the same manner and should follow the same procedure as a summary general court martial convened under the Indian Army Act, except that a Magistrate of the First Class or a Sessions Judge could be appointed a member of the Military Court and that a memorandum of the evidence and the statement of the accused should be recorded. The finding and sentence of a Military Court were subject to confirmation by the convening officer; a sentence of death was required to be reserved for confirmation by the General Officer Commanding-in-Chief.[43]

Every person accused of an offence before a Court constituted under the Ordinance was entitled to be defended by a legal practitioner.[44] In case a sentence of whipping was passed by a Court constituted under the Ordinance, such sentence was not to be carried out in public.[45]

On 5 March 1931, a settlement was reached between the government and Congress as a result of the Gandhi-Irwin pact or the Delhi Pact. The Gandhi-Irwin Pact was an agreement reached between Gandhi and

41 Sections 24-30, the Sholapur Martial Law Ordinance, 1930.

42 Sections 34-35, the Sholapur Martial Law Ordinance, 1930.

43 Section 37, the Sholapur Martial Law Ordinance, 1930.

44 Section 40, the Sholapur Martial Law Ordinance, 1930.

45 Section 41, the Sholapur Martial Law Ordinance, 1930.

Lord Irwin after months of political impasse as a result of Gandhi's Civil Disobedience Campaign. The agreement stipulated that in exchange for Gandhi suspending Civil Disobedience and agreeing to attend the next London Round Table Conference, the Government would undertake to permit peaceful picketing in favor of purchasing Indian goods, release political prisoners not found guilty of violent crimes, revoke the numerous declarations of emergency then employed throughout India, and lift bans on most political parties.[46]

Martial Law in Sindh

Martial law was proclaimed in certain parts of Sindh under the common law rule in 1942. Sindhi spiritual leader Pir Sibghatullah Shah Rashdi, popularly known as Soreh Badshah (brave king) started a powerful movement — the Hur[47] Resistance Movement — against the British colonial state during 1930-1943. The Hur movement's slogan, coined by Soreh Badshah, *Watanya Kafan, Azadiya Mout* (our land or a coffin, freedom or death), reflected the people's sentiments and their love for their motherland and national identity. Under the leadership of Soreh Badshah, thousands of his followers (both men and women) revolted against the British Raj and launched a struggle to oust the foreign rulers from Sindh. The hub of the Hur movement was the central and lower parts of Sindh especially the current Sanghar district.

The Hurs terrorized whole districts, committing murder, sabotage and dacoity, to such an extent that the civil authorities found it difficult to cope with the situation.[48] On 29 March 1942, Lahore Mail was derailed

46 "Gandhi-Irwin Pact 1931" in ParshotamMehra, 1985, *A Dictionary of Modern Indian History, 1707-1947,* Delhi: Oxford University Press, pp. 259-260.

47 Hur is an Arabic word meaning free. The Hurs are of Arab origin and are said to have migrated from Central Asia, initially settling along the Arabian Sea coast and then spreading all over the Province of Sindh. By 1900, the British authorities had declared the Hurs a 'Criminal Tribe,' under the Criminal Tribes Act of 1871, which operated on the presumption that criminality was the hereditary profession of various tribes of the Subcontinent. The Hurs were not resident in one place and kept moving on the orders of their leader Pir Pagaro. One of the reasons why the Criminal Tribes Act was promulgated was because of the British belief that any group of people who do not settle in one area, must be criminals. Ali Bhutto, The Last 'Hur'-rah, available at: https://newslinemagazine.com/the-last-hur-rah/.

48 In November 1939 riots started in Sukkur at the instigation of Soreh who felt that the Government was fully engaged in World War II and would not be in a position to put up resistance and hence he will be able to achieve his aim. With this end in view he directed all his efforts towards the creation of a serious law and order problem in the Province. In October 1941, Soreh was detained and later interned outside the Province.

at about 9 pm by removal of railway fish plates. The Hurs had apparently divided themselves into two parties, viz the raiding party and covering party. The former, under effective covering fire from the latter, entered the compartments and started looting and eliminating the passengers by the use of axes, guns and rifles. The total casualties being 32 killed and 100 wounded.

To crush the revolt by the Hurs, the British government not only used extreme violence but also imprisoned Soreh Badshah. In 1942, the Hur Criminal Act was passed by the British government in the Sindh Assembly. A special force of troops was sent to the area to aid the civil authorities in restoring order. Martial law was imposed in certain parts of Sindh on 1 June 1942. This proclamation was made under the common law rule which justified the repelling of force by force. Complete control of the civil administration was given over to Maj. Gen. R. Richardson, military commander who would have the advice and assistance of the civil authorities in the area concerned. During martial law, night curfew was imposed and orders were issued for depositing of arms and ammunition in the nearest police stations. The forces were allowed to shoot to death on sight any person suspected of being disciple of Soreh Badshah. The air reconnaissance was stepped up, huts and hamlets were destroyed by incendiary bombs and the Hurs, moving from well to well, were machine gunned from the air. To shatter their morale, the army was allotted the task of destruction of "Pir Jo Goth", the palace of Soreh Badshah. Thousands of followers of Soreh Badshah, including women and children, were confined to jails and concentration camps. During martial law, special courts were set up for trial of the Hurs. It is also alleged that thousands of Hur fighters were brutally tortured, imprisoned and killed or sentenced to death in order to subdue the uprising.

Prior to his removal from Karachi he managed to pass instructions to his Fakirs to play havoc in the area by carrying out large scale disruption activities so as to secure his release from detention. The Fakirs planned to paralyze the Government by looting, breaching canals, attacking railway stations and killing of staff, committing dacoity and eliminating trackers and informers working for the Government. For sobering and curbing the Hurs and other masses in the area, the police arrested a large number of people and put them through mock trials which resulted in exemplary punishments. Such an action did not deter the Hurs from carrying out their activities. Wisal M. Khan (retd Major General), Hur Operation in Sindh, Published in *Sindh Quarterly* in Five Parts in 1980 and 1981, p. 3, available at: http://www.sanipanhwar.com/HUR%20 OPERATIONS%20IN%20SINDH.pdf.

Soreh was imprisoned on different occasions from 1930 to 1943 in different jails.[49] In 1940, when the struggle was at its peak, he was again arrested from Karachi and was sent to Nagpur jail. On 14 January 1943, he was brought back to Sindh and shifted to Hyderabad jail. The British government tried him by a military court. The trial lasted only 26 days in which Soreh Badshah was sentenced to death for "abetting, conspiring and preparing to wage war against the King-Emperor". On 20 March 1943, he was hanged in Hyderabad jail. The death of Soreh provoked his followers and fuelled violence against the colonial government. In retaliation, violence, killings and torture against the followers of Soreh continued till 1946, though martial law was lifted on 31 May 1943. In July 1946, the Hurs planned to derail the Lahore Mail, but were unsuccessful as a goods train which was running ahead got derailed. Thousands of Hurs were arrested, killed and confined in camps and jails. The properties of Soreh Badshah and his followers were also confiscated.

The Martial Law (Indemnity) Ordinance, 1943 (XVIII of 1943) indemnified all servants of the Crown as well as persons who acted under orders of the servants of the Crown for any act done in the martial law area. The Ordinance specified the areas covered by the martial law order. Section 3 of the Martial Law (Indemnity) Ordinance, 1943 provided:

> No suit, prosecution or other legal proceeding shall lie in any court against any servant of the Crown for or on account of or in respect of any act ordered or done by him or purporting to have been ordered or done by him in the martial law area during the martial law period for the purpose of maintaining or restoring order or of carrying into effect any regulation, order or direction issued by any authority responsible for the administration of martial law in the said area to which he was subordinate; and no suit, prosecution or other legal proceeding shall lie in any court against any other person for or on account of or in respect of any act done or purporting to have been done by him under

49 Soreh Badshah was arrested on 28 August 1930 and was awarded eight years imprisonment for keeping his boy servant in a box and for being in illegal possession of arms and ammunition in spite of the fact that the witnesses failed to give evidence in the Court of Law to substantiate these allegations. The main reason for this state of affairs was that the British Government was bent on the arrest and punishment of the Soreh Badshah and hence every kind of evidence was concocted and fabricated and the witness failed to utter lies and corroborate evidence in the presence of the accused. Wisal M. Khan (retd Major General), Hur Operation in Sindh, Published in *Sindh Quarterly* in Five Parts in 1980 and 1981, p. 2, available at: http://www.sanipanhwar.com/HUR%20OPERATIONS%20IN%20SINDH.pdf.

any order of a servant of the Crown given for any such purpose as aforesaid:

Provided that the act was done in good faith and in a reasonable belief that it was necessary for the purpose intended to be served thereby. [50]

All orders for the seizure and destruction of property made by martial law authority were confirmed and all sentences passed, including those passed for offences committed before the martial law period, by the martial law courts during the period, were validated, whether the courts sat within or outside the martial law area.[51] The Ordinance also provided that no claim was maintainable in any court for compensation of the property seized, confiscated, destroyed or damaged in the course of operations conducted in the martial law area during the martial law period. All sentences passed during the martial law period were deemed to have been lawfully passed.[52]

50 Section 3 (2) of the Martial Law (Indemnity) Ordinance, provided that for the purposes of this section it shall be conclusive proof that an act was done under an order of a servant of the Crown given for one of the aforesaid purposes if the Central Government, in the case of an officer employed in connection with the affairs of the Central Government or the Provincial Government, so certifies; and an act shall be deemed to have been done in good faith and in a reasonable belief that it was necessary for the purpose intended to be served thereby unless the contrary is proved.

51 Sections 5 and 6, the Martial Law (Indemnity) Ordinance, 1943. A copy of the Martial Law (Indemnity) Ordinance, 1943, is placed at Appendix C of the book.

52 Hans Raj, 1989, *Executive Legislation in Colonial India 1939-1947: A Study of Ordinances promulgated by the Governor General of India*, Delhi: Anamika Prakashan, p. 78-79.

Chapter IIA

Martial Law of 1919 in India

Introduction

Martial law, an unconventional law that entails curbing enjoyment of various civil rights, is imposed in extraordinary situations. In the context of British India, the situation that led to the imposition of martial law was people's reaction to the enactment of Anarchical and Revolutionary Crimes Act of 1919, popularly known as the Rowlatt Act[1], as the Act was based on the recommendations of Sedition Committee chaired by Sir Sidney Rowlatt. This Act was passed hurriedly by the Imperial Legislative Council despite the united opposition of the Indian members and came

1 The Anarchical and Revolutionary Crimes Act, 1919 (Rowlatt Act), authorized the Government to exercise certain emergency powers to deal with anarchical and revolutionary movements. It supplemented the ordinary criminal law and specified in a schedule the offences brought under its purview. They included: (i) certain offences against the State such as waging war, conspiring to overthrow the government etc; (ii) certain offences of violence against person and property in connection with movements endangering the security of the State such as sedition, rioting with deadly weapons, murder, robbery, dacoity, damaging roads, and bridges, house breaking, criminal intimidation; and (iii) certain offences connected with the use of explosives and arms, provided that such offences were associated with anarchical and revolutionary movements. Any attempt or conspiracy to commit or any abetment of any of these offences was also included in the schedule. The Act was to extend to the whole of British India and was to continue in force for three years from the date of the termination of the war. The Act was divided into five parts, each enabling the Government of India to give to the local governments certain special powers, according to the nature and seriousness of the revolutionary activities in the area concerned. The Rowlatt Act was the occasion of much unrest in India. It was passed to counter anarchical and revolutionary crimes. This phrase in the Act was interpreted to mean "conspiracies, propaganda and agitations with the object of overthrowing the government, upsetting established order, and interfering with the administration of the laws." It was a measure intended to be used in an emergency and directed against a particularly dangerous class of offenders. It was repealed in 1922.

into force on 21 March 1919. It gave the government enormous powers to repress political activities and allowed detention of political prisoners without trial for two years.

A countrywide campaign was called by Mahatma Gandhi in 1919 in response to the Rowlatt Act. He wanted non-violent civil disobedience against such unjust laws, which would start with a hartal (closing of establishments in protest) on 6 April 1919. But before it could be launched, there were large-scale violent, anti-British demonstrations in Calcutta, Bombay, Delhi, Ahmadabad, etc. Especially in Punjab, the situation became volatile due to wartime repression, forcible recruitments, and ravages of disease. During the intense anti-British demonstrations, Punjab also witnessed the Jallianwala Bagh Massacre. The government declared martial law in the Punjab province and a few other parts on 15 April 1919. Mahatma Gandhi was overwhelmed by the atmosphere of total violence and suspended the civil disobedience campaign on 18 April 1919.

Hartal and Disturbance

During the protest, violence was reported from various parts in districts of Delhi, Ahmadabad, Amritsar, Lahore, Gurjanwala, and Lyalpur. The first outbreak occurred in Delhi on 30 March 1919 when *hartal* was observed throughout with great success, in the sense that shops, both Muslims and Hindus, were closed and business was brought to a standstill in the city. Early in the forenoon of 30 March, a considerable number of people went to the Railway Station, Delhi. There, the temporary arrest of the men appears to have evoked great excitement and caused number of people to invade the main building streaming across the platform, stopping all work, and using threats of violence. In police and military firing near railway station and town hall, eight persons were killed and about 12 were wounded. On 31 March, large processions attended the funeral services of those killed. Again on 17 April about 18 people were wounded in police firing, two of them died subsequently. Martial law was not proclaimed, though the situation was serious and the Chief Commissioner on 17 April applied to the Government of India for authority to declare martial law. Throughout the period of the disturbances, the civil authority received assistance from the military in the quelling of the disturbances, the patrolling of the streets and the maintenance of order.

The agitation against the Rowlatt legislation was vigorously maintained in the Ahmadabad and Kaira districts. Feelings of irritation and anger against the Government for the action they were taking were roused among the masses. The news of Mr. Gandhi's arrest on 10 April spread rapidly and caused great excitement. The mill-hands ceased work, and the shops in the city were closed. The number of rounds fired by the armed police and the troops in Ahmadabad was 748, and the number of ascertained casualties amongst the rioters was 28 killed and 123 wounded.[2] In Nadiad, the main incident was an attempt to wreck a train which was conveying British troops to Ahmadabad. The train was derailed but had a miraculous escape, as it was brought to a stand before running down a steep embankment. Several attacks were made on railway and telegraph communications, but no collision occurred between the people and the troops who were sent here as a precautionary measure. On 10 April, violent rioting took place at Amritsar and Lahore in the Punjab, and at Ahmedabad in the Presidency of Bombay, and distinct unrest manifested itself in a minor degree at places as far as Calcutta and Bombay.

On 9 April 1919, two nationalist leaders, Dr Saifuddin Kitchlew and Dr Satyapal, were arrested by the British officials without any provocation except that they had addressed protest meetings, and were taken to some unknown destination. This caused resentment among the Indian protestors who came out in thousands on April 10 to show their solidarity with their leaders. Soon the protests turned violent because the police resorted to firing in which 10 protestors were killed and many more were wounded.[3] Upon hearing news of the Indians shot dead by soldiers, the crowd attacked two Banks killing three British officials and also burned down a post office. A lady doctor, Miss Marcella Sherwood, who was also Superintendent of the Mission Day School for Girls was caught on her bicycle, beaten badly and left to die until some nearby Hindu shopkeepers took her to refuge. Sergeant Rowlands, an electrician to the Military Works, was killed by the crowd on his return from repairing telegraph wires. At around 2pm, the crowd attempted to break into the British civil lines, but the soldiers opened fire, killing 20-30 protesters. Angry members of the mob thereafter damaged telegraph wires and railway lines.

Jallianwala Bagh Massacre

On 13 April, a large crowd of people mostly from neighboring villages, unaware of the prohibitory orders in Amritsar, gathered in the Jallianwala Bagh. Brigadier-General Dyer arrived on the scene with his men. The

2 Disorders Inquiry Committee, 1919-1920: Report, Calcutta, Superintendent Government Printing, 1920, p. xvi.

3 Massey's Written Statement, *Evidence*, Vol. 3, 192, CAB 27/92; *Hunter Report,* 29, CAB 27/91.

troops surrounded the gathering under orders from General Dyer and blocked the only exit point and opened fire on the unarmed crowd. According to British Government report, 379 were persons were killed in firing and more than 1,000 unarmed men, women, and children were injured;[4] though other estimates suggest much higher casualties.[5] Many died when they leapt into a deep well to escape the gunfire. The situation in Punjab rapidly deteriorated and martial law was proclaimed on 15 April in the districts of Lahore and Amritsar, and shortly thereafter in three other districts.

Declaration of Martial Law

On 13 April 1919, the Lieutenant-Governor of the Punjab, with the concurrence of the General Officer Commanding the 16 Division and Chief Justice, High Court, requested the Governor General in Council to direct him to "suspend function of ordinary Criminal Courts in Amritsar and Lahore districts, to establish martial law therein and to direct trial of offenders under the Regulation of 1804, i.e., by courts martial."[6] The

4 Brigadier-General Dyer, having deployed his troops at once gave orders to open fire and continued a controlled fire on the dense crowd facing him in the enclosure (which he estimated at about 5,000 persons) for some 10 minutes until his ammunition supply was at the point of exhaustion. 1,650 rounds of 303 mark VI ammunition were fired. The fatal casualties as the result of this action are believed to be 379; the number wounded has not been exactly ascertained, but is estimated by Lord Hunter's Committee at possibly three times the number of deaths. Immediately after giving orders to cease fire, Dyer marched his troops back to police station at Ram Bagh without making any provisions for medical help to the wounded.

5 The current British Counter Insurgency Manual (Army Field Manual, *Part 1, Volume 10, Countering Insurgency*), published in April 2009 describes, "The first official linkage between general conflict, the civil authorities and the law came in 1914 when the British Manual of Military Law recorded some legal principles by which imperial policing was to be conducted. These principles seemed to satisfy the requirements of the day when General Sir John Maxwell was left to carry on without political instruction during the 1916 Easter Uprising in Dublin. However, they came under very great strain in 1919 after the rioting at Amritsar in India. Until then, the principle of 'minimum force' only applied if the situation was still under the control of the Civil Authorities. If civil control had been handed over, as was the case at Amritsar, the principle of minimum force was no longer mandatory. Fresh and updated principles were rapidly republished in the Manual of Military Law later that year. See: Army Field Manual, *Volume 1, Part 10, Countering Insurgency* (Army Code 71876, DCDC, 2009), p. 25.

6 Under the Bengal Regulation 10 of 1804, article 2, the Governor in Council was authorized to direct any public authority or officer to order the suspension (wholly or partially), of the functions of the ordinary Criminal Courts of Judicature within any part of the British territories subject to the Government and to establish martial law therein for any period of time while the British Government in India was engaged in war with

authority so asked was granted with the intimation that an Ordinance would be published the following day substituting for trials by courts-martial, trials by Tribunals similar to those under the Defence of India Act but with the powers of Field General Court Martial.

On 14 April 1919, the Martial Law Ordinance, 1919 was promulgated by Lord Chelmsford, bringing Lahore and Amritsar under martial law from the midnight between 15 and 16 April on the ground that the Governor-General was satisfied of the existence of a state of open rebellion against the authority of the government in certain parts of the Province of the Punjab. According to the Ordinance, every trial held under the Bengal State Offences Regulation of 1804, instead of being held by courts martial should be held by a Commission of three persons appointed by the local government. Two of them should be persons who had served as Sessions Judges or were qualified to be appointed Judges of a High Court. The Commission should follow in all matters the procedure regulating trials by Courts Martial prescribed by the Indian Army Act, 1911. The local government could, however, direct the Commission to follow the procedure prescribed for a Summary General Courts Martial under the Act, if such procedure was considered necessary in the interests of public safety. The finding and sentence of a Commission were not to be subject to confirmation by any authority. Section 7 gave retrospective operation to the Ordinance in that it stated that the provisions of the Ordinance would apply to persons who were charged with offences committed on or after 13 April 1919.

The Martial Law (Extension) Ordinance, 1919 extended the application of the previous Ordinance to the districts of Gujranwala, Gujarat and Lyallpur with the respective proclamations being made on 16, 19 and 24 April after applications for extending the Ordinance were made in respect of Gujranwala on 15 April, Gujarat on 18 April and Lyallpur on 20 April. Another Ordinance issued two days later, empowered any court martial or a Commission appointed under the Martial Law Ordinance, 1919 to sentence a person, when convicted, to transportation for life, or for any period not less than ten years or to rigorous imprisonment for a term between seven and fourteen years. A convicted person would not be liable to forfeiture of property, unless the Court or the Commission directed such forfeiture. Martial Law (Further Extension) Ordinance, 1919 issued on 21 April, gave further retrospective effect to the first Ordinance. By this

---

any native or other power, as well as during the existence of open rebellion against the authority of the Government, in any part of the territories aforesaid.

Ordinance, the local government was enabled to direct a Commission to try any person charged with any offence committed on or after 30 March, 1919. Martial Law (Trials Continuance) Ordinance, 1919 provided for the continuance and completion of trials pending before the Commissioners appointed under the first Martial Law Ordinance, though martial law had ceased to operate and the order suspending the functions of the ordinary criminal courts had been cancelled. In the category of pending trials were included trials for which an order had been made convening a Commission.

Martial law was withdrawn from Gujarat civil area and from certain parts of the other affected areas on 28 May 1919. At the conclusion of a Durbar held on 7 June at Amritsar, the Lieutenant-Governor announced that, except on the railway, martial law would be discontinued at midnight on 9 June in the districts of Amritsar, Gujranwala and Lyallpur and at midnight on 11 June at Lahore. It was finally withdrawn from railway lands on 25 August 1919.

Under section 3 of the Bengal State Offences Regulation of 1804, the only penalty that could be imposed by a court-martial upon a person found guilty of the crime of rebellion was death, a sentence involving forfeiture of all the criminal's property and effects. The Government of the Punjab pointed out to the Government of India that there would be many guilty persons whom it was not desirable to sentence to death and that provision should therefore be made by Ordinance for minor punishments. Accordingly, the Governor General issued Martial Law Ordinance No. III of 1919 providing that any Court-Martial or Commission convened under the previous Ordinances might, when convicting any person of any of the crimes specified in the Regulation of 1804, sentence such person to transportation for life or for any period not less than 10 years or to rigorous imprisonment for a term not less than 7 years and not exceeding 14 years. No person so convicted was to be liable to forfeiture of property unless such Court or Commission so directed.

The Governor General on 21 April passed Ordinance No. IV of 1919[7] which provided that "notwithstanding anything contained in the Martial

7 On 16 April 1919 the Government of the Punjab wired to the Government of India urging that Ordinance I should be amended so as to cover offences committed on or after 30 March, the date on which trouble began in Delhi. In a further wire on 19 April, they pointed out that the Amritsar murders occurred on 10th and those at Kasur on 12 April. Lieutenant-Governor considers it most desirable that these cases should be tried by commission under the Ordinance. Meetings which helped to prepare the ground for the rebellion took place on the 30 March at Amritsar and on 6 April at Lahore. The first riot in Lahore occurred on 10 and on 11 April; there was a mass meeting in the

Law Ordinance, 1919, the Local Government may by general or special order direct that any commission appointed under the said Ordinance shall try any person charged with any offence committed on or after 30 March 1919 and thereafter the provisions of the said Ordinance shall apply to such trials accordingly, and a commission may pass in respect of any such offence any sentence authorized by law."

Martial Law Proclamation

On 21 April 1919, the General Officer Commanding the 16th Division issued the following proclamation, which was published for general information:

> Whereas Martial Law has been proclaimed and is in force in the districts of Lahore, Amritsar and Gujranwala, it is hereby notified that until further intimation, the following Regulations will be enforced within the limits of the 16th Indian Division in all places to which Martial Law has been or may be extended:
>
> **No. l: Law and Tribunals**
>
> Martial Law has been declared subject to (a) the maintenance of ordinary courts for ordinary offences, and (b) the establishment under the Martial Law Ordinance, 1919, of Special Tribunals for offences specified in section 2 of the Bengal State Offences Regulation, 1804. The result of the establishment of Martial Law is that, subject to the said Ordinance, plenary power is vested in the General Officer Commanding the Division of prescribing offences, penalties, courts and procedure in regard to all matters connected with or arising out of the present disturbances and of taking all measures and issuing all orders that he may deem necessary for the suppression of these disturbances. In the exercise of these powers, the General Officer Commanding the Division is pleased to declare that a breach of any of the Regulations Nos. 2-15 below, shall be deemed to be an offence.
>
> **No. 2: Offences-Rebellion, aiding Rebels, endangering Public Safety**
>
> No person shall (a) be actively in arms against His Majesty, or (b) directly incite others to take up arms against His Majesty, or (c)

Shahi Mosque at which inflammatory speeches were made. Evidence also showed that emissaries from outside the province visited Punjab shortly before outbreaks in various places. His Honour fears that, if date 13 April is allowed to stand, it may be impossible to use the Ordinance against those with whom the real responsibility rests.

actively aid or assist the rebels, or (d) commit any overt act by which the safety of His Majesty's Forces or subjects is endangered.

No. 3: Assisting or harbouring Rebels

No person shall assist or harbour rebels by giving them information, or by supplying them with shelter, food, drink, money, clothes, arms, ammunition, stores, forage, or means of conveyance, or by assisting them in any way to evade apprehension.

No. 4: Failing to report Rebels

Every person (a) who receives information of gatherings or intended gatherings of rebels, or (b) who knows or has reason to believe that any of his relatives or dependants have joined or are about to join the rebels, shall without delay give full information thereof to the nearest Military or Civil authority.

No. 5: Seditious Language and Publications

1. No person shall make use of any language with the intention either (a) of raising or fomenting disaffection among His Majesty's subjects, or (b) of promoting hostility between different classes of such subjects.

2. No person shall print, publish, circulate, or have in his possession any publications containing seditious articles or articles likely to promote disaffection or bad feeling.

No. 6: Protection of Railways, Canals, and Telegraphs

No person shall (a) in any way interfere with the working of the railways or canals, (b) damage or tamper with any material or property connected with railways and canals, (c) damage or interfere with telegraph or telephone lines or apparatus of wireless telegraph installation, (d) tap with the intention of reading off messages any telegraph or telephone lines. The attempt to commit or the abetment of any breach of this regulation shall be punished as a breach of the regulation.

No. 7: Control of Transport

1. No person shall, save under a proper permit, have in his possession any motor vehicle.

2. Every person using any such vehicle shall pass any guard or sentry at a speed not exceeding 6 miles an hour, and shall stop the car if so ordered by any guard or sentry, and shall carry on such a vehicle a suitable light between the hours of sunset and sunrise.

These Regulations do not apply to Civil Officers of Government or to members of His Majesty's Forces (Naval, Military, or Air Force, Indian Defence Force or Police) in respect of any vehicles lawfully issued to them as such officers or members.

No. 8: Control of Travelling and Movements

Where any orders have been issued regarding the control of travelling and movements, no person shall enter or leave the area to which Martial Law has been extended or move to and fro within it, in contravention of such orders.[8]

No. 9: Control of Meetings

No person shall, save under a proper permit, convene or attend any meeting of more than five persons except in the case of (a) a meeting *bona fide* held for religious purposes in an authorised place of worship; (b) a meeting of a Municipal Committee or any other similar public body; (c) a meeting of persons residing in one house and gathering in such house.

No. 10: Escaping

No person shall (a) escape or attempt to escape from any prison or other custody in which he is for the time being confined or restrained under Martial Law; or (b) abet any other person in escaping or attempting to escape from any such prison or custody.

No. 11: Disobeying and obstructing Officers

No person shall (a) disobey or neglect to obey any order given by any Military or Civil Officer in the execution of his duty when administering Martial Law; or (b) obstruct, impede, or interfere in any manner with any Military or Civil Officer or other person who is carrying out the orders of any authority administering Martial Law, or who is otherwise acting in the execution of his duty under Martial Law.

8 This is amended text. The original text of Regulation 8 viz., "No person shall, save under such conditions as may be prescribed, enter or leave this area or move to and fro within it;" was amended by proclamation dated 21 April 1919.

No. 12: False News and Reports

No person shall disseminate false intelligence which he knows to be false, or spread reports calculated to create alarm.

No. 13: Defacing Martial Law Notices

No person shall destroy, deface, or in any way tamper with any notice exhibited under Martial Law while such notice is in force.

No. 14: Production of Permits

Every person shall, when required to do so, give his correct name and address, and produce his permit or pass to any Military or Civil Officer acting under the authority of these Regulations, or to any soldier, volunteer, or policeman in uniform.

No. 15: Miscellaneous Offences

No person shall commit any act or be guilty of any omission (a) which is to the prejudice of good order of the public safety; or (b) which is calculated to mislead, or hamper the movements of, or imperil the success of, His Majesty's Forces.

No. 16: Penalties

Any person who contravenes any of the foregoing Regulations 2-15 (inclusive) shall be liable to trial by an officer authorized to dispose of an offence summarily under Martial Law. Such an officer may sentence an offender to imprisonment, rigorous or simple, which may extend to two years or to fine not exceeding Rs. 1,000, or to both, and to six months' imprisonment in default of payment of fine, and may also inflict whipping in addition to, or in lieu of, any other punishment which he is empowered to inflict.

No. 17: Arrest and Trials

(a) For every offence against these Regulations the offender may be arrested with or without warrant from any officer authorized to dispose of offences. For minor offences against these Regulations the offender will not necessarily be arrested, but may be summoned to appear before such officer.

(b) Whenever a person is summoned to appear or is arrested under Martial Law, the charge against him shall without unnecessary delay be investigated by an officer authorized to dispose of an offence summarily under Martial Law or by some officer deputed by him and not under the rank of Captain, or, at his request, by a Civil Magistrate, or by the police.

(c) The investigating officer will dismiss a charge brought before him if in his opinion the evidence does not show that some offence under Martial Law has been committed, or if in his discretion he thinks the charge ought not to be proceeded with.

(d) At the conclusion of the hearing, if the investigating officer is of the opinion that the charge ought to be proceeded with, he shall without unnecessary delay, either (i) dispose of the case summarily; or (ii) in cases where he considers that the offence calls for a more severe punishment than he is empowered to inflict, refer the case to the Legal Remembrance to the Punjab Government, who after considering the evidence will decide whether to convene a Commission under the Martial Law Ordinance, 1919, for the disposal of the case or whether it should be remanded to the office referring it for disposal or to any other officer exercising powers under these Regulations; or (iii) remand the accused in custody while further inquiries are being made. In case (iii), if within reasonable time sufficient evidence is not forthcoming the accused person shall be discharged.

No. 18: Officer authorized to dispose of Offences summarily under Martial Law

The districts in which Martial Law has been declared shall be divided up into areas and for each such area an officer or officers will be authorized to dispose of offences summarily under Martial Law. Such officers shall be known as Area Officers.

In addition to the Area Officers, every officer commanding a station or regiment, every field officer and every officer nominated by a General Officer Commanding a Brigade, or by the Officer Commanding, Lahore Civil Area or by the Local Government, is hereby authorized to dispose of offences summarily under Martial Law.

Act of Indemnity: On 25 September 1919, an Act of Indemnity was passed to indemnify officers of Government and other persons in respect of certain acts done under martial law. In terms of this Act, no suit or other legal proceeding is to lie against any such person for any act done or purporting to be done for the purpose of maintaining or restoring order in any part of British India where martial law was enforced on or after

30 March 1919 and before 26 August 1919, provided such person acted in good faith and in a reasonable belief that his action was necessary for the said purpose. This Act is an enactment to indemnify all excesses committed by the concerned officers and other persons during period of enforcement of martial law.

Commissions

The Governor-General in Council under the Bengal State Offences Regulation, 1804, suspended the functions of ordinary criminal courts of judicature within the districts of Amritsar, Lahore, and Gujranwala for offences mentioned in section 4 of the Regulation. Four commissions were set up in Lahore to try offences under the Regulation of 1804 as extended by the Ordinances. They tried 114 cases involving 852 accused. Of these, 581 were convicted mostly of convictions being recorded under section 121 of the Indian Penal Code, which dealt with waging war against the King-Emperor. Of these, 108 persons were sentenced to death, 265 to transportation for life, 2 to transportation for other periods, 5 were sentenced to imprisonment for 10 years, 85 for 7 years and 104 for shorter periods.

The sentences passed by the Martial Law Commissions were considerably reduced by Government. Out of 108 death sentences, only 23 were maintained, and the remaining were commuted to transportation in some cases, and in the rest to sentences of imprisonment going down to one year. Out of 265 sentences of transportation, only two were maintained, five were commuted altogether, and the rest were commuted to imprisonments varying from 10 years to one year.[9] There was a great disproportion between the original sentences and those to which they

9 Substantial commutation of these sentences was made by the Local Government. Of the 108 death sentences, only 23, including 5 where execution were stayed pending an appeal to the Privy Council, had been maintained. Of the remaining 85 sentences, 23 were commuted to transportation for life, 26 to rigorous imprisonment for 10 years, 14 to 7 years, 1 to 6 years, 10 to 5 years and 11 to periods ranging from 1 to 4 years. Of the sentences of transportation for life, 2 only were maintained, in 5 the Government ordered immediate release of the convicts, while the remaining 258 sentences were commuted to terms of imprisonment, 2 of them for 10 years and the remainder for periods ranging from 1 to 7 years. Two sentences of transportation for 14 and 10 years respectively were reduced to 3 years' imprisonment. Of 191 effective sentences of imprisonment, the sentence was allowed to stand in 53 cases, in 2 cases the convicts were released and in the remaining 136 cases reductions were ordered, the average period of sentence before and after reduction being approximately 5 years 9 months to 1 year 9 months respectively.

were commuted, suggesting the severity of punishments awarded by the Commissions.

Summary Courts and Exclusion of Legal Practitioner

Under the authority of various Ordinances and the Notifications by the two General Officer's Commanding, the following courts were constituted during the period of martial Law:

- Tribunals composed of three Judges, which were empowered to try any person who was charged with any offence committed on or after 30 March. These tribunals tried only major offences in relation to disorders.
- Summary courts were presided over by Area Officers and Civil Officers authorized in that behalf to dispose of cases under Martial Regulations. Besides all officers designated as Area Officers, this term included every Officer Commanding a station or regiment, every Field Officer, every Officer Commanding a brigade, and all officers appointed by the General Officer Commanding the Lahore Civil Area or by the Local Government. These summary courts had powers to pass sentences of imprisonment of two years, fines up to Rs. 1,000 and also whipping.
- Summary courts presided over by officers nominated by the Lieutenant-Governor, who were authorized by the notifications of 5 May 1919, issued by the General Officers Commanding, to try offences against the ordinary law, arising out of the disturbances but committed before the declaration of martial law.

The notifications laid down the following limitations to the exercise of powers of those summary courts: (a) These courts shall take cognizance only of cases sent by the police; (b) These courts shall not try any person for an act which is not an offence under the ordinary law; (c) These courts shall not try any person for an offence exclusively triable by a Court of Sessions; (d) These courts shall not pass in respect of any offence any sentence which is not authorised by the ordinary law for that offence; (e) These courts shall not pass any sentence which could not be passed by a First Class Magistrate. The legal sanction for constituting the last class of summary courts with powers to try offences against the ordinary law committed before the proclamation of martial law and for clothing them with retrospective powers was not very clear. The legal practitioners from other places were denied their assistance to individuals undergoing trial at various forums. This was brought about by an order issued on 14 May by the General Officers Commanding the Lahore and Rawalpindi Division respectively:

> Notice is hereby given to all people concerned that legal practitioners whose ordinary place of residence is outside the Punjab will not be allowed to enter the martial law area without the permission of the martial law administrator.

Disorders Inquiry Committee

The administration of martial law in the Punjab was marked by brutality and was therefore evaluated by the Disorders Inquiry Committee or Hunter Committee.[10] The Hunter Committee took written statements from the major civil and military figures in each district that was affected by the disturbances. This included statements from Indian and British officials. It then interviewed each official based on what he had submitted in his written statement. The Committee heard evidence in Delhi, Lahore, Ahmadabad and Bombay. All evidence was heard in public except by the former Lieutenant Governor of Punjab, Michael O'Dwyer; Lieutenant-General Havelock Hudson, Adjutant General; Mr. J. P. Thompson (Chief Secretary to the Government of Punjab); and Mr Umar Hayat Khan, a Muslim notable. The Committee's conclusions were divided along racial lines between the Majority Report, comprised of all the European members, and the Minority Report, comprised of all the Indian members. The Indian

10 The Governor General in Council, with the approval of the Secretary of State, appointed Disorders Inquiry Committee to investigate the disturbances in Bombay, Delhi and the Punjab, their causes, and the measures taken to cope with them. Lord William Hunter, Senator of the College of Justice in Scotland was appointed as President of the Committee. Mr. H.G. Stokes, Secretary to the Government of Madras, and later Mr. Williamson served as secretary to the Committee. The Committee held their first meeting at Delhi on 29 October when the procedure to be adopted by them was discussed. The Committee heard the evidence of witnesses for 8 days at Delhi, for 29 days at Lahore, for 6 days at Ahmadabad and for 3 days at Bombay. All the witnesses, with the exception of Michael O'Dwyer, General Hudson, Mr. Thompson and Sir Umar Hayat Khan, who gave their evidence in camera, were examined in public. The Committee submitted their recommendations in the form of a majority and minority report. The majority report was signed by the President and four members of Committee, Mr. Justice Rankin, General Barrow, and Messrs. Rice and Smith. The minority report was signed by Sir C. H. Setalvad, Pandit Jagat Narayan and Sahibzada Sultan Ahmed Khan. While the majority report found that a state of rebellion existed, necessitating or justifying the adoption of that measure, the minority was of the opinion that the disorders did not amount to rebellion and that the disturbances could have been suppressed and order restored without abrogating the control of the civil authorities or calling in military force save as auxiliary to the civil power.

members of the Hunter Committee did not agree with the resolutions of the European members. According to Minority view, it appeared that regime was bent on exacting punishment rather than restoring order to the civil power.

The Indians members' Minority Report found discrepancies with the entire system of British rule in the province. Unlike the decision that there was no rebellion in Jallianwala Bagh to justify Dyer's actions, upon evaluating whether it was necessary to enforce martial law, the Hunter Committee's European Majority Report found that open rebellion did exist in the Punjab; hence, it declared that martial law was an appropriate action. The riots, it reasoned, targeted British persons, whether official or not, and spread to surrounding areas while sharing underlying causes, such as resentment over the Rowlatt Bills. Consequently, the committee's Majority Report, which did not include the opinion of any of the three Indian members of the Committee, concluded that the government was justified in declaring martial law. The Majority Report stated, "the element of rebellion as distinct from riot on the one hand and from political opposition to the Government on the other, can be traced throughout... An intention to paralyse the arm of Government by extensive destruction of Government buildings and of means of communication can hardly find vent in practice upon a considerable scale and at the same time fall short of open rebellion."

The Minority opinion held a different view. The Minority Report disapproved of most actions taken by civil and military officers because of their punitive and excessive nature. In other words, it found that the administration of martial law was marked by attempts to humiliate Indians and this led to embittered opinion. The Minority opinion also emphasized that no organized rebellion had been set alight in the Punjab and argued that to suggest that the Majority Report, was "an exaggerated view of the events." The Minority Report did not approve of the vast majority of actions by civil and military officers during the time in question because it considered them punitive, excessive and often designed to humiliate and embitter. The Minority Report's assessment appears accurate. There was no Punjabi conspiracy to overthrow the Raj. The violence was not intended to paralyze the Raj. Rather, it was a way to vent frustration with the treatment meted out to the Indians by a despotic government at a moment, when nationalism was becoming a mass movement, and rising expectations of self-government chafed against imperial intransigence. There was no wide-scale rebellion in the Punjab, but European members of the Hunter

Committee believed the statements of Punjab's administrators that the province was waging a war against the Raj. These officials based their perceptions not on evidence, but on uncorroborated rumors and general fears of conspiracy. Indian members of the Committee were less willing to accept this idea without evidence to substantiate it.[11]

Reasons for Martial Law and its Continuance

The Disorder Committee considered the question whether the Government of the Punjab was justified in applying to the Government of India for authority to declare martial law under the Bengal Regulation of 1804. According to the report of the Committee, Ordinance I of 1919 commenced with the recital that "the Governor General is satisfied that a state of open rebellion against the authority of the Government exists in certain parts of the Province of the Punjab." This recital was in terms of the Regulation and the language seems reasonably clear and free from technicality. According to the Committee, if there was room for any modification of its ordinary meaning when the Regulation was construed as a whole, the specific intention or particular value of the language must be left by for determination by a court of law. The Committee therefore, did not make any comment on this issue. According to the Committee, "if martial law has to be declared, it is still an evil which will be made worse if it is introduced irregularly. On the other hand, if there is statutory authority and provision covering the case, there is great advantage both for the people and for the Government in the use of a power which is regularized and can be the more readily examined." The Committee was of the opinion that it was right and wise to proceed as to this fundamental matter under statutory authority, if the provision was applicable to the facts.

According to Committee Report, what the Bengal Regulation of 1804 conferred was a power. That the power ensues only upon fulfillment of certain conditions is an element which does not convert discretion into a command. The power is given because, in the language of the Regulation itself, "it may be expedient" that it should be used. It does not seem impossible upon any view of what constitutes "open rebellion" that this condition should exist and yet should be confined to so few persons, or otherwise should be so little formidable, as not to justify the introduction of martial law. If, on the other hand, it was necessary and right to resort to martial law, the conduct of the Government is justified in principle and

11 See Shereen Fatima Ilahi, 2008, *The Empire of Violence: Strategies of British Rule in India and Ireland in the Aftermath of the Great War*, Unpublished Ph.D. Thesis, The University of Texas at Austin, pp. 402.

intention: any error which could be shown to exist is an error of method. Though not without a real importance as we have already shown, a mistake in method is of less importance: it would mean at most that a special Ordinance was necessary and should have been passed.[12]

Aerial Bombing of Gujranwalla

Gujranwalla, roughly 55 km from Lahore, had a population of about 30,000. It held a *hartal* on 6 April without any untoward incident. However, once news of Gandhi's arrest and the violence in Lahore, Amritsar, and surrounding areas reached the town on 12 April, another *hartal* was planned for 14 April in Wazirabad, a town roughly twenty miles away. A number of Indians had gathered at the train station to make the trip, but without enough trains to carry all of them, and the station stopped issuing tickets to the travelers. Also on the morning of 14 April, a dead calf was found hanging from Katchi bridge near the railway station. Although authorities had it removed and buried promptly, rumors spread that the police were responsible for the slaughter, in order to create divisions within the Hindu-Muslim unity movement. This further angered the crowd at the railway station, which by the late morning was preventing any passengers from traveling to Wazirabad by stoning the trains and by setting fire to the nearby railway bridge. The crowd also began cutting telegraph wires and set fire to the Katchi bridge.

When Mr. Heron, the Superintendent of Police, appeared and ordered them to disperse, they responded by throwing stones at him. After the police fired on the mob, few individuals were wounded. The mob withdrew to a safe distance, but continued to throw stones. Each time a mob was fired upon, it would disperse temporarily or reassemble elsewhere. Another crowd attempted to attack the local jail, but was dispersed by gunfire.

By 3.10 pm, airplanes began flying over the area. Major Carberry's plane arrived first and he dropped three bombs on a crowd of 150.[13] One bomb did not explode, but the others managed to kill a woman and a boy, and wounded many men. Major Carberry also fired 50 rounds from his machine gun to ensure that the crowd scattered. Then he dropped two

12 Report of the Committee Appointed by the Government of India to Investigate the Disturbances in the Punjab, etc., London: His Majesty's Stationery Office, 1920, p. 108.

13 The following instructions had been verbally given to Major Carberry by Lieutenant Colonel F. F. Minchin, D.S.O., M.C.: that the native city was not to be bombed unless necessary; that crowds were to be bombed if in the open; and that gatherings near the local villages were to be dispersed if coming or going from Gujranwala.

bombs on a group of 50 persons who had gathered about a mile away from the first bombsite, but there were no casualties. He dropped one more bomb on a crowd of 200 gathered near Khalsa High School and Boarding House where 160 boys lived. A second plane shot twenty-five rounds from its machine gun on a crowd of about 23 persons, but did not drop any bomb. In aerial bombing and gunfire, the total official count was 11 dead and 27 wounded.

On 15 April, Lieutenant Dodkins was ordered to use his plane to inspect the damage done to the railway lines to Lahore. While doing so, he opened fire on a crowd of 20 gathered in a field outside Gujranwalla, which dispersed without casualties. He found another crowd of 30 to 50 men standing outside a house listening to someone giving a speech, but they all ran inside upon seeing Dodkins' plane. In response, he dropped a bomb on the neighboring house, presumably because he missed the intended target. When evaluating whether this action was necessary, the Hunter Committee stated, "We have no information that this caused any casualties but no sufficient explanation has been given to us to justify the use of this aeroplane for purposes of offensive action." The total casualties in Gujranwala on 14 April including those killed by bombs and machine-guns and those shot by the police, were 11 killed and 27 wounded. Subsequently, martial law was imposed at midnight of 17 April 1919.

The Lt. Governor of the Punjab, Michael O'Dwyer, justified the use of aeroplanes for dropping eight bombs, of which two did not explode. According to him, the spread of disorder from Amritsar to Lahore to Kasur was alarming, and troops were not always readily available for deployment to quell the disturbances. He stated, "We knew a very dangerous situation had arisen in Gujranwalla; there were no troops there and very few police. The mob had burned the railway bridge necessary for troops from Lahore to reach the town, and it had destroyed two other bridges that troops from Sialkot, the other nearby garrison, would have used. Cut telegram lines made communication difficult, further impeding the transfer of soldiers."

In view of the Minority Report, actions of Major Carberry in dropping bombs on the Khalsa High School and on the people in the two villages were not justified as appropriate discretion was not exercised in executing the orders. Further, his action in firing from the machine gun into crowds in the street of the city was considered excessive. As regards, firing of 15 April by Lieutenant Dodkins over Gujranwala and its vicinity, the minority view was that unjustified orders were given by the authority and also Dodkins exceeded the instruction given to him by the superiors.

Firing from Armoured Trains

On 15 April, an armoured train which had machine guns and search lights, in charge of a British officer and British soldiers, was sent from Lahore to Sheikhupura. At Sheikhupura, Lala Sri Ram Sud, Sub-Divisional Officer, got into the train and proceeded to Chuharkana Station. Some of the residents of Chuharkana and other adjoining villages had on 14 and 15 April done considerable damage to the railway lines and the railway station. The armoured train proceeded slowly from Sheikhupura and arrived near Chuharkana Station in the early hours of 16 April. Near the distant signal they found an obstruction placed on the line. After removing this obstruction they were proceeding further when they found men about the line and opened fire, killing one individual. The armoured train then proceeded to the Chuharkana Station, but none of the rioters were there then. Lala Sri Ram Sud and the military escort got down from the armoured train and went into a factory where it was suspected that some men were in hiding. Some rifle shots were fired in the dark with a view to terrify the village people. There were no casualties. On the morning of 16 April, the armoured car proceeded a mile further and pulled up in the vicinity of Chuharkana market. From this point, the machine gun was fired from the armoured train into the village and later the party proceeded into the village and done some further firing. The people in the village who were fired at were not at that time engaged in any acts of violence. The armoured train in which Sri Ram Sud was, then returned to Sheikhupura where he alighted and from there went back to Lahore.

Again on the 18 April, the armoured train with Lala Sri Ram Sud went from Sheikhupura and pulled up near the village of Mahnianwalia. The party went to the village and fired into a crowd of about 25 people found there. These people were not engaged in any criminal activity or violent act. Justifying his action, Lala Sri Ram Sud stated ".... both the villages of Mahnianwalia and Pucca Dulla were concerned in the mischief and had looted that station. Myself and the officer commanding took counsel together and thought it advisable that some lesson must be taught to these villagers. Then we walked into the village. Myself, the officer commanding, and some soldiers walked together, and on the way a crowd that was on the fields was fired upon." According to minority view, Sub-Divisional Officer Lala Sri Ram Sud considered the whole village as guilty and resorted to firing with a view to inflicting punishment and making an impression. The firing from armoured car, in view of the minority report, was not justified.

Sentence of Flogging

There were 258 cases, where the sentences of whipping inflicted in the districts of Lahore, Kasue, Chuharkana, Gurjanwala, Amritsar and Gujrat under martial law, ranging from 5 to 30. In addition, the flogging was inflicted on the six boys at Kasur and the flogging inflicted on the six persons under trial for the attack on Miss Sherwood for the breach of Fort discipline. It does not include any flogging resorted to when the mobile columns visited the various villages. The normal procedure adopted was to strip the person to be whipped and to tie him to a framework and then lash him. It was also reported that a marriage party in Lahore Civil Area were arrested, because they were more than ten, in violation of the Martial Law Order 1, and some of them were flogged. The area officer in passing sentence on one of them made the following record, "He is young. Flogging will do him good." Initially, flogging was done publicly; but after 19 April it was carried out in Lahore in the Central Jail and court compounds. The sentences of flogging were defended by the British officers before the Committee on the ground that it was the most convenient and speedy way of dealing with offences under martial law, and that it was the ordinary punishment inflicted in the Army.

Arrests

During the period of martial law, both police and military arrested people on mere suspicion and kept in custody for considerable periods. Some of them were never brought to trial, and others brought before the court had to be discharged because there was absolutely no evidence against them.[14] A large number of individuals were kept for many days under arrest without being brought before a court and remanded, and facilities for bail were curtailed, even with regard to bailable offences. The military officer tried to justify arrest of certain leading people at Amritsar, Gujranwala,

14 Dr. Kedar Nath, an old-retired Assistant Surgeon, occupying considerable position in Amritsar, was arrested and handcuffed and kept under arrest for about a month, but without being brought to trial. Similarly Dr. Manohar Lal, a Barrister-at-Law of standing in Lahore, was arrested, apparently because he was one of the trustees of the paper "Tribune"; he was arrested and handcuffed and kept in the Lahore Jail for about a month, and released without being brought to trial. Mr. Gurdial Singh, a Barrister at Amritsar, at considerable risk to himself, did his best to prevent the crowd from getting unruly at the railway footbridge at Amritsar. He was also arrested and discharged. At Gurdaspur about eight pleaders were arrested and kept in custody for nearly six weeks, and were then released without being brought to trial. Report of the Committee Appointed by the Government of India to Investigate the Disturbances in the Punjab, etc., London: His Majesty's Stationery Office, 1920, p. 139.

Lahore, Wazirabad and Sheikhupura and stated that such arrests were likely to have most good effect. No arrest warrants were issued in these cases and they were arrested under the Defence of India Act. Lieutenant-Colonel O'Brien, who appeared before the Committee, stated that he had a conversation with the Chief Secretary over the telephone, and he was given to understand that if he took action hurriedly it would be legalized afterwards if it was done in good faith. In all, 789 persons were arrested during the period of martial law, and were never brought to trial.

Harassment and Illegal/ Fancy Punishments

During the martial law in various districts, over and above securing the maintenance of law and order, military commanders issues punitive orders to harass citizens. The Curfew orders, the restrictions on "travelling, the impressments of vehicles, the orders regarding roll calls involved serious inconvenience and humiliation to the people of Lahore.

In order to teach the population of Lahore a lesson, the military commander notified that all Indians to surrender their motor cars and other vehicles, electric lights and fans, and any misuse or waste of pipe water would be deemed a contravention of martial law. During inquiry, Lieutenant Colonel Johnson stated, "I thought it desirable to bring home to them all-loyal or disloyal alike - some of the inconveniences of martial law in the hope and belief that in future the weight of their influence will be whole heartedly thrown against seditious movements likely to lead to the introduction of martial law. In reference to taking of motor cars belonging to Indians and giving them to Europeans, Johnson, when he was asked whether it was the right thing to do, stated, "Yes, I wanted to teach them a lesson." By Order VIII issued on 16 April, Johnson notified, "All orders to be issued under martial "law will be handed to such owners of property as I may select, and it will be the duty of such owners of property to exhibit and to keep exhibiting all such orders. The duty of protecting such orders will, therefore, devolve on the owners of property and failure to "ensure the proper protection and continued exhibition of my orders will result in severe punishment." The selection of these properties were made on the recommendation of the Criminal Investigation Department police on the ground that the owners of the properties were not "notoriously loyal" or were suspected to be not very loyal.[15]

15 Report of the Committee Appointed by the Government of India to Investigate the Disturbances in the Punjab, London: His Majesty's Stationery Office, 1920, p. 119.

During the period of martial law, a notice was stuck on the compound wall of the Sanatan Dharm College. It was subsequently torn by somebody. Colonel Johnson ordered that every male person found in the precincts of the compound should be arrested. Sixty-five students and all the professors of that college were accordingly taken to the Fort, three miles away, and interned there for about 30 hours. They were then released after taking guarantees from the Principal that the defacing of notices would not happen again. Lieutenant-Colonel Johnson informed the Committee that he was waiting for an opportunity to show them the power of martial law; and he took this opportunity of doing so.

Lieutenant-Colonel Johnson also issued orders that the students of three colleges in Lahore should attend a roll-call four times a day for a period of nearly three weeks. This necessitated a large number of students (around 1,000) walking in the hot May sun of Lahore 16 miles every day. Johnson was under no misapprehension about it, and when his attention was drawn to the hardship involved he said, "No hardship at all for able-bodied young men. It was only a mild type of physical exercise for able-bodied young men." According Johnson, this order was passed not as a punishment, but for the purpose of keeping the students out of mischief. When it was put to him whether it ever occurred to him that this treatment of students was eminently calculated to make those young men very bitter with hatred towards the British Government for the rest of their lives, he answered that the atmosphere of the colleges was such that he could not make it worse.

Some of the students were expelled permanently from the college and were declared unfit to enter any college in future; others were punished by being rusticated for various reasons; and yet others had their scholarships and stipends stopped. Apparently, these punishments were awarded not after investigation into individual cases, but Johnson decided that a certain percentage of the students in each college should be punished. When the Principals of the various colleges sent up the lists of punishments, in cases in which he thought that the punishments were either not adequate or did not come up to the proper percentages, he remitted the list to the Principals concerned to bring up the lists to the proper percentage.[16]

Orders were issued, which were made applicable to the districts of Gujranwala, Gujrat, and Lyallpur, that students should attend roll-calls

16 Report of the Committee Appointed by the Government of India to Investigate the Disturbances in the Punjab, etc., London: His Majesty's Stationery Office, 1920, p. 120.

daily once or more often as the area officer determined, and there salute a British flag. These parades were to be attended also by the teachers. In the Gujrat area, the order also provided that "if any boy is absent without any proper cause, his father would attend in his place." These orders were enforced even in the case of infants of four and five years. The following humiliating order, which remained in force for one week, was issued by Major Smith on 19 May and all students were punished because two failed to Salaam:

> Whereas two students of over 14 years of age failed to salaam to me on the 16th instant, thereby contravening 'Notice under Martial Law No. 7,' and whereas it now transpires that they gave me their wrong names and addresses, I hereby direct that all students of over 14 years of age of the (1) Municipal Board School, Lyallpur; (2) Arya School, Lyallpur; Sanatan Dharm School, Lyallpur; (4) Government High School, Lyallpur, shall parade in front of my office in the public library at 0800 hours daily until the two offenders are given up, or failing this until such time as I consider necessary. They will be accompanied by a schoolmaster from each school, and will march past a Union Jack which will be erected in front of my office, and salaam to it as they pass, under the supervision of an officer appointed by me. The schoolmaster accompanying the boys of each school, will bring with him daily a nominal roll of all the boys of over 14 years of age at his school, signed as correct by the headmaster, and showing, against the name of each absentee from the parade, the reason for his absence. These parades will commence from Monday, 19th instant.

In Kasur,[17] the police rounded up almost every male resident and "paraded" them in front of witnesses. These men were gathered at the

17 Kasur, is a small town less than 40 miles outside of Lahore (within Lahore District) did not experience much anti-Rowlatt protest. In fact, no *hartal* took place at Kasur on 30 March or 6 April. But on 11 April, a crowd led by a local Muslim shopkeeper, Nadir Ali Shah, enforced a *hartal* by forcing a number of shopkeepers to close. The *hartal* continued the next day, April 12, and Nadir Ali Shah led another crowd toward the railway station. He carried with him a black flag to signify that they were bemoaning the loss of liberty, and this they did with an intensity rivaling the mourning rituals of the Muslim month of Muharram. Eventually crowd turned to violence and attacked parts of the railway station and the Telegraph Office. The mob turned toward a nearby train from Ferozepore upon which were few European passengers. They were attacked by the crowd but managed to escape to safety. One of the European warrant officers on the train was beaten to death with sticks. Riot ensued and the crowd burned down the post office before attacking the *tahsil* (revenue office), at which point police opened fire, killing four and wounding many. Troops arrived in Kasur the next day, the day of the shooting at Amritsar and martial law was imposed at midnight, 19 April 1919.

railway station, where they were kept for several hours in the sun, and made to dance about a small round arena in which certain Europeans were seated who inspected the faces of those who danced round them. Captain Doveton, the commanding officer, invented "fancy punishments" for minor crimes that he believed did not warrant courts-martial. Most commonly, he would sentence convicts to work on the railway, but one Indian was offered the choice between skipping and working. He chose to skip and from that point on, a number of individuals were sentenced to skipping. Another Indian who was also a poet received a sentenced to write and read in public a poem in praise of martial law. Doveton also ordered all convicts to salaam by touching their foreheads to the ground. The Captain explained to the Committee that the main object was to impress on the people that everybody was not his own master and they had got to conform to order. He meant to remind them that the British were their masters. Residents of Kasur were also flogged and many respectable residents of the town were arrested and kept in gaol without any reason. Some of them had to be released after several weeks when nothing incriminating could be found against them. In the town of 25,000, martial law administrators inflicted a total of 605 stripes upon the residents. Kasur was the only area in which the regulation "cat" was used for whipping rather than a cane.

There were reports that some of the students had taken part in the disturbances in Kasur, and two of them were identified as taking part in the riots and were subsequently arrested and sentenced. One schoolmaster represented that his boys had gone out of hand. Mr. Marsden, Sub-Divisional Officer, Kasur, suggested and Lieutenant-Colonel Macrae approved that certain boys should be picked out to bear punishment for the whole. Thereupon the headmasters were asked to select six boys and send them. When they were so sent up, they appeared to the authorities to be miserable looking. It was thereupon ordered that all the boys of the schools concerned should be paraded at the station, and the six biggest boys were selected. They were given six stripes each.

In two cases, individuals were shot dead by sentries in Kasur, one while running away and the other while resisting his arrest.

Threat of Reprisal: Orders for reprisals against the property of people who had left Gujranwala, Wazirabad, and Hafizabad, in order to avoid arrest, were issued. These orders (Orders Nos. 28 and 29) threatened reprisals not only against the property of those absconders but also against that of their fathers or nearest relations. In another case, at the town of Sheikhupura in the district of Gujrarnwala, three brothers had absconded.

Not only was their property confiscated, but their father was arrested and his property was also confiscated.

By his Order No. 1, Colonel Johnson intimated that if any fire-arm was discharged or bomb thrown at "the military or the police, the most drastic reprisals will instantly be made against the properties surrounding the outrage." Johnson clarified to the Committee that he called 100 leading men of the city and had explained to them that if any bomb fell or that if any British soldier or anybody was wounded or injured as a result of that bomb, that spot would be deemed the centre of a circle having a diameter of a hundred yards and that he would give them one hour to remove from that circle every living thing, and at the end of that time, the demolition of every building other than mosques or temples would take place inside that circle. He further intimated that the continuance of electric lights and water supply would depend on the good behaviour of the inhabitants and their obedience to the orders. Johnson frankly admitted before the Committee that these measures were designed to teach lesson.[18]

In the month of April during martial law, about Rs. 3,500 were collected from the inhabitants of Wazirabad, at the rate of one rupee per house, and the amount was used for supplying the wants of the soldiers stationed there.

Crawling Order

Most orders passed in Lahore were repeated in Amritsar, e.g., the curfew order, prohibition against gatherings and processions, restrictions on travelling, exhibition of martial law notices, impressments of cycles, declaration of stocks, fixing of rates of foodstuffs, etc. Among the orders passed by General Dyer at Amritsar, was an order that has been styled "Crawling Order." This order was passed on 19 April, eight days after General Dyer arrived and four days after the declaration of martial law. This order was passed with reference to a street where Miss Sherwood had been brutally attacked on the night of 10 April by a mob. The street was narrow, but of considerable length, and had abutting on it on both sides houses of different dimensions. The order was to the effect that no Indians should be allowed to pass through the street, except by crawling on all fours a distance of about 150 yards, between the two pickets which were

18 Report of the Committee Appointed by the Government of India to Investigate the Disturbances in the Punjab, etc., London: His Majesty's Stationery Office, 1920, p. 121.

placed at certain points in the street to enforce obedience to this order. The pickets had instructions to be there from 6 am to 8 pm.

Within a few minutes after crawling order was passed and pickets were placed, 12 persons had to be arrested for being insolent. Dyer ordered them to be taken into custody and the police took them through that street and the picket enforced the crawling order on them. General Dyer was pleased at this providential result. Unfortunately, many of the houses on the 150 yard long street had no back doors, forcing the residents to crawl every time they left their houses. When Sir Michael O'Dwyer noticed the crawling order, he ordered it to be immediately rescinded.

General Dyer further put up a triangle in this street for flogging people, and six persons who were under arrest in the fort for the assault on Miss Sherwood, on being found to have committed some breach of fort discipline, were brought and flogged there. These people were ultimately found guilty of the assault on Miss Sherwood, but at the time they were so flogged, they were merely under-trial prisoners. Among the other orders issued with martial law was an order from Dyer for all Indians to demonstrate respect to the commissioned civil and military officers of the British forces. The order was issued on April 22 in Gujranwala district and required all Indians to alight from their mode of transport, or stop what they were doing when a European Officer past by and provide Salaams in the form of the correct salute. This order was extended to the Lyallpur district on 30 April and to the Gujrat district on 2 May. These orders were calculated to humiliate the whole Indian population of those districts. The lawyers who were deemed the main instigators of the pro-independence rioting in Amritsar did not escape punishment by General Dyer. Fifty lawyers determined to be involved in the rioting were put to work as ditch diggers to clean up the mess present in the city. These "fancy punishments", as they were later described ensured that the incident was to remain highly emotive in the collective consciousness for many years to come.

In dealing with the events of Jallianwala Bagh, the Majority view, as regards General Dyer's failure to attend to the wounded, was that he had a very small force with him and, as he explained, the hospitals were open and no application was made to him for help. In conclusion, they did not accept the view that General Dyer's action saved the situation in the Punjab and averted a rebellion on a scale similar to the mutiny. The Minority view found that the notice prohibiting the meeting was not adequately published and they criticized General Dyer severely, (1) for suggesting that he would have made use of machine guns if they could have been brought into action, (2) for opening fire without warning and continuing after the crowd had begun to disperse until his ammunition was spent, (3) for firing not merely to disperse the crowd but to punish them and produce a moral effect in Punjab, and (4) for assuming that the crowd before him consisted of the persons guilty of the outrages of 10 April. They maintained that it was immaterial whether General Dyer thought he was doing right or not and that he could not avail the plea of military necessity, as this plea has always been used in justification of Prussian atrocities. The Minority did not agree with the majority that it was probable that the crowd could not have been dispersed without firing, citing General Dyer himself in support of their opinion: and they described his action as inhuman and un-British and as having caused great disservice to British rule in India. They attributed his conduct to a fixed idea that India must be ruled by force and they condemned his action in not taking steps for the removal of the dead and care of the wounded. Finally, they criticized the failure of the Punjab Government to ascertain without delay the number of casualties.[19]

Legal Cases

An appeal was preferred before the Privy Council by few individuals who were convicted by the Commissions in which, among other points, it is maintained that it was not within the power of the Governor General to give the tribunals set up by him power to try offences other than those mentioned in the Bengal Regulation or any offences committed after 30 March and before the first acts of violence occurred. In the case of *Bugga v The Emperor*,[20] an appeal was filed by special leave from a judgment dated 2 June 1919 of a Commission appointed under the Martial Law Ordinances of 1919 and sitting at Lahore. By that judgment, 20 of the 21 appellants were convicted of offences under Section 121 of the Indian Penal Code (IPC), i.e. waging or attempting to wage war against the King or abetting the waging of such war and were sentenced to death and forfeiture of property. However, in some of the cases the death sentence had been commuted. The remaining appellant, Ghulam Hassan, was convicted of an offence under section 412 of the IPC, i.e., receiving stolen property from dacoits, and was sentenced to rigorous imprisonment for seven years. The

19 Disorder Inquiry Committee 1919-1920, Report, Calcutta: Superintendent Government Printing, India, 1920, pp. xx-xxi.

20 *Bugga and others v Emperor* (1920) 22 BOMLR 609 decided on 20 February 1920 by the Bombay High Court.

question raised on the appeal was as to the competency of the Commission to try the appellants for those offences.

It was proved that during serious unrest in certain parts of the province of Punjab, the appellants (with possible exception of Ghulam Hassan), were members of the mob and took an active part in the attack on the National Bank.[21] There was evidence that some of them took part in the actual murder of the manager and assistant manager. Bugga and Ratan Chand appear to have been the ringleaders. Ghulam Hassan was found in possession of property looted from the Bank. Bugga was arrested on 12 April and the other appellants on subsequent dates. None of them were taken in arms or in the act of committing the offences with which they were charged.

On 13 April, the Governor-General in Council, acting under the Bengal State Offences Regulation, 1804 (which was extended to Punjab by the Punjab Laws Act, 1872), made an order whereby he suspended the function of the ordinary criminal courts within the districts of Lahore and Amritsar and established martial law there for the trial of persons for offences such as Bugga and others were charged with, and directed the immediate trial by court martial of all such persons. On 14 April, the Governor-General promulgated the Martial Law Ordinance (No 1 of 1919) providing that every trial in the above mentioned districts, instead of being tried by a court martial, should be tried by a Commission of three persons appointed by the local government. The provisions of the Ordinance were to apply to all the persons referred to in the Regulations who were charged with any of the offences therein described committed on or after 15 April 1919. In pursuance of the Ordinance No 1 of 1919, a Commission was appointed by the Local Government of the Punjab.[22]

From the above, it was clear that the appellants could not, if no further step had been taken, have been brought before the Commission for trial. They had not been taken in the act of committing any of the offences referred to in Regulation of 1804, and the offences with which they were charged were committed before 13 April, 1919, the date mentioned in Section 7 of the Ordinance. But on 21 April 1919, the Governor-General, acting under Section 72 of the Government of India Act, 1915, made a

21 *Bugga v. Emperor*, ILR (1919) I Lahore 326.

22 The Commission consisted of Lieutenant Colonel A. A. Irvine, District and Sessions Judge; F. W. Kennaway, Esq., District and Sessions Judge; and I. C. Lall, Esq. Report of the Committee Appointed by the Government of India to Investigate the Disturbances in the Punjab, etc., London: His Majesty's Stationery Office, 1920, pp. 176.

further Ordinance, i.e., Martial Law (Further Extension) Ordinance No IV of 1919, by which the Commissioners were empowered to try any person charged with offences committed after 30 March 1919. The Local Government of the Punjab was, instructed by the Government of India that the Commissions appointed under Ordinance No. IV were to be used only for the trial of offence arising out of the recent disturbances.

The appellants having been charged with offences under various sections of the India Penal Code, including section(s) 121, 302 and 412, as having been committed on 10 April, the Local Government, acting under Ordinance No. IV of 1919, directed that they should be tried by the Court of Commissioners appointed under Ordinance No. I sitting at Lahore with the powers of a Summary General Court-Martial, and convened the Commissioners for that purpose. The trial accordingly took place on 29 May and the following days, and judgment was pronounced on 2 June. The Commissioners, while convicting the appellants (other than Ghulam Hassan) of an offence under section 121, added that certain of the accused could also be convicted under section 302, i.e., for murder, but that they saw no necessity to discriminate, especially as in circumstances like those before them there was only one possible penalty for the offence or offences committed. Thereupon special leave was obtained from the Board to present this appeal.

It was contended by counsel for the appellants that Ordinance No. IV of 1919 was capable of being construed as intended only to extend the operation of Ordinance No. I to offences committed before the 13 April, but not earlier than 30 March, and accordingly that this Ordinance (like Ordinance No. I) applied only to persons taken in the act of committing one of the offences specified in Regulation X of 1804. It was then argued that, if Ordinance No. IV applied (subject to the direction of the Local Government) to any person and to any offence known to the law, it was invalid by reason of the provisions of Section 65, Sub-sections (2) and (3) of the Government of India Act, 1915.

Section 65 of the Government of India Act, while giving the Governor-General in Council a general power to make laws for British India, enacted by subsection (2) that he should not be able to make any law affecting the authority of Parliament or any part of the unwritten law or Constitution of the United Kingdom whereon might depend in any degree the allegiance of any person to the Crown of the United Kingdom or affecting the Sovereignty or dominion of the Crown over any part of British India, and by subsection (3) enacted that he should have no power without the previous approval of the Secretary of State in Council to make any law empowering any Court other than a High Court to sentence to the punishment of death any of His Majesty's subjects born in Europe or the children of such subjects or abolishing any court. The appellants, who were natives of India, were at the trial charged with offences under the Penal Code and some of them were sentenced to death.

The Lahore High Court held that Ordinance No IV could not be construed as intended only to extend the operation of Ordinance I to offences committed before 13 April, but not earlier than 30 March and therefore did not apply only to persons taken in the act of committing any of the offences specified in Regulation of 1804. It was clearly stated in the recital introducing the Ordinance that its operation was not confined to the persons and offences described in the earlier Ordinance. Ordinance IV of 1919, if it was repugnant to Section 65(3) of the Government of India Act, so far as British born subjects were concerned, was, under Section 2 of the Government of India (Amendment) Act, void to the extent of that repugnancy, but not otherwise. The appeal was therefore dismissed.

In *Kalinath Roy v. King Emperor*[23] the appellant, editor of *The Tribune* was convicted by a Court of Commissioners at Lahore under the Martial Law Ordinance I of 1919 of an offence under Section 124A of the Indian Penal Code, namely, of having by written words excited or attempted to excite disaffection towards His Majesty or the Government established by law in British India. He was sentenced to two years' rigorous imprisonment but afterwards reduced to three months' simple imprisonment and to a fine of Rs. 1,000. Special leave to appeal was granted by His Majesty in Council on 18 August 1919. The appellant in his case raised two grounds against his conviction, viz., (1) that his trial by the summary procedure of martial law was bad in law and wholly unconstitutional; and (2) that on a reasonable construction of the articles complained of, the appellant was not guilty of the offence of sedition as defined by section 124A of the IPC.

It was observed that the facts and Ordinances bearing on the first point raised by the appellant, viz., want of jurisdiction in the tribunal by which he was tried, were substantially the same as in the case of *Bugga v. The King-Emperor* (1920), the only distinction being that the order of the Lieutenant-Governor made under Ordinance IV of 1919, directing a trial before the Commissioners, did not (as in that case) name the accused who were to be so tried, but applied to "all persons charged with offences

23 (1920) 48 I.A. 96.

connected with the recent disturbances." The Privy Council held that the validity of the Ordinance being established by the decision of the Board in *Bugga v. King Emperor*, the Commissions Court had jurisdiction, although the order of the Lieutenant-Governor did not mention the names of the accused persons and that the court having applied the right principles of law in considering whether an offence under Section 124A had been committed, no interference with the conclusions was required.

Conclusion

A military commander administering martial law in a hostile country is weighed down heavily by burden of responsibility in particular, when he is compelled to exercise this responsibility over a population which owes allegiance and looks for protection to the Government which he himself is serving. A situation which is essentially military must be dealt with in the light of military considerations, which necessitates due appreciation of all the possible contingencies. There are certain standards of conduct which no civilized Government could neglect. Subject to the due observance of those standards, an officer administering martial law remains free to carry out the task imposed upon him in the manner which his judgment dictates to him as best and most effective, and may rely upon the unqualified support of his superiors when his task has been accomplished. The general principle is that martial law should remain in force no longer than the public safety demands, but beyond this there are no hard and fast criteria which can govern this decision. The original ordinance setting up Martial Law Commissions in the Lahore and Amritsar Districts gave the Commissions jurisdiction to try offences committed on or after April the 13th. Had this date remained unamended, it would have been impossible to try by Commission persons charged with actual participation in the murders, incendiarism and destruction of property which occurred on 10 April at Amritsar, or persons charged with participation in the riots at Lahore on 10-12 April, and in the murders at Kasur on 12 April 1919 on account of the principle of ex post facto law.

The trial of people who were not arrested for and charged with taking any part in the actual disturbances by special tribunals was unwise. People like Dr. Kitchlew and Dr. Satyapal, who had already been deported before the actual disturbances took place, and people like Lala Har Kishan Lal, Pandit Rambhuj Dutt Chaudhri and Lala Duni Chand, who were not charged with taking any part in the disorders of 10 April and subsequent dates, but were tried for, having by their previous acts and speech, being guilty of sedition, should have been left to be dealt with by the ordinary courts.

The course adopted by these courts was calculated to create the impression that they were prejudiced in getting a fair trial. In addition, all legal practitioners of their choice[24] were prevented from conducting their defence which further concretized such impression. The procedure adopted by summary courts, did not conform to that prescribed under the Indian Army Act, 1911 or for summary trials under the Criminal Procedure Code. These courts tried people for serious offences under the Defence of India Rules and for making seditious speeches and enforcing *hartal*. Offences such as cheating, perjury, false personating, adultery, which were not connected in any manner with the disturbances, were tried by summary courts under clause 15 of the Martial Law Proclamation as acts which were to the prejudice of good order and public safety. Bringing such offences within the purview of martial law, which was specifically enforced to dealing with the disturbances, with no option available to appeal against the decisions of summary courts, is not in line with the concept of fair trial.

Taking into consideration the acts committed under Martial Law regime, it could be concluded definitively that the terms of the Ordinances were too wide thus enabling unscrupulous officers to justify their arbitrary acts within the parameters of the Ordinance. There were excessive and unwarranted use of force on the people, such as the use of airplanes at Gujranwala for bombing on civilians and villages, the use of armoured train and indiscriminate firing. Floggings, which took place throughout the towns under martial law and 'crawling order' were humiliating punishments. It appears that martial law administrators were too eager to whip Indians for minor infractions, such as contravention of the curfew order, for failure to salaam a commissioned officer, for disrespect to a European, for taking a commandeered car without leave, for refusal to sell milk, and for other similar contraventions. To British officials, it was an expedient way to put Indians in their place, thereby restoring order. According to Majority view, Martial Law was not being administered in an enemy country, but in a country where on the restoration of normal

24 They engaged legal practitioners from Calcutta, Bombay, Allahabad, and Patna, but were denied their assistance by an order on the eve of their trial.

conditions it was advisable that martial law administration should leave behind as little as possible feeling of bitterness and unfairness. Some of the orders issued were injudicious. They served no good purpose and were not drawn with sufficient tact to prevent undue annoyance to the civil population.

Chapter III

Indemnity Act

Introduction

Imposition of martial law may entail commission of acts that violates fundamental rights of the citizens. In ordinary circumstances, violation of fundamental rights by state action would invite judicial review of such act. However, since martial law is imposed and enforced by the executive to tackle extraordinary situations, there is no provision for judicial review of acts done during imposition of this law but accountability lies before the Parliament which may indemnify acts done in connection with maintenance or restoration of order in such area by the executive by passing a legislation in this regard[1].

Once military has suppressed rebellion or insurrection, the Parliament gives statutory sanction to the measures adopted by the military and other authorities during martial law and the sentences imposed by military court martial or commissions. This is done by passing an Indemnity Act which debars judicial examination of the martial law measures and sentences. According to Frederick Pollock, "An Act of Indemnity is merely a measure of prudence or grace". The act of indemnity is the postlude to a regime of martial law; its significance rests in that it maintains parliamentary control over the executive in the exercise of his emergency authority.[2]

During the British rule in India, it was customary to follow up a proclamation of martial law, with an act of indemnity with retroactive effect, affording judicial protection to those agents of the government who,

1 This is precisely in sync with the principle of checks and balances among the three organs of the state.

2 Rossiter Clinton L.,1948, *Constitutional Dictatorship—Crisis Government in the Modern Democracies*, Princeton University Press, p. 143.

though acting in good faith, were guilty of breaches of private right. The Act of Indemnity provides a general sanction for everything done under a regime of martial law and thus debars judicial scrutiny and retribution in the case of clearly wanton exertions of authority for those actions undertaken in "good faith"--- an elastic standard to protect the actions of executives. The object of an Act of Indemnity is to make legal transactions which when they took place were illegal, or to free individuals to whom the statute applies from liability for having broken the law.[3] The Act of Indemnity may also provide for compensation to innocent victims who suffered injury or award compensation to individuals whose property was used or damaged during martial law.[4]

Indemnity Act

The Indemnity Act is a retrospective statute protecting all persons who have acted, or have intended to act, under the powers given to the government by the statute. A statute of this kind is the last and supreme exercise of Parliamentary sovereignty. It legalizes acts which are primarily illegal; it affords the practical solution of the problem which perplexed the State. The protection to be derived from the Act by men who have been guilty of irregular, illegal, oppressive, or cruel conduct, depends on the terms of the Act of Indemnity, which may be either narrow or wide.

The Indemnity Act passed by the British Parliament in 1801, gave a very limited amount of protection to official wrongdoers. It provides, indeed, a defence against actions or prosecutions in respect of anything done, commanded, ordered, directed, or advised to be done in Great Britain for apprehending, imprisoning, or detaining in custody any person charged with high treason or treasonable practices. Such an Act would cover any irregularity or formal breach of the law, but any act of spite or extortion, done under cover of the Suspension Act, which would expose the offender to actions or prosecutions, could not be justified under the terms of the Indemnity Act. An Act of Indemnity, though it is the legalization of illegality, is after all a law and, therefore, operates within limits set by the principles and premises on which law is founded. Reckless cruelty to apolitical prisoner, or the arbitrary punishment, or the execution of a

3 Dicey, A. V., 1885, *Introduction to the study of the law of the Constitution*, London, p 10.

4 Sebastian V.D., Martial Law and Defence of Constitutional Order in India, *Kerala University Law Review*, Vol. 1(2), 1971, pp. 172-195.

political prisoner, between 1793 and 1801, would, inspite of the Indemnity Act, make men concerned in martial law liable to suffer punishment.[5]

The Act applies to proceedings in the courts against the government or any government servant or any person acting under the direction or with the approval of the government, and it applies both to proceedings already pending and those that may be instituted in future. The Act provides that no civil or criminal proceedings may be instituted or continued in any court of law against the State, its employees or its appointees in respect of acts done in good faith whilst acting for the purpose of, or in connection with, the suppression of insurrection or maintenance of public order. A written certificate by the government agent or minister that the action was taken for the suppression of insurrection is deemed to be conclusive proof in any court of law that the act was done for this purpose. Thus, no court could question the certificate even if it could be proved that the act in question had nothing whatsoever to do with the suppression of insurrection or rebellion. The Government alone decides what constitutes "good faith", "action necessary to suppress insurrection or rebellion", "public order", and "national interest". The courts are prohibited from questioning the validity of any certificate issued. Review jurisdiction of the courts is expressly excluded. No reasons for the issuing of the certificate need be given.

For instance, the 1847 Ordinance for Indemnifying Officers of Her Majesty Forces for all acts done by them under certain Proclamations of Martial Law in New Zealand provided: ".....that all and singular the officers of Her Majesty's Forces and others who shall have duly acted under the authority of the said recited Proclamations, or any of them, shall be and they are hereby respectively freed indemnified and discharged of from and against all actions and prosecutions which they respectively may have been or may become liable or subject to for or by reason or by means of or in relation to any act matter or thing done by any such officer or person by virtue or under the authority of the said Proclamations or any of them; and that no act matter or thing done by any such officer or person under or by virtue of any such Proclamation shall be questioned in the Supreme Court or any other Court whatsoever within the Colony of New Zealand."[6]

5 Dicey, A. V., 1885, *Introduction to the study of the law of the Constitution,* London, p. 145.

6 Victoria II, Sess. VIII, Ordinance No, XIII, dated 14 October 1847.

The imposition of martial law in Jamaica, a British Colony, in 1865 engaged public attention, and raised alarming controversy in which some of the most distinguished men in Britain took opposite sides.[7] Martial law was proclaimed on 13 October 1865. On 9 November an Act of Indemnity (29 Vic., c.1) was passed. The second paragraph of the Act stated: " And it is hereby also enacted, That his Excellency Edward John Eyre, Esquire, Captain-General and Governor-in-Chief, and all officers and other person who have acted under his authority, or have acted bona fide for the purposes and during the time aforesaid, whether such acts were done in any district in which Martial Law was proclaimed, or in any district in which Martial Law was not proclaimed, are hereby indemnified in respect of all acts, matters, and things done in order to put an end to the said rebellion; and all such acts so done are hereby made and declared to be lawful, and are confirmed." [8] The imposition of martial law and subsequent trials by court martial came under severe criticism. It caused debates in Parliament and prosecutions in the courts. As regards the Indemnity Act of 1865, the Secretary of State stated:

> "Her Majesty's Government are advised by the law officers of the Crown, that the effect of the Indemnity Act will not be to cover acts done, either by the Governor or by subordinate officers, unless they are such as (in the case of the Governor) he may have reasonably, and in good faith, considered to be proper for the purpose of putting an end to the insurrection, or such as (in the case of subordinates) have been done under, and in conformity with, the orders of superior authority, or (if done without such orders) have been done in good faith, and under a belief, reasonably entertained, that they

7 *Jamaica* was an English colony from 1655 or 1670 and a *British* Colony from 1707 until 1962. In the late 1830s and '40s, the Royal Governor, the Jamaican legislature, and Parliament had many bitter disagreements regarding taxation and government expenditures. The Governors Sir Charles Metcalfe and James Bruce attempted to improve the economy by bringing in thousands of plantation workers from India (rather than paying higher wages to former slaves) and creating the island's first railway. In spite of those programmes, the plantation system collapsed, leading to widespread poverty and unemployment. In 1865, impoverished former slaves rioted in the town of Morant Bay, killing the chief magistrate and 18 others of European ancestry. The Jamaican assembly, dismayed, ceded its power to Governor Edward John Eyre, who declared martial law, suppressed the rioters, and hanged the principal instigator, Paul Bogle, and his alleged co-conspirator, assembly member George William Gordon. Many West Indians applauded Eyre's actions, but amid public outcries and an official investigation in Britain, he was recalled and dismissed from his position.

8 Clode Charled M., 1869, *The Military Forces of Crown: Their Administration and Government*, Vol. II, London: John Murray, p 495.

were proper for the suppression of the insurrection, and for the preservation of the public peace of the island. As regards all acts done by or under military authority, Her Majesty's Government are advised that the proclamation of martial law, under the Island Statute of 1844, operated within the proclaimed district to give as complete an indemnity as the Indemnity Act itself. But: 1. For any acts done beyond the proclaimed district, the authority of the Act of 1844, and of the proclamation, is inapplicable. 2. Civilians who may have acted bona fide for the suppression of the rebellion, although without military authority, would have a protection secured to them by the Indemnity Act, which they might not obtain from the mere operation of martial law. 3. Under the Indemnity Act, the certificate of the Governor is conclusive for the protection of subordinates. I have already directed you, and your own judgment doubtless would have led to the same conclusion, how careful you must be in giving these certificates; and, with this precaution taken, her Majesty's Government have determined that the Act of Indemnity ought to be left to its operation."[9]

In *Phillips* v. *Eyre*, Chief Justice Cockburn has made certain observations about the legal import and character of Indemnity Act:[10]

> There can be no doubt that every so called Indemnity Act involves a manifest violation of justice, in as much as it deprives those who have suffered wrongs to their vested right of the redress which the law would otherwise afford them and gives immunity to those who have inflicted those wrongs, not at the expense of the community for whose alleged advantages the wrongful acts were done, but at the expense of individuals who, innocent possibly of all offence, have been subjected to injury and outrage often of the most outrageous character. It is equally true as was forcibly urged on us, that such legislation may be used to cover acts of most tyrannical, arbitrary and merciless character, acts not capable of being justified or palliated even by the plea of necessity, but prompted by local passions, prejudices or fears -acts not done with the temper and judgement which those in authority are bound to bring to the exercise of so fearful a power, but characterized by reckless indifference to human suffering and an

9 Finlason W.F., 1869. *The History of the Jamaica Case: Being an account founded upon official documents of the rebellion of the Negros in Jamaica, the causes which led to it and the measures for its suppression*, London: Chapman and Hall, pp. 185-186.

10 *Phillips* v. *Eyre* (1869) 4 QB 225, p. 242-243.

utter disregard of the dictates of common humanity. On the other hand, however, it must not be forgotten that against any abuse of local legislative authority in such a case protection is provided by the necessity of the assent of the Sovereign, acting under the advice of Ministers, themselves responsible to Parliament. We may rest assured that no such enactment would receive the royal assent unless it were confined to acts honestly done in the suppression of existing rebellion, and under the pressure of the most urgent necessity. The present indemnity [The Act of Indemnity passed by the legislature of Jamaica after the rebellion of 1865] is confined to acts done in order to suppress the insurrection and rebellion, and the plea contains consequently the necessary averments that the grievances complained of were committed during the continuance of the rebellion, and were used for its suppression, and were reasonably and in good faith considered by the defendant to be necessary for the purpose; and it will, therefore, be incumbent on the defendant to make good these averments in order to support his plea."

Indemnity Acts in India under British Rule

Under the East India Company and the British rule, martial law was imposed on many occasions in different territories in India.[11] There is no available record to show whether indemnity acts were issued after martial law ceased to exist in the territories under the East India Company. However, under the British rule, indemnity acts were issued by the government.

11 The early charters issued to the East India Company for India during the British period contained provisions for executing martial law. However, the scope of such martial law was limited to the maintenance of discipline among the armed forces maintained by the company (This in real sense was 'military law' for governing the forces of the Company and not martial law at it is understood now). After the company established itself as a territorial power in India and after the British Parliament passed statutes to regulate the Company's government of Indian territories, the power to establish martial law was given by regulations framed under statutory powers. The Bengal State Offences Regulation, 1804, (X of 1804) (commonly referred to as the Martial Law Regulation) and the Madras Regulation VII of 1808 empowered the establishment of martial law. These regulations also authorized the trial by court martial of persons taken in rebellion. Under the East India Company rule, martial law was proclaimed in Cuttack (1817-18), in Vishakhapatnam and Palkonda in 1832, in Kimedi in 1833, in Gumsur in 1835, in Savantawadi in 1844 and in various other places in 1857 following the Mutiny. Under the British Government rule, martial law was established in the Punjab in 1919, in Malabar in 1921, in Sholapur in 1930, and in Sind in 1942. For more details see: Sebastian V.D., Martial Law and Defence of Constitutional Order in India, *Kerala University Law Review*, Vol. 1(2), 1971, pp. 172-195; Minattur Joseph, 1962, *Martial Law in India, Pakistan and Ceylon*, The Hague: Martinus Nijhoff, p. 16.

On 13 April 1919, the British government had put most of the Punjab under martial law.[12] The legislation restricted a number of civil liberties, including freedom of assembly which banned gatherings of more than four people. The Indemnity Act of 1919 [13] was passed to indemnify military and civil officers of Government and other persons in respect of certain acts done under martial law which was declared and enforced in some districts in the Punjab. The Act indemnified all officers of Government and other persons in respect of the acts done under martial law for the purpose of maintaining or restoring order, provided that such acts, matters or things were ordered or done in good faith and in a reasonable belief that they were necessary for the said purposes.[14] Section 2 of the Act indemnified all Government officers and other persons for certain acts, stating:

> "No suit or other legal proceedings whatsoever, whether civil or criminal, shall lie in any court of law against any officers of government, whether civil or military, or against any other person acting under the orders of any such officer for or on account of or in respect of any act, matter or thing ordered or done or purporting to have been ordered or done for the purpose of maintaining or restoring order in any part of British India where martial law was enforced, on or after 30 March 1919 and before 26 August 1919 by any such officer or person; provided that such officer or person has acted in good faith and in a reasonable belief that his action was necessary for the said purposes. If any such proceeding has been instituted before the passing of this Act it is hereby discharged."

For the purposes of Section 2, a certificate of a Secretary to Government that any act was done under the orders of an officer of Government was to be conclusive proof thereof, and all action taken for the aforesaid purposes was deemed to have been taken in good faith and in a reasonable belief

12 See Chapter IIA of the book for more details.

13 Act No. XXVII of 1919, passed on 25 September 1919. A copy of the Indemnity Act, 1919 is placed at Appendix D to the book.

14 The Acts issued by the British Government in India indemnified every government official after Jallianwala Bagh massacre in 1919. As expected, General Dyer walked clean except that he was called back to England after resigning. The British Parliament welcomed Dyer as a hero in the House of Lords. On his deathbed suffering from the arteriosclerosis, he reportedly said, "So many people who knew the condition of Amritsar say I did right, but so many others say I did wrong. I only want to die and know from my Maker whether I did right or wrong." After suffering a series of strokes Dyer died of a cerebral haemorrhage in 1927. Available at: https://cityonpedals.com/blog/jallianwala-bagh-massacre-facts-and-a-century-later.

that it was necessary, unless the contrary was proved. The Act, under section 3, provided for the continuance of sentences awarded to convicted persons by special courts or authorities appointed under martial law. It stated, "Every person confined under and by virtue of any sentence passed by a court or other authority constituted or appointed under martial law and acting in a judicial capacity shall be deemed to have been lawfully confined and shall continue liable to confinement until the expiration of such sentence or until released by the Governor-General in Council as otherwise discharged by lawful authority."

Under Article 5 of the Act, provisions were made for allowing reasonable compensation for property taken or used by any officer of government. It provided that when under martial law the property of any person has been taken or used by any officer of government, whether civil or military, the Governor-General in Council shall pay to such person reasonable compensation for any loss immediately attributable to such taking or using, to be assessed upon failure of agreement by a person holding judicial office not inferior to that of a District Judge to be appointed by the Government in this behalf.

In 1942, martial law was proclaimed in certain parts of Sind where Hurs—a designated criminal tribe—had terrorized the entire districts, committing murder, sabotage and dacoity, which the civil authorities found it difficult to govern. A special force of troops was sent to the area to aid the civil authorities in restoring order. The Military Commander was instructed to take all necessary steps to restore civil security and order with all possible speed. The Military Commander proclaimed martial law under which Special Courts were established to punish the Hurs.[15] The Martial Law (Indemnity) Ordinance, 1943[16] indemnified all servants of the Crown and other persons in respect of acts done by them under martial law. The Ordinance specified the areas covered by the martial law order. It provided that no suit, prosecution or any other legal proceedings shall be instituted in any court against any servant of the crown for any act done or orders issued in martial law area during the martial law period for the purposes of maintaining or restoring order, etc.; provided that act was done in good faith and in a reasonable belief that it was necessary for the purpose

15 Complete control of the civil administration was given over to the Military Commander who would have the advice and assistance of the civil authorities in the area concerned. This proclamation was made under the common law rule which justified the repelling of force by force. Martial law continued in force for eleven months, from 1 June 1942 to 3 May 1943·

16 Ordinance XVIII of 1943, issued on 31 May 1943.

intended to be served thereby. It was also provided that no prosecution or legal proceedings shall be instituted in any court on an allegation that the act complained was not done in good faith etc. except with the permission of the central government. The Ordinance also provided that no claim was maintainable in any court for compensation of the property seized, confiscated, destroyed or damaged in the course of operations conducted in the martial law area during the martial law period. All sentences passed including those passed for offences committed before the martial law period, by the Special Courts during the period, were validated, whether the courts sat within or outside the martial law area.[17]

Constitutional Provision relating to Indemnity Act

Martial law had been invoked on many occasions under the British Rule in India and elsewhere. The framers of Indian Constitution were aware about the concept of martial law, though they have not made any express provision about the proclamation under the Constitution. Article 34 of the Constitution makes provision for the passing of an Act of Indemnity by the Parliament in respect of acts done under martial law.[18] The article was not part of the original Draft Constitution, the debates on which ended on the 17 October 1949. It was added at the revision stage by the Drafting Committee. The letter of 3 November 1949 from the members of the Drafting Committee, forwarding the Revised Draft Constitution to the President of the Constituent Assembly pointed out that "the Fundamental Rights in the Constitution might prevent validation by the Legislature of acts done during the period when martial law is in force and also prevent the indemnifying of persons in the service of the Union or of a State in respect of action taken by them during such period," and this Article was suggested to cover that contingency.[19]

On 14 November 1949, Article 34 as formulated by the Drafting Committee, along with all the other revisions and alterations that came

17 Hans Raj, 1989, *Executive Legislation in Colonial India 1939-1947: A Study of Ordinances promulgated by the Governor General of India*, Delhi: Anamika Prakashan, p. 78-79.

18 The experience in Sind of proclaiming and administering martial law without resort to legislation seems to have inspired Article 34 of the Constitution of India which makes provision for the passing of an Act of Indemnity by the Parliament in respect of acts done under martial law. Minattur Joseph, 1962, *Martial Law in India, Pakistan and Ceylon*, The Hague: Martinus Nijhoff, p. 40.

19 Pal Samaraditya, 2016, *India's Constitution: Origin and Evolution, Vol. III, Articles 29 to 51A*, Gurgaon: Lexis Nexis, p. 681.

up for consideration before the Constituent Assembly. During the debate on the Revised Draft Constitution, Professor Shibban Lal Saxena wanted the Article deleted. He thought that the Article would encourage officers working in martial law area to commit excesses and be in hope of indemnification by law made by Parliament. Shri H.V. Kamath moved two amendments, one of them to restrict the application of Article 34 to only public servants and not to 'any other person' as he thought would be far too sweeping. During the debate on Article 34, Shri H. V. Kamath raised a question as to why the indemnification of persons other than public servants was visualized in this article. The issue was clarified by Dr. B. R. Ambedkar: ".... that when martial law is there it is not merely the duty of the Commander-in-Chief to punish people, it is the duty of every individual citizen of the State to take the responsibility on his own shoulder and come to the help of the Commander-in-Chief. Consequently if it was found that any person who was an ordinary citizen and did not belong to the Commander-in-Chief's entourage, so to say, does any act it is absolutely essential that he also ought to be indemnified because whatever act he does he does it in the maintenance of the peace of the State and there is a no reason why a distinction should be made for a military officer and a civilian who comes to the rescue of the State to establish peace."[20]

Dr. Ambedkar opposed the amendments stating that the movers of the amendments had not understood the purpose of Article 34 and explained that the Article could be best explained if read with Article 20(1) and Article 21. He said the presence of these two Articles without the qualification mentioned in Article 34, would make it impossible for martial law to be declared at all, thereby making it impossible for the state to restore order quickly in an area engaged in rebellion. Dr. Ambedkar clarified the issue in relation to criticism to the proposed Article 34:[21]

> This article, too, has been subjected to some strong criticism. I am sorry to say that Members who spoke against article 34 did not quite realize what article 20, clause (1) and article 21 of the Constitution propose to do. Sir, I would like to read article 20, clause (a) and also article 21, because without a proper realization of the provisions contained in these two articles it would not be possible for any

20 Pal Samaraditya, 2016, *India's Constitution: Origin and Evolution, Vol. III, Articles 29 to 51A*, Gurgaon: LexisNexis, p. 686.

21 Constituent Assembly Debates on Revised Draft Constitution, Vol. XI, pp. 468-470 and 577-578; Debated on 14 November and 16 November 1949, are at Appendix E of the book.

Member to realize the desirability of---I would even go further and say the necessity for---article 34. Article 20, clause (1) says:

"No person shall be convicted of any except offence for violation of a law in force at the time of the commission of the act charged as an offence."

Article 21 says:

"No person shall be deprived of his life or personal liberty except according to procedure established by law."

Now, it is obvious that when there is a riot, insurrection or rebellion, or the overthrow of the authority of the State in any particular territory martial law is introduced. The officer in charge of martial law does two things. He declares by his order that certain acts shall be offences against his authority, and, secondly, he prescribes his own procedure for the trial of persons who offend against the acts notified by him as offence, is quite clear that any act notified by the military commander in charge of the disturbed area is not an offence enacted by law in force, because the Commander of the area is not a law-making person. He has no authority to declare that a certain act is an offence, and secondly the violation of any order made by him would not a be an offence within the meaning of the phrase "law in force", because "law in force" can only mean law made by a law-making authority. Moreover, the procedure that the Commander-in-Chief or the military commander prescribes is also not procedure according to law, because he is not entitled to make a law. These are orders which he has made for the purpose of carrying out his functions, namely, of restoring law and order. Obviously, if article 20 clause (1) and article 21 remain as they are, without any such qualification as is mentioned in article 34, martial law would be impossible in the country, and it would be impossible for the State to restore order quickly in an area which has become rebellious.

It is therefore necessary to make a positive statement or positive provisions to permit that notwithstanding anything contained in article 20 or article 21, any act proclaimed by the Commander-in-Chief as an offence against his order shall be an offence. Similarly, the procedure prescribed by him shall be procedure deemed to be established by law. I hope it will be clear that if article 34 was not in our Constitution, the administration of martial law would be quite impossible and the restoration of peace may become one of the impossibilities of the situation. I therefore submit, Sir, that article 34 is a very necessary article in order to mitigate the severity of articles 20(1) and 21.

> Subsequently two amendments were withdrawn and the rest were out to vote and negatived. Article 34 as contained in Part III of the Constitution reads as follows:
>
> **Restriction on rights conferred by this Part while martial law is in force in any area**:- Notwithstanding anything in the foregoing provisions of this Part, Parliament may by law indemnify any person in the service of the Union or of a State or any other person in respect of any act done by him in connection with the maintenance or restoration of order in any area within the territory of India where martial law was in force or validate any sentence passed, punishment inflicted, forfeiture ordered or other act done under martial law in such area.

Article 34 seeks to indemnify public servants and other persons for acts done by them in connection with the maintenance or restoration of order in any area within the country where martial law has been declared. The article carries the heading, "restrictions on rights conferred by this Part while martial law is in force in any area;" and contrary to general belief amongst the members of civil society, it does not specifically indemnifies military personnel, but everyone, including the civilians who might have played a role in restoration of order in a disturbed area.

In India, there has not been any occasion after independence when martial law was enforced. The provision of Article 34 is worded similar to the indemnity law existing at the time of the British rule. However, since elaborate fundamental rights have been enshrined in the Constitution and jurisprudence in this area has been developed through judicial interpretation, it is pertinent to examine the ambit and scope of this provision so as to know whether the excesses committed through this provision during the colonial rule can be repeated in today's context or not.

The title of Article 34 indicates that it is meant to constitutionally validate abrogation of fundamental rights while martial law is in force in any area. It starts with a non-obstante clause, 'Notwithstanding anything in the foregoing provisions of this Part'. The meaning of the non-obstante clause i.e. 'notwithstanding' has been explained by the Apex Court in the case of *Chandavarkar Sita Ratna Rao* v. *Ashalata S. Guram* (1987) in the following words:

> A clause beginning with the expression 'notwithstanding anything contained in this Act or in some particular provision in the Act or in some particular Act or in any law for the time being in force, or in contract' is more often than not appended to a section in the beginning with a view to give the enacting part of the section in case of conflict an overriding effect over the provision of the Act or the contract mentioned in the non-obstante clause. It is equivalent to saying that in spite of the provision of the Act or any other Act mentioned in the non-obstante clause or any contract or document mentioned the enactment following it will have its full operation or that the provisions embraced in the non-obstante clause would not be an impediment for an operation of the enactment. [22]

In other words, the non-osbtante clause gives overriding effect of the indemnity law that may be passed by the Parliament over the fundamental rights which are guaranteed in Part III of the Constitution.

The indemnification of acts done in violation to provisions of Part III extends to all persons, including those who are not in the service of the State, as long as those acts have been done in connection with the maintenance or restoration of order in an area where martial law is in force. The phrase 'in connection with' means 'with reference to or concerning'. This phrase, if read with the words that follow it, shows that the acts done in area under martial law may be validated by the Parliament provided that those acts has reference to or concerns with maintaining or restoring order there; irrespective of the fact whether the act was deemed necessary to maintain or restore order or not. In short, it could cover wide range of acts, if we look at the literal meaning of the words used in this Article. But the moot question is – whether this is the correct approach or not.

A look at the interpretation of the fundamental rights, particularly the right to life and liberty provided in Article 21, shows how the judiciary had read into it in *Maneka Gandhi* v. *Union of India* [23] the elements of 'due process clause' which was purposely avoided by the Drafters of the Constitution. So, it is germane to examine how judiciary has interpreted this provision too.

It may be noted that the high courts have not considered Article 34 independently in any case, may be because of the fact that martial law has

---

22 *Chandavarkar Sita Ratna Rao* v. *Ashalata S. Guram* 1987 AIR 117 : 1986 SCR (3) 866.

23 *Maneka Gandhi* v. *Union of India,* 1978 SCR (2) 621.

never been imposed in any part of India after independence. There have been only three cases when the Supreme Court has made observations on Article 34 while considering the entire spectrum of Fundamental Rights under the Constitution. The Supreme Court in *ADM Jabalpur* case held:[24]

> Now, under our Constitution there does not appear to be any express provision conferring power on the executive to declare martial law. But it is implicit in the text of Article 34 of the Constitution that the Government may declare martial law in any area within the territory of India. What are the legal implications and consequences of declaration of martial law is not provided anywhere in the Constitution. It is, therefore, obvious that merely declaring martial law would not, by itself, deprive the courts of the power to issue the writ of *habeas corpus* or other process for the protection of the right of the individual to life and liberty. In our country, unlike England, the right to life and liberty is secured as a fundamental right and the right to move the Supreme Court for enforcement of this right is also guaranteed as a fundamental right. Also the power to issue a writ or order in the nature of *habeas corpus* has been expressly conferred on the High Courts by a constitutional provision, namely, Article 226. Therefore, the declaration of martial law, which is not even expressly provided in the Constitution, cannot override the provisions of the Article conferring the right to life and liberty as also of Articles 32 and 226 and, unless the right of an individual to move the courts for enforcement of the right to life and liberty can be suspended or taken away by or under an express provisions of the Constitution, the individual would be entitled to enforce the right to life and liberty under Article 32 or 226 or by resorting to the ordinary process of law, even during martial law. That would be contradictory of the basic and essential feature of martial law and make it impossible to impose effective martial law anywhere at any time in the territory of India. Such a consequence could never have been imagined by the constitution-makers. They could never have intended that the Government should have the power to declare martial law and yet it should be devoid of the legal effect which must inevitably follow when martial law is in force. Moreover, Article 34 itself presupposes that acts contrary to law may be committed by the military authorities or the executive during the time when martial law is in force and that is why it provides that after the martial law ceases to be in force,

24 *ADM Jabalpur v. S.S. Shukla*, (1976) 2 SCC 512: 1976 AIR 1207: 1976 SCR 172 [5 Judge Bench].

> Parliament may by law indemnify "any person in the service of the Union or of a State or any other person in respect of any act done by him in connection with the maintenance or restoration of order in any area-where martial law was in force or validate any sentence passed, punishment inflicted, forfeiture ordered or other act done under martial law in such area." This provision clearly postulates that during the time that martial law is in force, no judicial process can issue to examine the legality of any act done by the military authorities or the executive in connection with the maintenance or restoration of order.

A 13-Judge Bench of the Supreme Court in *Kesavanand Bharti* case expressed the view that under Article 33 Parliament may by law modify rights conferred by Part III in their application to Armed Forces. Parliament may restrict or abrogate any of the rights conferred by Part III so as to ensure the proper discharge of the duties of the Armed Forces and the maintenance of discipline among them. Therefore, Article 33 shows that citizens can be denied some of these rights. If these are natural rights these cannot be abrogated. Under Article 34, the Parliament may by law indemnify any person in respect of any act done by him in connection with the maintenance or restoration of order in any area where martial law was in force or validate any sentence passed, punishment inflicted, forfeiture ordered or other act done under martial law in such area. Article 34 again shows restriction on rights conferred by Part III while martial law is in force in any area. This again is a case where the security of the country is the main consideration. Citizens have to undergo many restrictions in the interest of the country. The dominant concept is social good. Where there is no restraint the society fails.[25]

The *non-obstante* clause in Article 34 makes it clear that all the other provisions of the Constitution are subject to this provision.[26] Article 34 was also considered in the case of *Golak Nath v. State of Punjab*, wherein the Supreme Court held:[27]

> It will, therefore, be seen that fundamental rights are given transcendental position under our Constitution and are kept beyond the

25 *His Holiness Kesavanand Bharti Sripadagalavaru v. State of Kerala*, (1973) 4 SCC 225: (1973) Supp SCR 1: AIR 1973 SC 1461 [13 Judge Bench].

26 Pal Samaraditya, 2016, *India's Constitution: Origin and Evolution, Vol. 3: Articles 29 to 51A*, Gurgaon: Lexis Nexis, p. 688.

27 *Golak Nath (I.C.) v. State of Punjab*, (1967) 2 SCC 762: AIR 1967 SC 1643 [11 Judge Bench].

reach of Parliament. At the same time Parts III and IV constituted an integrated scheme forming a self-contained code. The scheme is made so elastic that all the Directive Principles of State Policy can reasonably be enforced without taking away or abridging the fundamental rights. While recognizing the immutability of fundamental rights, subject to social control, the Constitutional itself provides for the suspension or the modification of fundamental rights under specific circumstances, for instance, Article 33 empowers Parliament to modify the rights conferred by Part III in their application to the members of the armed forces, Article 34 enables it to impose restrictions on the rights conferred by the said parts while martial law is in force in an area, Article 35 confers the power on it to make laws with respect to any of the matters which under clause (3) of Article 16, Clause (3) of Article 32, Article 33 and Article 34 may be provided for by law. The non-obstante clause with which Article 34 opens makes it clear that all the other provisions of the Constitution are subject to this provision. Article 32 makes the right to move the Supreme Court, by appropriate proceedings for the enforcement of the rights conferred by the said Part a guaranteed right. Even during grave emergencies Article 358 only suspends the provisions of Article 19 and Article 359 enables the President by order to declare the right to move any court for the enforcement of such of the rights conferred by Part III as may be mentioned in that order to be suspended; that is to say, even during emergency, only Article 19 is suspended temporarily and all other rights are untouched except those specifically suspended by the President.

Article 34 merely empowers Parliament to make an Act of Indemnity to cover illegalities, if any, committed during the operation of martial law. It says nothing of the suspension of *habeas corpus* which may not *ipso facto* follow from a mere declaration of martial law.

Indemnity Act under Military Law

The Manual of Military Law of the Indian Army, dealing with the Act of Indemnity provides, "When law and order has been restored, and civil authority resumes charge, civil courts may inquire into the legality of acts of military authorities while martial law was in force. For this reason, it is necessary to protect persons from actions and prosecutions, who have been administering martial law. This is done by an Act of Indemnity passed by the Parliament (under Article 34 of the Constitution). Such an Act would make transactions legal which were illegal when they took place; free the individuals concerned from legal liability, and make the judgment of military courts valid, without which sentences passed by them could only be executed within the martial law areas and would automatically cease on the withdrawal of martial law." The Manual further clarifies, "It is to be borne in mind that production is afforded under an Act of Indemnity only to those where acts were bonafide and performed in the honest belief that they were part of their duty."[28]

The object of the Act of Indemnity is thus to make legal transactions which, when they took place, were illegal, or to free individuals to whom the statute applies from liability for having broken the law. This Act has no application to conduct which, however severe, is strictly lawful. A magistrate who, under proper circumstances, causes an unlawful assembly to be dispersed by force, or an officer who, under proper circumstances, orders his troops to fire on a mob and thereby, in dispersing the mob, wounds or kills some of the crowd, need not be indemnified. They are sufficiently protected by the law if, in discharge of their duty, they used the force necessary to maintain order and peace. A military commander or a magistrate, or a police officer, on the other hand, who, whether in time of war or in time of peace, does without distinct legal justification, any act which injures the property or interferes with the liberty of an citizen, would incur the penalties to which every man is liable who commits a breach of the law. The lawbreaker's motives may be in the highest degree patriotic, his conduct may be politically sagacious, and may confer great benefit on the public. However, his actions will not, in the absence of legal justification, save him from liability to prosecution.[29] If the military commander does some act altogether beyond the power conferred upon him by martial law, so that it could never, under any state of circumstance have been his duty to do it, he would be responsible for the violation; and even if the doing of that illegal act was the salvation of the country, it would not be a bar to his criminal prosecution.

According to Finlason (1866), martial law is something entirely arbitrary, uncontrollable by ordinary law. Martial law involves the "suspension of all law", thus conferring "an absolute discretion for the doing of anything which possibly could be deemed necessary or expedient". It follows that anything done during the period of martial law is by definition not illegal. Indeed, strictly speaking there was no need for an

28 The Manual of Military Law, 2010, Vol. I, Chapter VII, para 19.

29 Dicey, A. V., 1885, *Introduction to the study of the law of the Constitution,* London, p. 406.

Act of Indemnity following a declaration of martial law. Even if excessive acts were done, this was not something "material to their legality" and those who did them could not be legally liable.[30] Authorities, according to Michael Head (2009), have exploited vague and elastic phrase such as 'emergency', essential' and 'security' to intervene militarily, or to act without clear legal authorization, and if necessary, obtain retrospective indemnity.[31] For instance, between 1796 and 1800, seven Indemnity Acts were passed to protect authorities against legal liability for their unlawful acts.

When martial law exists, the civil courts have no authority to call in question the actions of the military authorities. However, it is for the courts to decide, if their jurisdiction is invoked, whether a state of war exists which justifies the application of martial law. The powers of the military authorities cease and those of the civil courts are resumed *ipso facto* with the termination of the martial law, and, in the absence of an Act of Indemnity, the civil courts may inquire into the legality of anything done during the state of war. Even if there is an Act of Indemnity couched in the usual terms, malicious acts may not be permitted. However, indemnity legislation could be passed to exonerate those who acted in good faith to suppress any uprising.[32] The British Government had passed such an Act of Indemnity to cover 1920 declaration of martial law in areas of Ireland.

A voluntary wrongful act cannot, as a rule, be excused as occurring in the exercise of military duties even if committed in good faith. The rule that acting on duty does not excuse unlawful acts or orders applies in emergencies as well as otherwise, even where a state of martial law or of war has been formally declared. However, in such cases good faith can be claimed as a defence.[33] The concept of command responsibility has also evolved over a period of time. A military commander can be held liable for unlawful acts of his subordinates, where he had the knowledge that his subordinates are likely to commit the act, but he fails to take remedial

30 Finlason, W.F., 1866, *A Treatise on Martial Law: As Allowed in Time of Rebellion; with Practical Illustrations Drawn from the Official Documents in the Jamaica Case and the Evidence Taken By The Royal Commission of Enquiry with Comments, Constitutional and Legal*, London: Stevens & Sons, pp. 100-107.

31 Head Michael and Scott Mann, 2009, *Domestic Deployment of the Armed Forces: Military Powers, Law and Human Rights*, England: Ashgate, p. 28.

32 De Smith S.A., 1981, *Constitutional and Administrative Law*, London: Longmans, p. 514.

33 Ehrenzweig Albert, Soldiers' Liability for Wrongs Committed on Duty, *Cornell L. Rev.*, Vol. 30, 1944, pp. 179-217.

measures. Whether acting under emergency conditions or not, a soldier is liable for wrongs committed in obedience to an order, if such order was manifestly illegal. The military law in India is very categorical in this respect and a military person can refuse an order which is not related to military duty or is illegal.[34] A military guard on duty during a public disorder if kills an innocent man, in obedience to an order to "shoot to kill" anyone failing to halt when so directed; could not be held liable because his first duty was obedience, in view of the serious situation, and he had no ground for doubt as to the legality of the order to shoot.[35]

In modern time, a number of difficulties may arise with the passing of an act of indemnity by the government. While suppressing insurrection or rebellion, acts of atrocity and extreme brutality can be committed in good faith. For instance, a military person could commit acts of torture upon a prisoner and could be acting in good faith in order to extract what that person believes to be vital security information. Since the terms "good faith" and "in national interest" remains undefined for the purposes of the suppression of insurrection or maintenance of public order, there could be no limit of the unlawful violence that may be perpetrated upon individual under martial law regime. The questions which arise are: Can a constitutional court be deprived of its jurisdiction to deal with cases of wrongdoing arising out of military operations during martial law? Can a person who is injured by wrongdoing find himself without a remedy as a result of the indemnity legislation? Can persons injured by *mala fide* action pursue their claims before the Courts? Could such person claim compensation from the government for *mala fide* injuries? Can the government reject the application for compensation claim without giving any reasons? We have to seek answers to these questions from the international human rights law.

The Remedy for Violation of Rights

A fundamental principle is that a State responsible for a wrongful act bears the duty to make full reparation for the injury caused by that act. The individual right to a remedy is contained in several human rights treaties. Article 8 of the UDHR states that: "everyone has the right to an

34 The Army Act, 1950, section 41 provides that the command must relate to military duty, it must be a specific command to an individual i.e., it must be capable of individual execution by the person to whom it is addressed, and justified by military, as well as by civil, law and usage.

35 Ehrenzweig Albert, Soldiers' Liability for Wrongs Committed on Duty, *Cornell L. Rev.*, Vol. 30, 1944, pp. 191-192.

effective remedy by the competent national tribunals for acts violating the fundamental rights granted to him by the constitution or by law." ICCPR article 2 paragraph 3 acknowledges the right to a remedy for violations of the rights set forth therein. The UN General Assembly has adopted the Basic Principles and Guidelines on the Right to a Remedy and Reparation for Victims of Violations of International Human Rights and Humanitarian Law in 2005.[36] The Basic Principles contain 27 principles and thirteen paragraphs. The first two paragraphs recall the obligation "to respect, ensure respect for, and implement international human rights law and international humanitarian law", and identify means and methods by which States can fulfill that obligation. Paragraph three recalls the duty to investigate gross violations of international human rights law and serious violations of humanitarian law in case these violations constitute crimes under international law. Paragraph seven, article 11, formulates a victims' right to remedies: "Remedies for gross violations of international human rights law (IHRL) and serious violations of international humanitarian law (IHL) include the victim's right to the following as provided for under international law: (i) Equal and effective access to justice; (ii) Adequate, effective and prompt reparation for the harm suffered; and (iii) Access to relevant information concerning violations and reparation mechanisms." Principle 11 follows the assumption that a remedy is owed only if there is: a breach of obligation, in case gross violations of IHRL or serious violations of IHL; resulting harm, indicated by "harm suffered"; and lastly, an injured party which is in this case the victim of gross violation of international human rights law or serious violations of humanitarian law.

The Basic Principles define the term 'victims' in paragraph 8 of the text as, "persons who individually or collectively suffered harm, including physical or mental injury, emotional suffering, economic loss or substantial impairment of their fundamental rights, through acts or omissions that constitute gross violations of IHRL, or serious violations of IHL." Further, "where appropriate, and in accordance with domestic law, the term victims also includes the immediate family or dependents of the direct victim or persons injured in assisting direct victims." The term, "equal and effective access to justice," is elaborated in paragraphs 12 to 14 of the Basic Principles, which provides that, "a victim ....shall have equal access to an effective judicial remedy as provided for under

36 The UN General Assembly Resolution 60/147 of 16 December 2005: Basic Principles and Guidelines on the Right to a Remedy and Reparation for Victims of Gross Violations of International Human Rights Law and Serious Violations of International Humanitarian Law, UN Doc. A/RES/60/147.

international law. Other remedies available to the victim include access to administrative and other bodies, as well as mechanisms, modalities and proceedings conducted in accordance with domestic law."

Access to justice is a basic human right conferred by the common law and exists unless it is taken away under any valid exercise of statutory or constitutional power by the legislature. It is generally accepted that States may reasonably impose limitations on the access to a court by statutes of limitations, jurisdiction and granting of immunities. The right of access to justice may be limited; however, must not be disproportionately restricted to the extent that they impair the very essence of the right. Article 12 of the Basic Principles further recommends States to: "disseminate information about available remedies, take measures to ease access for victims, protect victims against interference, intimidation and retaliation, provide proper assistance to victims seeking access to justice and make available appropriate legal, diplomatic and consular means to ensure that victims can exercise this right."

India is a signatory to the most IHRL and IHL treaties and has obligation to respect the international law and treaties.[37]The right to adequate, effective and prompt reparation for harm suffered is elaborated in Article 18 of Basic Principle, which states that: "In accordance with domestic law and international law and taking account of individual circumstances, victims of gross violations of IHRL and serious violations of IHL should, as appropriate and proportional to the gravity of the violation and the circumstances of each case, be provided with full and effective reparation, as laid out in principles 19 to 23, which include the following forms: restitution, compensation, rehabilitation, satisfaction and guarantees of non-repetition." Therefore, an Act of Indemnity, if passed by the Parliament (in future), should not deny access to justice to the victims who have suffered gross violation of human rights under martial law regime.

---

37 The Preamble to the Indian Constitution declares that India is a sovereign Democratic Republic. Article 253 of the Constitution dealing with the legislation for giving effect to international agreements, provides that the Parliament has power to make any law for the whole or any part of the territory of India for implementing treaty, agreement or convention with any other country or countries or any decision made at any international conference, association or other body. Article 51 is considered the concrete provision dealing with the relation of Indian Constitution and international law. The Article mandates the State to endeavour to promote international peace and security, to maintain good relations with other nations, to respect international law and to settle international dispute by peaceful means. Clause (c) of Article 51 obligates India to respect international law.

The Constitutional courts in India may also be approached to determine whether military courts or commissions constituted under martial law regime for trial of civilian were independent and impartial. The European Court of Human Rights has examined the conformity of the martial law tribunals in Turkey with article 6(1) of the European Convention on Human Rights (ECHR).[38] In the *Yalgin* case,[39] for instance, two of the applicants submitted that their right to a fair hearing had been breached as a consequence of their conviction by the Ankara Martial Law Court which lacked independence and impartiality. The European Court noted that the Martial Law Court had been set up to deal with offences aimed at undermining the constitutional order and its democratic regime. It concluded, however, that it was not its task to determine *in abstract* whether it was necessary to set up such courts in a Contracting State or to review the relevant practice, but to ascertain whether the manner in which one of them functioned infringed the applicants' right to a fair trial.

The Martial Law Courts in Turkey have five members: two civilian judges, two military judges and an army officer. The question of the independence and impartiality of the military judges and the army officer were considered together, while the independence and impartiality of the two civilian judges were not challenged. The military judges selected for the Courts were appointed with the approval of the Chief of Staff and by a decree signed by the Minister of Defence, the Prime Minister and the President of the Republic. The army officer, a senior colonel, was appointed on the proposal of the Chief of Staff and in accordance with the rules governing the appointment of military judges. This officer was removable on the expiry of one year after his appointment. With regard to the existence of safeguards to protect the members of the Martial Law Court against outside pressure, the European Court noted that the military judges undergo the same professional training as their civilian counterparts and they enjoy constitutional safeguards identical to those of civilian judges. They may not be removed from office or made to retire early without their consent; as regular members of a Martial Law Court they sit as individuals. According to the Constitution, they must be independent and no public authority may give them instructions concerning their judicial activities or influence them in the performance of their duties. However, three other aspects of

38 Article 6(1) of the ECHR says that in the determination of his civil rights … everyone is entitled to a fair and public hearing within a reasonable time by an independent and impartial tribunal established by law.

39 *Case of Yalgin and others v. Turkey*, judgment of European Court of Human Rights of 25 September 2001.

their status calls into question their independence and impartiality: (i) the military judges are servicemen who still belong to the army, which in turn takes orders from the executive; (ii) as the applicant rightly pointed out, they remain subject to military discipline and assessment reports are compiled on them for that purpose. They therefore need favourable reports both from their administrative superiors and their judicial superiors in order to obtain promotion; (iii) decisions pertaining to their appointment are to a great extent taken by the administrative authorities and the army". Lastly, the army officer sitting in the Martial Law Court was subordinate in the hierarchy to the commander of the martial law and/or the commander of the army corps concerned and was not in any way independent of these authorities. The European Court then observed that: "even appearances may be of some importance. What is at stake is the confidence which the courts in a democratic society must inspire in the public and above all, as far as criminal proceedings are concerned, in the accused. In deciding whether in a given case there is a legitimate reason to fear that a particular court lacks independence or impartiality, the standpoint of the accused is important without being decisive. What is decisive is whether his doubts can be held to be objectively justified."[40]

The Court further considered that in this case, the tribunal's members included persons who were in a subordinate position, in terms of their duties and the organization of their service, *vis-à-vis* one of the parties, accused persons may entertain a legitimate doubt about those persons' independence. Such a situation seriously affects the confidence which the courts must inspire in a democratic society. In the light of all these considerations, the Court was of the opinion that the applicants tried in a Martial Law Court on charges of attempting to undermine the constitutional order of the State, could have legitimate reason to fear about being tried by a bench which included two military judges and an army officer under the authority of the officer commanding the state of martial law. The Court therefore concluded that there had been a violation of article 6(1) of the ECHR as the Martial Law Court's lacked independence and impartiality.

In India, the military courts or commission which may be established during martial law regime would be composed of military officers and a civilian judge.[41] Right to a fair trial by an independent and impartial

40 *Case of Yalgin and others v. Turkey*, judgment of European Court of Human Rights of 25 September 2001, para 45.

41 The Manual of Military Law, 2010, Volume I, Chapter VII, para 18 provides, "Military courts under Martial Law are convened under the orders of the Administrator. One

tribunal is part of article 6(1) of the ECHR; but in India there are glaring deficiencies in the safeguards provided to the accused and in the attitude of those administering the military justice system. The military tribunals are not independent of the chain of command and the military officer convening a court martial exercises influence over it at every stage.

The evolving basic rights of human beings, notably the right to life and the right to physical and moral integrity of the human person under international law dictate that the states must provide effective remedy against serious violations of human rights even during state emergencies. A victim of a gross violation of human rights should have access to an effective judicial remedy. Therefore, once the law and order has been restored, the government must establish courts or other tribunals presided over by independent, impartial and competent individuals to ensure that victims have access to an effective judicial remedy.

Conclusion

When a state of war or of insurrection or rebellion exists, the government may use the amount of force necessary in the circumstances to restore order. A proclamation of martial law is not necessary. Once the military has achieved its aim and the law and order has been re-established, the government issues an indemnity act which applies to proceedings in the courts against the government or any other person acting under the direction or with the approval of the government. The Act has retrospective effect and applies both to proceedings already pending and those that may be instituted in future. The Act provides that no civil or criminal proceedings be instituted in any court of law against the state, its employees or its appointees in respect of acts done in good faith whilst acting for the purpose of, or in connection with, the suppression of insurrection or maintenance of public order. A written certificate by the concerned minister or the officer of the government would suffice that the act was done for the suppression of insurrection. The civil and criminal proceedings already instituted can be terminated on the basis of the certificate issued by the concerned officer of the ministry. When proceedings are terminated by the issue of a certificate, the courts are prohibited from ordering the legal costs already incurred by the claimants to be paid by the Government. If the court is of the opinion that such proceedings should not have been instituted

civil member having judicial experience should, if possible, be appointed to each court. These courts will deal with all offences including breaches of Martial Law Regulations."

because the injury arose out of *bona fide* action to suppress insurrection or to maintain public order, it can also terminate such proceedings without ministerial certificate.[42]

Over the last seven decades, there have been substantial progresses in identifying the fundamental norms of human rights that are accepted by all nations and peoples across the world. Prohibitions against torture, summary execution, prolonged arbitrary detention, and enforced disappearances; are violations of the Universal Declaration of Human Rights, and other international Conventions and have found their way into customary international law. The States have a serious responsibility to investigate such cases if reported during martial law.[43]

Under article 4 of the ICCPR, the government can impose restrictions on certain rights, including freedom of movement, expression, and association, during states of emergency, but only "to the extent strictly required by the exigencies of the situation." The martial law comes to an abrupt end with the restoration of order. The Common Law rules regarding criminal liability are relatively simple; a member of the armed forces who commits a crime while assisting in maintaining civil order is not protected from criminal prosecution because of his military status. The military authorities cannot take protection of misleading statement---*silent enimleges inter arma* [in time of war, the law is silent].[44] Once normalcy returns, the government may have to prove to the court[45] that the conditions were extraordinary which justified imposition of martial

42 Feltoe G., Legalising Illegalities, *The Rhodesian Law Journal*, October 1975, Vol. 15, Part 2, pp. 167-176.

43 For more details on the subject see: Roht-Arriaza Naomi, State Responsibility to Investigate and Prosecute Grave Human Rights Violations in International Law, *California Law Review*, Vol. 78, 1990, pp. 449-513.

44 Michael F. Noone, Legal Liability of the Armed Forces When Dealing With Internal Disturbances: The Unsatisfactory Anglo-American Approach, CUA Law Scholarship Repository, 1991, pp. 9.

45 The role of the Court in the context of martial law is only to the extent of maintaining proper relationship between the military and civil authority and to ensure that the military does not usurp the power of civilian authority. The military necessity, even when approved by the executive, could not be a self-justifying plea. The military remains responsible not only to his superiors and the government, but to the law and the courts. The military must act, at least when dealing with citizens within the country, within the confines of the Constitution and subject to civil, that is, judicial control. Jacobusten Broek, Wartime Power of the Military over Citizen Civilians within the Country, *California Law Review*, Vol. 41, No. 2, 1953, pp. 167- 208.

rule and the measures adopted were warranted by the exigencies of the situation. The government must also ensure that any measure taken under the martial law is strictly proportionate to the aim pursued and that these powers are not applied in a discriminatory manner.

Chapter IV

Habeas Corpus and Martial Law

In the preceding Chapters, it is seen that martial law is imposed in a specific area in order to suppress a rebellion or insurrection and entails commission of acts which may infringe rights of the people. Arresting rebels with or without warrant and detaining them is a common measure adopted to suppress such rebellions or insurrections. A detained person loses enjoyment of almost all the rights including his right to life and liberty. In this context, the writ of *habeas corpus* plays a significant role in ensuring production of arrested person before the court and examining the validity of the detention, so that he can be released, if invalidly detained. In view of the correlation between martial law and *habeas corpus*, this chapter discusses the possibility of arrest and detention of an offender during martial law regime, the application of the rights to *habeas corpus* in such circumstances and the power of courts to issue the writ of *habeas corpus* under the Constitutions of various countries.

During the British rule, when martial law was declared in any territory in India, the military authorities had the power to arrest and detain any person who was engaged in activities prohibited under the Martial Law Ordinance or was violating the martial law order. The military authorities had the power to interrogate the arrested person and prosecute him in the special military court constituted under the Ordinance. There were very few instances in British-India where petitions were filed on behalf of detained persons in the courts for the issuance of the writ of *habeas corpus*.[1] For instance, in 1921, in *Re*

1 The original purpose of the writ of *habeas corpus* is to bring a person before a court to ensure that the person's imprisonment or detention is not illegal. In addition to being used to test the legality of an arrest or confinement, the writ may be used to obtain judicial review of (i) the regularity of the extradition process, (ii) the right to or amount of bail, or (iii) the jurisdiction of a court that has imposed a criminal sentence. Garner Bryan A., Black's Law Dictionary, Third Edition, 2014, Thomson Reuters, p. 825.

Kochunni Elaya Nair[2], an application for the issuance of writ of *habeas corpus* was made for the release of the prisoner who was alleged to have been illegally detained. It was contended on his behalf that the accused could not be legally arrested for an offence committed inside the Martial Law Area when he was at the time of his arrest outside the Area. Secondly, the magistrate, before whom he was brought and who refused to release him on bail, had no jurisdiction to exercise his powers, since Clause (6) of the Martial Law Ordinance No. II of 1921 provided for the constitution of summary courts of criminal jurisdiction in any administration area that may be proclaimed as Martial Law Area.

There is no express provision in the Indian Constitution for declaration of martial law and it has not been proclaimed in India since independence. However, Article 34 provides that the Parliament may by law indemnify any person in the service of the Union or of a State or any other person in respect of any act done by him in connection with the maintenance or restoration of order in any area within the territory of India where martial law was in force or validate any sentence passed, punishment inflicted, forfeiture ordered or other act done under martial law in such area. Therefore, it is implicit in the text of Article 34 of the Constitution that the government may declare martial law in any area within the territory of India.

Martial law is unlike civil law because it is not statutory in nature. It is the will of the military commander, subject to a few regulations. It has been proclaimed in a number of democracies only when necessary and is the law resorted to in times of state/national emergencies. While unfettered military power may be necessary to preserve the State in times of emergencies, however, this power cannot be absolute and balance has to be struck between necessity and use of such military power.

Habeas Corpus

The writ of *habeas corpus* has been described as a great constitutional privilege or the first security of civil liberty. The writ provides a prompt and effective remedy against illegal detention. The writ of *habeas corpus,* which predates the Magna Carta, is closely linked to martial law, though the exact nature of this relationship is difficult to ascertain because of the difference of opinion amongst the scholars about the nature and the use of writ itself.[3] *Habeas corpus*, translated literally from Latin, means "you

2 AIR 1922 Madras 215.

3 Rankin Rober S., 1935, *When Civil Law Fails: Martial Law and its Legal Basis in the*

have the body". Initially the King's court developed *habeas corpus* to centralize judiciary and collect revenue.[4] This writ which originated as a tool of power later on became a tool to secure individual's liberty.[5] The writ of *habeas corpus* of the court gave judges the power to command the presence of a person before the court.[6] By issuing a writ, a judge or court may compel those holding a prisoner to produce the prisoner and prove that they have legally incarcerated the individual. The writ provides a prompt and effective remedy against illegal detention as to enable the Court to decide the validity, jurisdiction or justification for such detention. The writ of *habeas corpus* is an important check against an inordinate concentration of power in the executives as it allows the judiciary to quash illegal detentions. The principal aim of the writ is to ensure swift judicial review of alleged unlawful detention on liberty or freedom of the person which is one of the most fundamental guarantees of personal liberty.

Habeas Corpus under the American Law

The American doctrine of *habeas corpus* finds its origin in the common law of England. When the US Constitution was being drafted, the writ and its common law protections were placed in the first article of the Constitution. Article I, Section 9, Clause 2 of the Constitution provides: "The privilege of the writ of *habeas corpus* shall not be suspended unless when in cases of rebellion or invasion the public safety may require it." By placing this provision in the first article of the Constitution, the founders allowed only the Congress to hold the power to suspend the privilege of *habeas corpus* and therefore the prohibition is directed to the Federal Government of the Unites States. There are two conditions precedent to the suspension of the writ. These are: (i) The existence of rebellion or invasion, and (ii) Grounds of public safety. These two conditions must co-exist before the writ can

---

United States, Duke University Press, p. 35.

4 See, Anthony Gregory, 2013, *The Power of Habeas Corpus in America: From the King's Prerogative to the War on Terror*, Cambridge Press, p.11.

5 *Ibid.*

6 The writ of *Habeas corpus*, or written order of the court, gave judges the power to command the presence of a person before the court. This power worked two ways: (1) the writ was an order for the government and the accused to appear before the court; and (2) it required the government to explain why a person was being detained. If the court was not satisfied by the government's explanations for holding a person, the judges had the power to free the prisoner. People in England believed that *habeas corpus* was an important protection against the government holding people as prisoners simply for political or personal reasons. Carolyn Pereira and Nisan Chavnik, *Habeas Corpus* and Enemy Combatants, *Social Education*, Vol. 72(5), 2008, pp 236–245.

be suspended. Once the writ has been suspended, the executive may arrest any person without giving grounds, and such arrests go without a judicial remedy. The suspension of the writ does not legalize arrests and detention. The person who is responsible for the arrests and detention may be held liable for illegal actions, if any.

In spite of the clarity of both the common law and the United States' Constitution, the writ of *habeas corpus* has not always been well respected and at times the courts have resisted these abuses. During the Civil War, President Lincoln declared martial law in many areas and ordered suspension of the privilege of *habeas corpus*.

In 1861, John Merryman was arrested at two o'clock in the morning without any warrant by the armed forces. He was then conveyed to Fort McHenry, where he was imprisoned by the commanding officer, without warrant from any lawful authority. When Chief Justice Roger B. Taney, then sitting on the Circuit Court for Maryland, issued a writ of *habeas corpus*, the commanding officer of the fort, General George Cadwalader, in his return to the writ, stated that Merryman was arrested by order of General Keim of Pennsylvania, and conveyed as a prisoner to Fort McHenry by his order, and placed in his (General Cadwalader's) custody and detained by him as a prisoner. A copy of the warrant or order under which the prisoner was arrested was demanded by his counsel but refused. It appeared that prisoner was arrested upon general charges of treason and rebellion, without proof, and without giving the names of the witnesses, or specifying the acts which, in the judgment of the military officer, constituted these crimes. When a *habeas corpus* was served on the commanding officer, requiring him to produce the prisoner before a Justice of the Supreme Court, in order that he may examine into the legality of the imprisonment, the answer of the officer was that he is authorized by the President to suspend the writ of *habeas corpus* at his discretion, and, in the exercise of that discretion, suspends it in this case, and on that ground refused obedience to the writ.

In response to this arrogant usurpation of the legislature's sole authority to temporarily suspend *habeas corpus*, Justice Taney issued his opinion in *Ex parte Merryman*:

> I understand that the President not only claims the right to suspend the writ of *habeas corpus* himself, at his discretion, but to delegate that discretionary power to a military officer, and to leave it to him to determine whether he will or will not obey judicial process that may

be served upon him. No official notice has been given to the courts of justice, or to the public, by proclamation or otherwise, that the President claimed this power, and had exercised it in the manner stated in his return. And I certainly listened to it with some surprise, for I had supposed it to be one of those points of constitutional law upon which there was no difference of opinion, and that it was admitted on all hands that the privilege of the writ could not be suspended, except by act of Congress.

From the concluding part of the opinion, it appears that the Chief Justice not only denied the right of the President to suspend the writ of *Habeas corpus,* and the right of General Cadwalader to decline compliance with the command of the writ requiring him to appear with the prisoner and show the cause of the detention, but he also denied the right of the military authority to make searches, seizures, and arrests without warrant. In this opinion, the justice traced the common law origins of *habeas corpus*, showing that it was always held that only the Parliament could suspend the writ. The Chief Justice insisted:

And these great and fundamental laws, which even Congress itself could not suspend, have been disregarded and suspended, like the writ of *habeas corpus,* by a military order, supported by force of arms. ..... I can only say, that, if the authority which the Constitution has confided to the Judiciary Department, and judicial officers, may thus, upon any pretext and under any circumstances, be usurped by the military power at its discretion, the people of the United States are no longer living under a government of laws, but every citizen holds life, liberty, and property at the will and pleasure of the army officer in whose military district he may happen to be found.

Unfortunately, the Lincoln Administration and his armed forces ignored this decision. For the next two years, Lincoln asked Congress to pass measures authorizing his suspension of *habeas corpus*, but Congress refused to do so. Finally, the Congress passed the *Habeas Corpus* Suspension Act on 3 March 1863 legalizing President's long-standing illegal actions and giving them Constitutional legitimacy.

In 1866, the Supreme Court decided the case *Ex parte Milligan*. In this case, Lambdin P. Milligan, a resident in the loyal State of Indiana, had been tried before a military tribunal convened at Indianapolis during the latter part of the Civil War. The charges were conspiracy against the government, aiding the rebels, and various other offenses. Milligan was found guilty and sentenced to be hanged. He petitioned for *habeas corpus*, and on a certificate of disagreement in the circuit court, the case came before the Supreme Court.

The Supreme Court overturned the conviction of Milligan by a military tribunal because the civilian courts were still open in Indiana and Indiana was not a war zone. Writing for the Court, Justice Chase noted, "The Constitution of the United States is a law for rulers and people, equally in war and in peace, and covers with the shield of its protection all classes of men, at all times, and under all circumstances." The Court held that the military commission was not a court within the meaning of the Constitution.

According to Court, one of the main constitutional provisions was infringed when Milligan was tried by a court not ordained by Congress. Another guarantee was violated when Milligan was denied a jury trial. Members of the military service might lawfully be tried otherwise. In the opinion of the Court, "All other persons, citizens of states where the courts are open, if charged with crime, are guaranteed the inestimable privilege of trial by jury." Later that year, the Chief Justice of the United States Supreme Court, sitting as justice of the federal Circuit Court of Appeals for Maryland held that the power to suspend *habeas corpus* was vested in Congress and, therefore, the President lacked the authority to suspend.

After the Merryman and Milligan cases, there were some minor developments in the doctrine of *habeas corpus* mostly dealing with procedural questions. On 7 December 1941, after the Pearl Harbor attack, the Governor of the Territory of Hawaii invoked powers vested in him by the Organic Act [48 USC 532 (1940)], suspended the privilege of the writ of *habeas corpus* and placed the territory under martial law to be administered by military commander. The President subsequently approved the action. Military tribunals were established in Hawaii to try civilians for violating the laws of the US and the Territory of Hawaii and rules, regulations, orders and the police of the Military Government. In awarding punishment, the military tribunals were to be guided by the penalties authorized by the Manual of Court Martial, the laws of the United States, the Territory of Hawaii, the District of Columbia, and the customs of war. As a result, the military authority promulgated orders from time to time and regulated the daily activities of the civilians. The sentences imposed by the military tribunals could not be reviewed by the appellate court, since they were not part of the judicial system of the United States.

During martial law regime, provost courts levied and collected fines in excess of $1,000,000.[7]

In April 1944, an individual convicted of assault by a military court petitioned the US District Court Hawaii for a writ of *habeas corpus*.[8] The court sustained the writ, held that martial law did not exist despite the executive proclamation, and discharged the petitioner.[9] The Supreme Court affirmed the district court's ruling that martial law did not exist when there was no immediate threat of invasion and the civilian courts were open. It did not, however, decide whether the continued suspension of *habeas corpus* was lawful since *habeas corpus* had been restored before the case reached the court. The decision of the Supreme Court in *Hirabayashi* v. *United States* made it clear that any regulation or order, which at the time of its issuance, is reasonably necessary in the judgment of the military commander to resist threatened injury or damage, will be upheld.[10]

Martial Law under the State Constitutions in the Unites States: In the United States, apart from the proclamations of martial law by the Federal Government, martial law has also been resorted to by the state authorities. In some cases, not the governor or military authority, but the mayors of the city of have declared martial law. For instance, in 1906 martial law was declared on an outbreak of fire at San Francisco by the Mayor. During the flood in Ohio, when martial law was imposed, a company of the Ohio National Guard established a picket line surrounding a portion of the affected district with a view to prevent individuals going there without a military pass. An individual, who defied the order and crossed the line to take some pictures, was arrested. On a petition for *habeas corpus*, the court of the Common Pleas held that the commanding officer could issue regulations for the protection of life and property and arrest any person trying to violate such orders. The constitutions of four states expressly recognize the power to declare martial law. Besides, the Organic Acts governing Hawaii, the Philippines and Puerto Pico contain express grant of power to the executive to declare martial law. The constitutions of nearly

7 Anthony Garner, Martial Law, Military Government and the Writ of *Habeas Corpus* in Hawaii, *California Law Review*, Vol. XXXI, No. 5, December 1943, p. 481.

8 Duncan, a civilian worker employed in the navy yard at Honolulu, was arrested after two years of martial rule. He was engaged in a brawl with two armed Marine sentries, tried by a military tribunal and sentenced to six months imprisonment. See: *Duncan* v. *Kahanamoku*, 327 U.S. 304, 310-11 (1945).

9 *Ex parte Duncan*, 66 F.Supp.976, 981-82 (D. Haw. 1944).

10 *Hirabayashi v. Unit States*, (1943) 63 Sup. Ct. 1375, 87 L. Ed. Adv. Ops. 1337.

twenty states provide that laws can be suspended only by the legislature. The exercise of martial law by the state authorities can be challenged before a Federal court and if it finds the exercise of power under a declaration of martial law contrary to the provisions of the Constitution of the United States, it can declare such martial rule illegal and unconstitutional.[11]

***Habeas Corpus* and Terrorism**: After terrorists attack of World Trade Towers on 11 September 2001, a large number of persons were detained in military facilities at the US military base in Guantanamo Bay, Cuba. Shafiq Rasul and Asif Iqbal were two British citizens were captured in Afghanistan and subsequently transferred to Guantanamo Bay. In 2002, they and two Australian citizens, Mamdouh Habib and David Hicks, as well as 12 Kuwaiti citizens, challenged the legality of their detention. Through their relatives, they filed various actions in Federal court alleging that none of them had ever been a combatant against the US or had ever engaged in any terrorist acts. Instead, they claimed that they had been turned over to the US for various reasons, including prisoner bounties and captures by other governments or the Northern Alliance, a coalition of Afghan groups opposed to the Taliban. The detainees claimed that none of them had been charged with any wrongdoing, nor permitted to consult with legal counsel, nor provided access to the courts or any other tribunal. They claimed that denial of these rights violated the Constitution, international law, and treaties of the United States.

In the case of *Shafiq Rasul v. George W Bush* (2004), the Bush administration argued that the United States' court system did not have jurisdiction to issue writs of *habeas corpus* for the Guantanamo prisoners since the base at Guantanamo Bay was (as stated in the deed under which the land was leased to the United States) the property of Cuba. The Supreme Court held that in this case, it had jurisdiction over the *habeas corpus* rights of detainees at the Guantanamo base because the US exercised "exclusive jurisdiction and control" over the military base.

In 2006, Supreme Court heard the case of *Salim Ahmed Hamdan v. Donald H. Rumsfeld*. The Court declared that the Military Commissions were unconstitutional, as they were formed by the Department of Defence, rather than by the Congress, and their procedures and charges were different from those sanctioned in either the Uniform Code of Military Justice or the Geneva Conventions.[12] In response to this decision, the Bush

11 Munim, P. K. Md. Ahdul, Martial Law in the Indo-Pakistan Sub-continent, Unpublished Ph.D, Thesis, University of London, 1960, p. 135-139.

12 Hamdan's military commission violated the Uniform Code of Military Justice (UCMJ)

administration came up with the Military Commissions Act of 2006 which attempted to counter each of the reasons that the Supreme Court based its *Hamdan* decision. It clearly defined the new status of "illegal enemy combatant" and described the process for determining if any non-citizen detainee could be classified as such. It also set up the exact procedures and standards for the operation of Military Commissions to try illegal enemy combatants and defined a new set of charges which would be available for such Commissions to try. The Act also declared that "No court, justice, or judge shall have jurisdiction to hear or consider an application for a writ of *habeas corpus* filed by or on behalf of an alien detained by the United States." [13]

The Supreme Court in *Boumediene v. Bush* (2008), again ruled in favour of the detainees at Guantanamo Bay addressing the entitlement of these detainees to the constitutional privilege of *habeas corpus*. Although Congress had enacted the Detainee Treatment Act of 2005, which provided certain procedures for review of the detainees' status, the Court held that "those procedures are not an adequate and effective substitute for *habeas corpus*." Again in *Munaf v. Geren* (2008), the Supreme Court unanimously concluded that United States courts had jurisdiction over *habeas corpus* petitions filed on behalf of citizens.[14]

---

and the 1949 Geneva Conventions on two counts. First, Hamdan's military commission violated the UCMJ's uniformity principle, which required that the procedures for military commissions and courts–martial be the same insofar as practicable. Second, the military commission violated Common Article 3 (CA3) of the Geneva Conventions, applicable by way of Article 21 of the UCMJ's reference to the law of war, because it did not satisfy CA3's requirement of trial before a regularly–constituted court. John Ip, The Supreme Court and House of Lords in the War on terror: *Inter Arma Silent Leges? Michigan State Journal of International Law,* Vol. 19, No.1, 2010, pp. 1-62.

13 Military Commissions Act, 2006.

14 This case concerned two American citizens, Munaf and Omar, who had voluntarily travelled to Iraq, and subsequently been detained by Multinational Force Iraq after allegedly committing crimes there. Petitions for *habeas corpus* were filed on behalf of both men by family members. In the lower courts, Omar had obtained a preliminary injunction barring his transfer to Iraqi custody. Munaf's petition had been dismissed for lack of jurisdiction. The Supreme Court concluded that United States courts had jurisdiction over *habeas corpus* petitions filed on behalf of citizens such as Munaf and Omar, who were held by American forces operating as part of a multinational force. Both were in the immediate physical custody of American forces answering only to the American chain of command. This was enough to determine the issue of jurisdiction under the *habeas corpus* statute. John Ip, The Supreme Court and House of Lords in the War on terror: *Inter Arma Silent Leges? Michigan State Journal of International Law,* Vol. 19, No.1, 2010, pp. 20.

In fact these decisions have served as a reminder of the sanctity of the right to *habeas corpus* in Anglo-American jurisprudence.[15] The writ of *habeas corpus* remains a critical tool in maintaining the balance between the rights and liberties of individuals and the responsibilities of the federal government to protect the welfare of the nation.[16] In the United States, suspension of *habeas corpus* is justified by the grave threat to the public safety posed by terrorist organizations. There is little that the judiciary can do if the executive chooses to unilaterally suspend *habeas corpus* and ignore any such writs issued by the courts, except protests by the press and a couple of human rights organizations.[17]

Habeas Corpus in Israel

Israel has faced large number of terrorists' attacks on its soil. Israeli armed forces have occupied the West Bank and Gaza since its victory in the Arab-Israeli War of 1967. These territories are administered by the military government, where legislative powers are held by the military commander and judicial power exercised by military courts.[18]Israel has incorporated common-law adversarial procedure after its independence in 1948. The Israeli Supreme Court has jurisdiction to review actions of the military government. In the context of terrorism, the Israeli law provides for arrest as well as administrative detention in both Israel and the occupied territories. The Israel Knesset has passed the Incarceration of Unlawful Combatants Law in 2002 authorizing the detention of "enemy combatants" whose release would harm state security, even if that individual does not pose any actual security threat. Under these conditions, the detained person was

15 Farrell Brian, From Westminster to the World: The Right to *Habeas Corpus* in International Constitutional Law, *Mich. St. U. Coll. L. J. Int'l L.*, Vol. 17, No. 3, 2009, p. 551-565.

16 Carolyn Pereira and Nisan Chavkin, *Habeas Corpus* and "Enemy Combatants", *Social Education*, Vol. 72(5), 2008, pp. 236-245.

17 Tor Ekeland, Suspending *Habeas Corpus*: Article I, Section 9, Clause 2, or the United States Constitution and the War on Terror, *Fordham Law Review*, Vol. 74, 2005, p. 1519.

18 Military courts of first instance are distinguished by number of judges (one or three) and the maximum sentencing power. One-judge courts handle simple cases involving charges with lesser sentencing power. Three-judge courts handle hard cases and are empowered to pass sentences up to the maximum of life in prison or death penalty. Although a number of death sentences were awarded by the military courts, but were subsequently commuted to life sentence. The military court of appeals is composed of three-judge panel, although there is a provision of five-judge panel. Hajjar Lisa, *Courting Conflict: The Israeli Military Court System in the West Bank and Gaza*, Berkeley: University of California Press, p. 255.

entitled to a review of the lawfulness of his detention by an independent judicial officer. Both within Israel or the occupied territories, a detention order upheld at the first judicial review may be appealed to a court of appeals and, finally to the Israeli Supreme Court.

In Israel, criminal suspects are entitled to judicial review within 24 hours, whereas for administrative detainees the period is 48 hours. In the occupied territories, judicial review of criminal and administrative detentions must take place within a period of eight days. Orders of detention for enemy combatants pursuant to the 2002 law must be reviewed by a civilian district court within 14 days. In April 2002, the Israeli Defence Forces issued MO 1500 reaffirming the policy to allow for 18 days of incommunicado detention. This order instituted a blanket prohibition of lawyers' right to meet client for 18 days. Following the initial detention for 18 days, it can be extended by order of a judge for up to six months. There is no requirement that an arrested person be informed of the reason for his arrest at the time he is taken into custody.

In Israel, the judicial review of detention has been granted even if the detention occurs outside of Israel or the occupied territories. Israel maintains a detention review regime in spite of a declared emergency which remains functional in the occupied territories as well as during armed conflict.[19] The High Court of Justice (HCJ) in Israel is authorized under section 15(d)(1) of Basic Law to release persons unlawfully detained or imprisoned (e.g., the authority to issue an order of *habeas corpus*). While in ordinary practice, such claims are usually handled within the framework of regular criminal procedure, this section retains symbolic importance, stressing the role of the HCJ as the safeguard of civil liberties. A careful examination of *habeas corpus* jurisprudence in Israel shows a decline in its legal status and significance.

Habeas Corpus in Canada

In 1982, Canada adopted the Canadian Charter of Rights and Freedoms. This constitutional document has much in common with the American Bill of Rights, but differs on few counts. Section 10 of the Charter states that everyone has the right on arrest or detention ....to have the validity of the detention determined by way of *habeas corpus* and to be released if the

19 Brian Farrell, *Habeas Corpus* in Times of Emergency: A Historical and Comparative View, *Pace International Law Review Online Companion*, Vol. 1, No. 9, April 2010, pp. 74-95.

detention is not lawful.[20] Under section 33, this right can be suspended by legislation only. While a law suspending *habeas corpus* can be challenged on constitutional grounds, the courts can uphold such a law if it finds that law to be demonstrably justified in a free and democratic society. However, even if a law suspending *habeas corpus* is declared to be unconstitutional by a court, that decision can be overridden by Parliament if it expressly declares that the impugned law shall operate notwithstanding the provisions of the Charter. This provision was inserted in the Charter to preserve the principle of Parliamentary supremacy, but it has never been invoked at the Federal level.

The substantive law in Canada respecting *habeas corpus* and other prerogative writs or forms of judicial relief was derived from the laws of England and Wales and still contains many similar substantive features. However, Canada has developed its own procedures for applying the principles of *habeas corpus*. In criminal cases, applications for writs of *habeas corpus* can be filed with a trial court and an appeal from the decision of that court can be taken to the highest provincial courts, the Courts of Appeal. A final appeal to the Supreme Court of Canada is possible if leave is obtained.[21] The Criminal Code provides that an appeal in *habeas corpus* matters shall be heard by the court to which the appeal is directed at an early date, whether in or outside of the prescribed sessions of the court. The Federal Court Act gives the Federal Court of Canada exclusive original jurisdiction to hear applications for writs of *habeas corpus* with respect to members of the Canadian Forces serving outside of the country. Appeals can be taken first to the Federal Court of Appeal and then to the Supreme Court of Canada with leave. In these cases, the provincial courts are not involved.[22]

The Supreme Court of Canada in a recent case[23] has pronounced, "*Habeas corpus* is a fundamental and historic remedy which allows individuals to seek a determination as to the legality of their detention.... Although our legal system continues to evolve, *habeas corpus* remains as fundamental to our modern conception of liberty as it was in the days of King John and any exceptions to its availability must be carefully limited."

20 Constitution Act, 1982, pt.I, s. 10(c).

21 Criminal Code, R.S.C. ch. C-46, s. 784 (1985).

22 Federal Courts Act, R.S.C. ch. F-37, s. 18 (1985).

23 *Minister of Public Safety and Emergency Preparedness and Attorney General of Canada v. Tusif Ur RehmanChhina*, 2019 SCC, [Canadian Supreme Court] decided on 10 May 2019.

The respondent in this case had entered Canada under a pseudo name and obtained refugee status. Later, his refugee status was vacated and he was declared inadmissible to Canada due to misrepresentations in his refugee application and his involvement in criminal activity. Thus, a deportation order was issued against him. He was placed in immigration detention in a maximum security unit. Immigration officials reviewed his detention on a monthly basis, each time upholding the decision that he should be detained. Respondent filed a *habeas corpus* application under Section 10 (c) of the Canadian Charter of Rights and Freedoms on the ground that his detention had become unlawful, because it had become lengthy and indeterminate and the conditions of his detention were inappropriate, breaching his rights under Sections 7 and 9 of the Charter. The Chambers Judge declined to consider respondent's application on the basis that the scheme set out in the Immigration and Refugee Protection Act, 2001 (IRPA) satisfied the Peiroo exception.[24] The Court of Appeal reversed this decision and allowed the respondent's application. The Court, by a majority of 6:1, noted that there are only two exceptions to the availability of *habeas corpus*: (i) challenging the legality of a criminal conviction where a statute provides for a right of appeal; (ii) it is not available in matters of immigration law, because Parliament has put in place a complete, comprehensive and expert statutory scheme which provides for a review as broad as that available by way of *habeas corpus*. The Supreme Court dismissed the appeal filed by Minister of Public Safety and Emergency Preparedness against the judgment of Court of Appeal whereby the detained immigrant's application for *habeas corpus* was allowed.

24 *Peiroo v. Canada (Minister of Employment & Immigration,* (1989), 69 O.R. (2d) 253: The Parliament has put in place a complete, comprehensive and expert statutory scheme providing for review of detention that is at least as broad as, and no less advantageous than *habeas corpus* review, superior courts should decline to exercise their *habeas corpus* jurisdiction in favour of that statutory scheme. It was opined that IRPA was a complete, comprehensive and expert scheme for immigration matters generally, but the statutory scheme set out in the IRPA did not provide for review as broad and advantageous as *habeas corpus* with respect to the specific basis upon which the respondent had challenged the legality of his detention, i.e., the length, uncertain duration and conditions of his detention. It was held that the IRPA scheme fell short in at least three important ways: (i) the onus in detention review was less advantageous to detainees than in *habeas corpus* proceedings; (ii) the scope of immigration detention review before the Federal Courts was narrower than that of a superior court's consideration of a *habeas corpus* application and; (iii) *habeas corpus* provided a more timely remedy than that afforded by judicial review. Therefore, the appeal was dismissed.

Habeas Corpus in France

In France, the preservation of liberty is proclaimed by article 2 of the 1789 Declaration of the Rights of Man, which has been incorporated into the present Constitution of 1958. Article 7 of such Declaration also provides that "No individual may be accused, arrested, or detained except where the law so prescribes, and in accordance with the procedure it has laid down." The Constitution in Article 66 further states that "No one may be arbitrarily detained. The judicial authority, guardian of individual liberty, ensures the observance of this principle under the condition specified by law." France is also a signatory of the European Convention for the Protection of Human Rights and Fundamental Freedoms (ECHR). Article 5 of the ECHR provides that everyone has the right to liberty and sets forth permissible circumstances under which people may be deprived of their liberty and procedural safeguards in case of detention. In particular, it states that "anyone deprived of his liberty by arrest or detention shall be entitled to take proceedings by which the lawfulness of his detention shall be decided speedily by a court and his release ordered if the detention is not lawful."

The Code of Criminal Procedure contains several provisions implementing the constitutional guarantees set forth above. It provides, for example, that "any person arrested by virtue of a warrant who has been held for more than 24 hours without having been interrogated shall be considered as arbitrarily detained. Any judge or civil servant who has ordered or knowingly tolerated arbitrary detention shall be punished with the penalties stated in articles 432-4 to 432-6 of the Penal Code." These articles of the Penal Code deal with infringements on individual liberty by persons exercising governmental authority or who are entrusted with a public service mission. They set forth very harsh penalties.[25]

Furthermore, as a general rule, police cannot detain a suspect more than 24 hours. The public prosecutor may extend this period for another 24 hours. Other extensions must be authorized by a specialized judge, the judge of liberties and detention, or by an investigating judge. Warrants are required for arrests. When placed on provisional detention during a formal

25 Article 432-4, for example, reads as follows: "A person exercising governmental authority or entrusted with a public service mission who, in the performance or on the occasion of performing his or her duties or mission, arbitrarily orders or performs an act prejudicial to individual liberty is punishable by seven years imprisonment and a fine of €100,000. When the prejudicial act is a confinement or detention for a period longer than seven days, the penalty is increased to thirty years imprisonment and a fine of € 450,000."

judicial investigation, in addition to appealing the detention orders to the Investigating Chamber, a suspect or his attorney may file a petition for his release at any time during such investigation. The competent judge or court must rule within eight days from the date of the filing of the appeal (Article 148). Finally, judgments rendered by the Investigating Chamber (including detention orders) and judgments rendered by the Courts of Final Instance in criminal matters may be quashed, in the event of a violation of the law, upon a request filed before the Court of Cassation, France's Supreme Court for civil and criminal matters (Article 567).

Habeas Corpus in Germany

The 1982 German Constitution in Article 104 provides that deprivations of liberty may be imposed only on the basis of a specific enabling statute that contains procedural rules also. Article 104, paragraph 2 requires that any arrested individual be brought before a judge by the end of the day following the day of the arrest. For those detained as criminal suspects, Article 104, paragraph 3 specifically requires that the judge must grant a hearing to the suspect in order to rule on the detention. Restrictions on the power of the authorities to arrest and detain individuals also emanate from Article 2 of the Constitution which guarantees liberty and requires a statutory authorization for any deprivation of liberty. In addition, several other articles of the Constitution have a bearing on the issue. For instance, Article 19 generally requires a statutory basis for any infringements of the fundamental rights guaranteed by the Constitution while also guaranteeing judicial review. In addition, a constitutional obligation to grant remedies for improper detention is required by article 19, of the Constitution which provides, "should any person's right be violated by public authority, he may have recourse to the courts. If no other jurisdiction has been established, recourse shall be to the ordinary courts."

In federal law, the constitutional guarantees against improper detention are incorporated primarily in the Code of Criminal Procedure and the Act on Court Proceedings for Deprivations of Liberty. The Act is applicable on a subsidiary basis to all detentions imposed by federal law, if the specific enabling provisions are not sufficient. In the states, these constitutional guarantees are incorporated in the laws governing the police. The Code of Criminal Procedure applies to all criminal proceedings and it requires that a detained person be brought before the judge on the day of detention as a rule, but at the latest on the day following detention. In addition, this Code provides that a detained person may at any time submit a complaint challenging the detention, by claiming either that the detention was unlawful to begin with or that it is no longer required on the basis of law.

Habeas Corpus in Japan

The Constitution of Japan, which was drafted by Americans when Japan was under the Allied Occupation from 1945 to 1952, was strongly influenced by the US Constitution. Article 34 of the Constitution has a provision, which relates to *habeas corpus*. Article 34 reads: No person shall … be detained without adequate cause; and upon demand of any person such cause must be immediately shown in open court in his presence and the presence of his counsel. The *Habeas Corpus* Act was enacted in 1948 during the Occupation and is implemented through the *Habeas Corpus* Rules. The purpose of the Act is "to enable the people to recover the liberty of a person actually unlawfully deprived of liberty in a prompt and easy manner through a judicial procedure." Further, "any person whose personal liberty is under restraint without due process of law may apply for relief pursuant to the provisions of this Act." It is pertinent to note that the *Habeas Corpus* Rules limit the grounds for obtaining a writ of *habeas corpus* to (a) the absence of a legal right to place a person in custody, and (b) manifest violation of due process, that too after exhaustion of all other remedies. Accordingly, the UN Human Rights Committee criticized Japan for impairing the effectiveness of the remedy for challenging the legality of detention because of the *Habeas Corpus* Rules.[26]

Habeas Corpus in Russia

The right to freedom and personal inviolability is guaranteed by the Russian Constitution. Article 22 of the Constitution provides that arrest or detention shall be authorized by a judicial ruling. Without a judicial ruling, no person may be subjected to detention for a period of more than 48 hours. The legal grounds for taking and holding a criminal suspect or an accused individual in detention are defined by the Code of Criminal Procedure of 2002. Detention as a measure of restraint in regard to the person accused or suspected of committing a crime can be selected by a prosecutor, investigator, or a person conducting the inquiry, if there is a possibility that the individual may obstruct the investigation, hide from the authorities, continue his criminal activities, or threaten witnesses and other participants of the investigation process. Detention of an individual suspected or accused of a crime is allowed only in those cases where the

26 United Nations, Concluding Observations of the Human Rights Committee: Japan, CCPR/C/79/Add.102, 19 November 1998.

minimum punishment established by law for such a crime is no less than two-year imprisonment.[27]

Habeas Corpus in Britain

In England, after the Norman Conquest in 1066, a centralized court system was followed all over the previously existing localized system. For these centralized courts to exercise their judicial functions, a procedure was developed to command a sheriff to bring a party physically into court. Thus, by 1230, the writ of *habeas corpus* was established in this role and continued to be employed over the following centuries. In the subsequent period, this process of the writ was transformed into a guarantee of personal liberty.[28] This in due course transformed *habeas corpus* into a system to test the legality of imprisonment. After a number of unsuccessful attempts to strengthen *habeas corpus*, the British Parliament passed the *Habeas Corpus* Act in 1679.

The Act of 1679 was a significant piece of legislation.[29] It applied to all criminal cases and provided the following reforms: In case any British

27 The following procedure is adopted for extension of period of detention: In such cases, the official who conducts the inquiry, the prosecutor or an investigator, is required to submit a detention request to the judge for judicial approval of the detention order within 48 hours before the expiration of the detention period. The request is considered by an individual judge during *in camera* hearings within eight hours after receipt of the request. The hearing is attended by the detainee, prosecutor, and defence attorney, if retained. The detention order can be issued in absentia only if the suspect/accused is reported for an international search. The detainee is allowed to provide explanations to the judge. After hearings, the judge decides whether to authorize the detention, to deny the detention request and release the individual, or to extend the detention for the next 72 hours in order to let the investigator build the case for the next detention hearings. The judge's ruling can be appealed to the higher court within three days. Amendments to the Code of Criminal Procedure, adopted in 2008, did not affect the rights or status of individuals during the pretrial detention period.

28 In England, mid-fourteenth century cases reveal instances of the writ of *habeas corpus* being issued upon petition of a defendant who has been imprisoned while awaiting trial in private actions. These cases mark two significant developments in *habeas corpus* jurisprudence: (i) these writs were issued on petition of the detained person, rather than *suasponte* by the court; and (ii) issuance of the writ implied the court wished to inquire into the cause and legitimacy of imprisonment ordered by a lower court. These developments were largely a result of efforts by centralized courts to divest older local courts of jurisdiction. For more details see; Farrell Brian, From Westminster to the World: The Right to *Habeas Corpus* in International Constitutional Law, *Mich. St. U. Coll. L. J. Int'l L.*, Vol. 17, No. 3, 2009, p. 551-565.

29 In England, *Darnel's Case* (1627) 3 How. St. Tr. 1 (KB) marked the emergence of the writ of *habeas corpus* to challenge the legitimacy of an executive detention. In 1627,

subjects was committed to prison in any criminal matter, the said person shall not be moved to other places of confinement, unless specifically provided by the writ of *habeas corpus* or any other legal writ under the Act (section VIII).For preventing illegal imprisonments in Prisons beyond the Seas, the imprisonment of subjects in Scotland, Ireland, the islands, or "places beyond the seas" was made illegal (section XI).The Courts of Lord Chancery, Exchequer, Common Pleas and King's Bench were all authorized to issue the writ of *habeas corpus*. The Judges were required to consider petitions for writ of *habeas corpus* even outside of regular court terms under threat of fine (section II and IX). A sheriff or jailer served with a writ of *habeas corpus* was required to make return and produce the individual before the court within three days (section 1).[30] The Judges were required to discharge the person if no cause was shown, release the individual on bail, or, remand the person to prison within two days of production (section II). No person discharged pursuant to a writ of *habeas corpus* could be recommitted for the same offence without court order, under threat of fine. Violators of this provision were liable to pay fine of five hundred pounds (section V). Persons not eligible for release were issued assured trial in a timely manner (section VI). Limitation period of two years was fixed for prosecution for offences under the Act (Section XVI).

By the end of the seventeenth century, *habeas corpus* was a fundamental part of English law. The British Government did not extend the *Habeas Corpus* Act of 1679 to Britain's colonies until the nineteenth century. However, in most colonies including India, the common law version of *habeas corpus* was available once courts were established with the same jurisdiction as the English superior courts. At the onset of WW

Charles I detained subjects that refused to contribute to a loan needed to fund a war with France and Spain. At the time of *Darnel's Case,* there was little doubt that the sovereign had long exercised a power of arbitrary committal where there was thought to be a threat to the safety of the realm. However, when judges refused to bail the prisoners, widespread outrage at the decision led to the Petition of Right of 1628, which prohibited imprisonment without express charges. In 1629, Charles I began flouting *habeas corpus* despite the Petition of Right. This led to the passage of the *Habeas Corpus* Act of 1640. The Act of 1640 was ineffective, and was eventually replaced by the *Habeas Corpus* Act of 1679, under which the legality of an executive detention could be challenged. Tor Ekeland, Suspending *Habeas Corpus*: Article I, Section 9, Clause 2, or the United States Constitution and the War on Terror, *Fordham Law Review*, Vol. 74, Issue 3, 2005, pp. 1475-1519.

30 The time was extended to 10 days if the person was imprisoned 20 miles or more from the court, and to 20 days if imprisoned 100 miles of more from the court (section 1).

II, a Defence Regulation [31] was promulgated in Britain, which provided: "If the Secretary of State has reasonable cause to believe any person to be of hostile origin or associations, or to have been recently concerned in acts prejudicial to the public safety or the defence of the realm, or in the preparation or instigation of such acts, and that by reason thereof it is necessary to exercise control over him, he may make an order against that person directing that he be detained." The Regulation also provided that a "person detained in pursuance of this regulation shall be deemed to be in lawful custody." Thus, *habeas corpus* was not available where the Secretary had reasonable belief that a detainee presented a security threat.

In the UK, the first legislative response to the 9/11 attacks was the enactment of the Anti-Terrorism, Crime and Security Act, 2001 (ATCSA). It contained a number of provisions relating to counter–terrorism measures and authorized indefinite detention of a person who was suspected to be a terrorist.[32] However, Part 4 of the ATCSA was controversial, because it infringed Article 5 of the European Convention for the Protection of Human Rights and Fundamental Freedoms 1950 (ECHR), which protects the right to liberty and security of the person. Part 4 of the ATSCA necessitated the British government to lodge a formal derogation from Article 5 in accordance with Article 15 of the ECHR, which the British Government avoided. A number of individuals who were suspected of terrorism related activities (as certified by the Home Secretary) and were detained at Belmarsh Prison in London, challenged the lawfulness of their detention. The House of Lords ruled that the ATCSA detention regime was incompatible with the ECHR.[33] In response, the British Government came out with the Prevention of Terrorism Act 2005, which created a new legislative framework for detention by empowering the Home Secretary to impose control orders upon both citizen and non-citizen terrorist suspects

31 The Defence (General) Regulations, 1939.

32 Part 4 of the ATCSA authorized the Home Secretary to certify a person a suspected international terrorist for the purposes of the ATCSA if the Home Secretary reasonably believed that the person's presence in the UK was a risk to national security and suspected that the person was a "terrorist." In cases where legal or practical considerations barred the UK from removing a non–citizen certified as a suspected international terrorist, Section 23 of the ATCSA authorized indefinite detention. The Home Secretary's decision could only be scrutinized in proceedings before SIAC, which could cancel a certification if it concluded that there were no reasonable grounds for suspecting the person to be a terrorist as defined in Section 21(1).

33 The House of Lords quashed the derogation order and declared Section 23 of the ATCSA incompatible with Articles 5 and 14 of the ECHR. *Belmarsh* case: *A v. Secretary of State for the Home Department* [2005] 2 A.C. 68.

involved in terrorism-related activities. Thereafter, the House of Lords has scrutinized the government's actions on matters of national security in its decisions concerning control orders 252 and the use of evidence obtained through torture.[34]

The common law version of *habeas corpus* came to India initially with the establishment of the Supreme Court by the Regulating Act of 1773. The *habeas corpus* was statutorily established in India through the Criminal Procedure Code (Cr PC) of 1872. Section 81 of the Cr PC provided that any European subject who was detained in custody by any person, might apply to the High Court for an order directing the person detaining him to bring him before the court and to abide by such order as might be made by it. The provision, however, applied to British European subjects only. The provisions were continued in the Cr PC, 1875, 1882, 1898 and the repealing Act of 1914. Under the Criminal Law Amendment Act, 1923 any High Court could pass an order in respect of persons within the territorial limits of its appellate criminal jurisdiction.

Habeas Corpus in British-India

The modern Indian legal system was largely based on the English model established during the colonial period. The *Habeas Corpus* Act of 1679 was incorporated into Indian law in the late nineteenth century. The High Court had the power, apart from section 491 of the Cr PC, 1914 to issue a writ of *habeas corpus*. However, in colonial India the writ suffered a regressive history.[35] In the late nineteenth century, there were a number of legislative enactments and the power of the judiciary to issue writ against the executive actions was very limited.[36]In 1775, the first writ of *habeas corpus* was issued in India for one Kemaluddin Khan, a revenue collector held by the East India Company over the issue of late payments. The First War of Independence in 1857 was a transformative event in the history of British India. The Indian Council Act, 1861 gave the Governor-General

34 For more details see: John Ip, The Supreme Court and House of Lords in the War on terror: *Inter Arma Silent Leges? Michigan State Journal of International Law,* Vol. 19, No.1, 2010, pp. 1-62.

35 Hussain Nasser, 2003, *The Jurisprudence of Emergency: Colonialism and the Rule of Law*, The University of Michigan Press, p. 73.

36 Under the East India Company there were two parallel judicial systems: (i) Crown courts, instituted directly by the monarch through charter and letter patents which held jurisdiction over both the European as well as natives in the Presidencies; and (ii) Company's courts having jurisdiction over the natives in the mofussil. Warren Hasting reformed the system in 1772 and the Regulating Act, 1773 further altered the institutional structure of judicial system in the British India.

broad legislative power and executive control. The Indian High Courts Act, passed in the same year, created the high courts by combining the powers and jurisdiction of the Crown and Company courts and the scope of *habeas corpus* were also enlarged.

In 1870, a petition was filed for issue of a writ of *habeas corpus*.[37] In this case, *Ameer Khan* was arrested in Calcutta in July 1869 and taken to moffusil jail. A warrant of arrest had neither been furnished nor was the prisoner's counsel advised of the charges against the prisoner. It was informed by the superintendent of the jail that the person was held under special orders covered by Regulation III of 7 April 1818.[38] It was argued for the petitioner that if Regulation III did authorize an arbitrary detention, it would have to be considered a bad law, as no colonial legislature could pass an Act repugnant to section 29 of the Magna Carta. On the other hand, the advocate argued that this detention was an act of state over which the court could claim no jurisdiction. Justice Norman of the Supreme Court of Calcutta, the presiding judge, however, issued a rule *nisi*, calling on the superintendent of the jail to show why a writ of *habeas corpus* should not be issued. The Advocate General argued that all of English law had never been introduced into the colony, and therefore, the *Habeas Corpus* Act was inapplicable. According to Advocate General, the English had inherited absolute power from their Mughal predecessors. The Mohamedan law gave the sovereign absolute power over the subject, and the Governor-General has the same power when Regulations III of 1818 was issued. Justice Norman justified the suspension of the *habeas corpus* on the grounds that the British constitution has a "flexible character"; and if the British Parliament could temporarily suspend the *Habeas Corpus* Act in the time of public distress or danger, the Indian Legislature is also justified in exercising exceptional power. An Act for the suspension of the *habeas corpus* in such time is no violation of constitution, observed Justice Norman.

In 1898, the Code of Criminal Procedure (Cr PC) provided that the High Courts could issue directions in certain matters "in the nature of a

37 *Re Ameer Khan*, [1870], 6 Bengal Law Reports, 392.

38 The Regulations for the Confinement of State Prisoners, Regulations III, 1818 provided: "Whereas reasons of State ....occasionally render it necessary to place under special restraint, individuals against whom there may not be sufficient ground to institute any judicial proceedings, or when such proceedings may not be adapted to the nature of the case, or may for other reasons be inadvisable or improper."

habeas corpus" but could not interfere in cases involving "State Prisoners" or "State Offences."[39]

In 1921, martial law was imposed in certain parts of India during the Moplah rebellion. In the case of *Re Kochunni Elaya Nair*[40] an application for issue of a writ of *habeas corpus* was made for the release of the prisoner who was alleged to have been illegally detained. It was contended on his behalf that the accused could not be legally arrested for an offence committed inside the Martial Law Area when he was at the time of his arrest outside the area. Secondly, the magistrate before whom he was brought and who refused to release him on bail had no jurisdiction to exercise his powers, since Clause (6) of the Martial Law Ordinance No. II of 1921 provided for the constitution of summary courts of criminal jurisdiction in any administration area that may be proclaimed as Martial Law Area. However, Clause 16 of the Martial Law Ordinance II, 1921, which excluded the interference of other courts, did not refer to the jurisdiction of the High Court which could issue such a writ, if the summary military court acted without jurisdiction.[41]

On the question whether a police officer can arrest a person outside the Martial Law Area for an offence committed inside it, it was held that, under the provisions of Section 177 of the Cr PC, the rule as to jurisdiction was that it was the area within which the offence was committed and not the place where the offender was found which determined the jurisdiction of the Court. Section 54 of the same Code authorized any police officer to arrest without a warrant and without an order from a Magistrate a person concerned in any cognizable offence. Section 50 authorized a police officer for the purpose of arresting without warrant any person whom he was authorized to arrest to pursue such person into any place in British India. Section 60 directed a police officer making an arrest without a warrant to take the person arrested without unnecessary delay before a Magistrate having jurisdiction in the case. Spencer J. said that there was no alteration of the law in this respect inconsequence of the constitution of the Martial Law courts and the provisions of the Cr PC were not abrogated or suspended by the introduction of Martial Law. On the contrary, Clause (12) and the other clauses of the Ordinance No II for 1921 indicated that the courts constituted under it were to follow, as far as possible, the

39 The Code of Criminal Procedure (Cr PC), 1898, section XXXVII.

40 AIR 1922 Madras 215.

41 Minattur Joseph, 1962, *Martial Law in India, Pakistan and Ceylon*, The Hague: Martinus Nijhoff, p. 27.

procedure laid down in the Code. The police should, as early as possible, take the prisoner into the Martial Law Area and obtain orders of a Court constituted under the Ordinance. This could be done without any order of the nature of an extradition order, in as much as the whole of the Malabar district was under the administration of the British Indian Government. As the petitioner's counsel failed to show that the police acted without jurisdiction, the first contention failed.

The next issue was that, when the petitioner was produced before the Magistrate outside the Martial Law Area, an application for bail was summarily rejected without even hearing the counsel. Under the provisions of Section 167 of the Cr PC, the nearest Magistrate to whom an offender may be brought has authority to order his detention in such custody as he may think fit for a term not exceeding fifteen days or, if he has no jurisdiction to try the case, he may order the offender to be forwarded to a Magistrate who has jurisdiction. According to Spencer J., there was nothing illegal in the procedure adopted by the Magistrate in this case in summarily rejecting the application for bail. This was the only course open to a Magistrate who lacked the jurisdiction to try the offence. To deal with terrorist movements mainly confined to Bengal, the Executive was armed with extraordinary powers of arrest, detention and trial by several special enactments.

In *Eradu Padinharedil Govindan Nair v. Emperor*,[42] which was also related to the Martial Law Ordinance, 1921, a petition for a writ of *habeas corpus* was made on behalf of two persons undergoing a sentence of 18 months for alleged participation in the Moplah rebellion.[43] They were tried outside the martial law area by a summary military court constituted under the Ordinance. The question considered by the Court was: Whether the Court has any power to interfere by issuance of a writ of *Habeas Corpus* to the Jailor of the jail in this Presidency in which the petitioners are confined? The Madras High Court decided that there was no right at all to hold a summary military court except in martial law area and the jurisdiction of

42 *Eradu Padinharedil Govindan Nair v. Emperor*, AIR 1922 Madras 499, Criminal Misc P. No. 31 of 1922 decided by Madras High Court on 4 May 1922.

43 The two individuals were charged with rioting under Section 147, Indian Penal Code, an offence cognizable by the ordinary courts. It was alleged that they had assisted the rebels in destroying a bridge. This they admitted, but stated that they were compelled to do so under threat of death. They alleged, owing to the trial being summary and taking place away from the scene of action and far from their homes they were not in a position to substantiate this defence by evidence which they could have called if the trial had taken place under the ordinary law and in its proper place.

such a court was local. Further, outside the area, the ordinary rules of law would prevail and there was nothing in the Ordinance to prevent the High Court from interfering with the decision of any court outside that area purporting to exercise a criminal jurisdiction which it did not possess. The Court concluded, "In our judgment, this Court has the power to issue this writ and in this case it is its duty to do so."

In *Chennappa and others v. Emperor,*[44] *habeas corpus* application was made by the relatives of 17 persons who were under detention after their conviction by the military court at Sholapur.[45] The common feature to all these cases was that each petitioner was charged and convicted at Sholapur between 12 May and 18 May 1930 of offences against Martial Law Regulations and each petitioner was sentenced by military court or tribunal acting under those Regulations. Section 11 of the Sholapur Martial Law Ordinance had validated all sentences passed by any officer acting in the exercise of military control between 12 May and 18 May, as if they were sentences passed under the Ordinance. It provided:

> Where, on or after 12 May 1930, and prior to the proclamation of Martial Law under Section 2 in any administration area, any sentence has been passed by any officer acting in the exercise of military control for the purpose of providing for the public safety or the restoration or maintenance of order in respect of any contravention of a Regulation or order made or issued within the same period by any such officer, such sentence shall be deemed to be as valid as if it were a sentence passed under this Ordinance in respect of an offence against a Regulation or a Martial Law order in force in that area under this Ordinance.

44 (1931) AIR Bombay 57.

45 After the arrest of Mahatma Gandhi on 6 May 1930, riots took place in Sholapur on 8 May 1930. A toddy shop was wrecked, toddy trees were cut down, and when persons were arrested the Police Lorries were obstructed on the road and stones thrown. The Police fired, some persons were wounded, and the crowd thereupon revenged itself by attacking an unarmed Police station and murdered an Excise Inspector and two Police Constables. The unarmed Police were disorganized. The Court buildings were burnt. A company of military arrived on 8 May. No further outrages took place although the District Magistrate was apprehensive of trouble in two other towns, Barsi and Pandharpur. Further military assistance arrived on 12 May and at 8.30 pm on 12 May the Military took charge of the town from the civil authorities and proclaimed Martial Law. On 13 May Martial Law Regulations were published. On 30 June 1930 the Martial Law Ordinance was withdrawn.

Therefore, the question whether martial law was properly proclaimed on 12 May did not arise in deciding the petition in *habeas corpus* because all that courts could do was to give effect to the Ordinance which had the same force and effect as an Act of the Legislature of India.

The Court observed, "According to English constitutional law, where state of war or insurrection amounting to war exists, it is competent for the Crown, in the exercise of its prerogative, to place the country affected under Martial Law. Martial Law in that sense, as has often been said, is no law at all ....and the effect of Martial Law .... is to substitute for the ordinary law of the land the will of the Military Commander. The liberty, property and even the lives of the persons in the effected area are placed at the mercy of the military. But, as by the law of England, which applies in India, the Crown is not above the law, the Crown can only declare Martial Law in cases of absolute necessity, and when the necessity ends normal legal conditions are automatically restored. Where Martial Law has been declared it is competent for the Courts--and is indeed the duty of the Courts if called upon--after the restoration of normal conditions to decide whether and to what extent Martial Law was justified." The Court observed that the state of martial law was not to determine with the necessity for it, but was to continue until brought to an end by a notification in the Gazette of India. The Chief Justice Beaumont further opined, "The ordinary rule is clear that sentences passed by Military Tribunals in time of war are not justiciable. Section 11 of the Ordinance does not provide that sentences of the military are to be treated for all purposes as if passed under the Ordinance but only that they shall be deemed as valid as if passed under the Ordinance. They are left as the sentences of Military Courts, and cannot, in my opinion, be treated as sentences of the ordinary Criminal Courts subject to the usual rules as to appeal and revision."

Habeas Corpus under the Indian Constitution

Following independence in 1947, the right to *habeas corpus* has been guaranteed in the Indian Constitution. Article 21 provides that no person shall be deprived of his life or personal liberty except according to a procedure established by law. Article 22 contains further provisions for protection against arrest and detention in certain cases. The writ of *habeas corpus* has been provided as one of the constitutional remedies to which a person is entitled as a matter of his Fundamental Right. By virtue of Article 32 of the Constitution, the Supreme Court may issue directions, orders or writs in the nature of the writ of *habeas corpus*. The High courts under Article 226, may issue directions, orders or writs in the nature of *habeas corpus* for the enforcement of the right to life and personal liberty.

The right to personal liberty faced serious threat when the President of India declared a state of emergency on 25 June 1975 on the advice of the Prime Minister Indira Gandhi, citing national security concerns and an economic crisis. The government postponed elections and civil liberties were curtailed. Among the rights suspended by the proclamation was the right to liberty, found in Article 21. Many people were detained by police pursuant to the Maintenance of Internal Security Act (MISA), and a number of them filed petitions for *habeas corpus* challenging their detention. The government argued that *habeas corpus* was unavailable due to the suspension of Article 21. Nine of India's high courts rejected this argument, holding that even if the fundamental right to liberty was suspended, a detainee was entitled to a judicial determination that the order of detention complied with the law and was made in good faith. The Supreme Court in *ADM Jabalpur v. Shrikant Shukla*[46] reversed the decision of the High court and held that no person had standing to even petition for *habeas corpus* in light of the Presidential Order declaring the emergency. Given the suspension of the right to liberty, it reasoned that a detainee could not even inquire as to which provision the detention was authorized under, or question whether the formalities of that provision had been complied with. It was held that not only was there no longer a right to liberty, but that no legal source was necessary to authorize detentions.[47] Justice Khanna, in dissent, wrote, "The power of the courts to issue a writ of *habeas corpus* is regarded as one of the most important characteristics

46 *ADM Jabalpur vs Shrikant Shukla* (1976) 2 SCC 521. In this case, during the time of National Emergency of 1975, a large number of persons had been arrested by the Government on the ground that their activities were prejudicial to the security of the State. The detention orders were challenged in the court and it was contended on behalf of the detenu that their detention was contrary to the principles of common law, justice and fair play. It was argued that the concept of rule of law in India is wider in its scope and that it should not be interpreted restrictively with reference to the provisions of Articles 21 and 22 only, rather, a wider interpretation should be given to the concept so as to give greater protection to the rights of the individuals. Rejecting the contention of the detenu, the Supreme Court held that the rule of law in India is what is already there incorporated in the Constitution. There is nothing outside the provisions of the Constitution to be treated as part of the concept of Rule of Law. The judgment of the Supreme Court in this case was severely criticized as taking away the safeguards to the persons' life and liberty under the Constitution and laws of the country.

47 During the Emergency (1975-77), the high courts kept up the tradition, while the Supreme Court of India failed miserably in its duty. Noorani A.G., *Habeas corpus* law: A sorry decline, *Frontline*, 25 October 2019.

of democratic states under the rule of law. The principle that no one shall be deprived of his life or liberty without the authority of law is rooted in the consideration that life and liberty are precious possessions." A person was, therefore, entitled to find out what authority the government was acting on, and to ensure the government complied with that authority, even when he could be lawfully detained.

In early 1977, the Emergency ended and Prime Minister, Indira Gandhi had to call for elections under public pressure, and was defeated. Before leaving office, she advised the President to withdraw the proclamation. The Constitution of India was amended by the 44th Amendment Act 1978. The effect of 44th Amendment was that: (i) The Presidential Order cannot suspend the enforcement of rights conferred by Article 20 and 21. In the result even during the proclamation of emergency, the individual's right to move the Supreme Court or High courts to challenge either a law or an executive order on the grounds of contravention of the rights guaranteed by Article 20 and 21 shall survive. This superseded the view taken in *ADM Jabalpur* that when Article 21 is suspended by an order under Article 359, the persons imprisoned or detained loses his *locus standi* to regain his liberty on any ground. (ii) Even as regards fundamental rights other than those under Article 20 and 21, unless the law which affects the aggrieved individual contains a recital to the effect that such law is in relation to the "Proclamation of Emergency", neither such law nor any executive action taken under it shall have any immunity from challenge from violation of a fundamental right during operation of an emergency. As a result, in situations where the military and police have broad powers pursuant to emergency legislation, *habeas corpus* has been singled out as the "only remedy available" for the protection of the individual.

Article 34 of the Constitution merely empowers Parliament to make an Act of Indemnity to cover any irregularity committed during the operation of martial law. It says nothing about the suspension of *habeas corpus* which would not *ipso facto* follow from a mere declaration of martial law. The only provision for suspension of *habeas corpus* is Article 359 of the Constitution.[48] But since the 44th Amendment Act, Article 21 cannot be suspended by an Order under Article 359. Hence, even though Article 32 is suspended, a person who is detained without authority of law would be competent to move for *habeas corpus*.

48 *ADM Jabalpur v. Shukla Shivakant*, AIR 1976 SC 1207.

The right to *habeas corpus* has spread worldwide in the past two centuries as a result of the influence of Anglo-American law and the inclusion of *habeas corpus* principles in post-World War II international and regional human rights instruments. Today, *habeas corpus* is considered a fundamental guarantee in domestic legal systems all over the world including India.

Habeas Corpus in International Law

International human rights law is a system of international norms designed to protect and promote the human rights of all persons. These rights, which are inherent in all human beings, have been expressed and guaranteed by law in the form of treaties, customary international law, general principles and soft law. Human rights entail both rights and obligations. International human rights law lays down the obligations of states to act in certain ways or to refrain from certain acts, in order to promote and protect the human rights and fundamental freedoms of individuals or groups. Under international human rights law, it is possible for states to derogate from certain human rights obligations and to impose limitations on the exercise of certain rights[49].

The Universal Declaration of Human Rights (UDHR): The UDHR is an inspirational document having highest moral status. It has been referred to in numerous national constitutions, international and regional human rights instruments, and international and domestic jurisprudence. The UDHR was adopted by the UN General Assembly on 10 December 1948. In the initial draft of the Declaration, the right to *habeas corpus* was included, which stated: "Every one (sic) who is detained has the right to immediate judicial determination of the legality of his detention. The State has the duty to provide adequate procedures to make the right effective."[50] However, it was removed during the third session of the drafting Commission in June 1948 when the entire declaration was reduced from 33 articles to 28.[51] In October 1948, Article 8 was added, providing, "Everyone has the right to an effective remedy by the competent national

49 Article 4 of the International Covenant on Civil and Political Right, 1966.

50 John Humphery, 1984, *Human Rights and the United Nations: A Great Adventure*, New York: Transnational Publishers, p. 32.

51 The separate *habeas corpus* provision was omitted during the third session of the 18-member Commission on Human Rights, the body that last considered the draft Declaration. The Declaration was not debated before approved by the Economic and Social Council. Economic and Social Council Res. U.N. Doc. E/1046 dated 26 August 1948.

tribunals for acts violating the fundamental rights granted to him by the constitution or by law." This provision, though is more general in its scope than a separate *habeas corpus* article, incorporates the right to judicial review of the legality of detention. The UDHR remains the primary source of global human rights standards, and its recognition as a source of rights and law by states throughout the world distinguishes it from conventional obligations. A number of human rights scholars agree that Article 8 of the UDHR includes the right to *habeas corpus*[52] and the broader remedy of *amparo*.[53]

The International Covenant on Civil and Political Rights (ICCPR): The ICCPR elaborates on the right to *habeas corpus* contained in the UDHR. Article 9(4) of the ICCPR provides:

> Anyone who is deprived of his liberty by arrest or detention shall be entitled to take proceedings before a court, in order that court may decide without delay on the lawfulness of his detention and order his release if the detention is not lawful.

As a source of international human rights law, the ICCPR differs from UDHR in two ways: (i) the ICCPR is a treaty ratified by 173 states whereas UDHR is a declaration,[54] and (ii) its provisions are in a much more detailed form than the UDHR. The monitoring body of the ICCPR, the Human Rights Committee has also interpreted Article 9(4) in a number of cases and held that restrictions on the applicability of *habeas corpus* are generally not permissible.[55] The Committee in its general comments has stated:

52 The International Criminal Tribunal for Rwanda in appellate decision in *Barayagwizi v. Prosecutor*, Case No. ICTR-99-54, decision dated 3 November 1999, held that the right to *habeas corpus* is enshrined in Article 8 of the UDHR.

53 On 12 October 1948, a new proposal for inclusion in the declaration was introduced by Mexico. The proposed article related to a brief procedure whereby the courts will protect an individual from acts of authority that, to his prejudice, violate any fundamental constitutional right. The language of the proposed article reflected Latin American remedy of *amparo*, which had been part of Mexican law since 1847. The use of *amparo* to enforce constitutional rights was inspired by the concept of judicial review in the US. Farrell Brian R., 2018, *Habeas Corpus in International Law*, Cambridge: Cambridge University Press, pp. 40-46.

54 The Covenant was opened for signature at New York on 19 December 1966. As on 31 December 2019, it has been ratified by 173 states.

55 Farrell Brian R., 2018, *Habeas Corpus in International Law*, Cambridge: Cambridge University Press, p. 59.

> ...in particular the important guarantee laid down in Article 9, paragraph 4, i.e. the right to control by a court of the legality of the detention, applies to all persons deprived of their liberty by arrest or detention. Furthermore, States parties have, in accordance with article 2(3), also to ensure that an effective remedy is provided in other cases in which an individual claims to be deprived of his liberty in violation of the Covenant.

Also if so-called preventive detention is used, for reasons of public security, it must be controlled by these same provisions, i.e. it must not be arbitrary, and must be based on grounds and procedures established by law [Article 9, para 1], information of the reasons must be given [para 2] and court control of the detention must be available [para 4] as well as compensation in the case of a breach [para 5].[56]

The ICCPR guarantees access to *habeas corpus* proceedings for a person deprived of his liberty by arrest or detention. The Human Rights Committee has found that Article 9(4) applies to persons in military service,[57] to persons placed under extra-judicial arrests and held incommunicado by agents of the state,[58] guarantees the right of a detained person to bring proceedings before a court, but it does not contemplate the initiation of proceedings by a third party on behalf of an individual. The Committee found that an administrative official or military officer does not constitute the "court" within the meaning established by the ICCPR; however, a military court could be considered a "court" when exercising jurisdiction over military personnel.[59] The decision of the court reviewing a *habeas corpus* petition must be without delay, and period of delay should be considered on a case-by-case basis.[60] The Human Rights Committee found that the delay of nine and half months in passing the resolution against constitutional challenge violated the requirement of "without delay".[61] The court must be empowered to order release, if detention is unlawful.[62]

---

56 General Comment No. 8: Article 9 (Right to liberty and security of persons), Sixteenth Session, 1982.

57 *Voulanne v. Finland*, No. 265/1987, UN Doc.A/44/40, 29 September 1989.

58 *Bleier v. Uruguay*, No. 7/30, UN Doc.A/37/40, 29 March 1982.

59 *Voulanne v. Finland*, No. 265/1987 in UN Doc. A/44/40 dated 29 September 1989.

60 *Ines Torres v. Finland*, No. 291/1988, UN Doc. CCPR/C/38/D/291/1998 dated 5 April 1990.

61 No. 1051/2002, UN Doc. CCPR/C/80/D/1051/2002dated 29 March 2004.

62 *A. v. Australia*, No. 560/1993, UN Doc. CCPR/C/59/D/560/1993 dated 3 April 1997.

The Human Rights Council's Working Group on Arbitrary Detention attaches particular importance to effective internal control mechanisms over the legality of detention. According to the report of the Working Group, "The remedy of *habeas corpus* is one of the most effective means of preventing and combating arbitrary detention. Procedural guarantee must not be suspended or rendered impracticable in states of emergency. Further, the Subcommittee on Prevention of Torture has recommended that "the effectiveness and absolute non-derogability of *habeas corpus* be guaranteed in states of emergency."[63] In addition, the Committee on Enforced Disappearances has recommended the adoption of "the necessary measures to establish that the right to apply for *habeas corpus* may be neither suspended nor restricted under any circumstances, even when a state of emergency or siege has been declared, and to guarantee that any person with a legitimate interest may initiate the procedure."[64]

Regional Conventions: There are three regional human rights systems established in Europe, Americas and Africa. The foundations of these three systems are human rights treaties[65] enforced by regional human rights courts. The European Convention for the Protection of Human Rights and Fundamental Freedoms (ECHR) guarantees the right to *habeas corpus* in Article 5(4). It provides:

> Everyone who is deprived of his liberty by arrest or detention shall be entitled to take proceedings by which the lawfulness of his detention shall be decided speedily by a court and his release ordered if the detention is not lawful.

Article 5(4) of the ECHR has been the subject of numerous cases before the European Court of Human Rights (ECtHR). Article 5(4) requires that

63 The Subcommittee also recommended: (i) The senior authorities in the institutions responsible for implementing *habeas corpus* take the requisite steps to ensure the effectiveness of this fundamental safeguard against torture or other cruel, inhuman or degrading treatment or punishment; and (ii) A central *habeas corpus* register, under the auspices of the Supreme Court, be created as a matter of urgency. Optional Protocol to the Convention against Torture and Other Cruel, Inhuman or Degrading Treatment or Punishment, Report of the Subcommittee on Prevention of Torture, CAT/OP/HND/1 dated 10 February 2010, para 137.

64 Report of the Working Group on Arbitrary Detention, UN General Assembly Doc. A/HRC/27/47 dated 30 June 2014, paragraph 25.

65 The European Convention for the Protection of Human Rights and Fundamental Freedoms, The American Declaration of the Rights and Duties of Man, 1948, and the African Charter on Human and Peoples' Rights, 1986 also known as "the Banjul Charter".

habeas corpus is applicable to all forms of detention. The availability of a remedy in law does not satisfy Article 5(4), if it is not available in practice.[66] Under the ECHR,[67] the proceedings can be initiated before a "court", that is, an independent and impartial decision-making body,[68] which must be able to decide on the lawfulness of the measure and order release if the detention is not lawful. The right to institute proceedings must be real and effective, i.e. it must exist with an adequate degree of certainty. Further, the court must monitor compliance with the procedural requirements essential to "lawfulness" within the meaning of the Convention.[69] The ECtHR has held that Article 5(4) requires the availability of proceedings to review the lawfulness of a person's detention.[70] Further, every person is entitled to *habeas corpus* proceedings regardless of whether the detention is, in fact, legal; and non-availability of *habeas corpus* can result in violation of Article 5(4) even if person is lawfully detained under Article 5(1).[71]

In *Chahal v. United Kingdom*, the ECtHR clarified that the remedy of *habeas corpus* is also available to an alien.[72] Only limitation which is placed on the access to *habeas corpus* is that the individual seeking the remedy must be deprived of his liberty by arrest or detention.[73] The European law of *habeas corpus* is fairly developed and has a substantial body of case laws related to Article 5(4) of the ECHR.

In Europe, conventional wisdom shows that compliance with the Court rulings is very high. The Inter-American human rights system[74] is

66 *Sakik and others v. Turkey* 1997-VII ECtHR 2609.

67 The European Convention originally established two enforcement mechanisms: a European Commission of Human Rights, for first review, and a European Court of Human Rights (ECtHR). With the introduction of Protocol 11 to the Convention in 1998, the Commission was abolished and the Court was restructured and made permanent.

68 European Court of Human Rights (ECtHR), 4 July 2000, *Niedbala v. Poland*, No. 27915/95, 29 March 2001.

69 Renucci Jean-Francois, Introduction to the European Convention on Human Rights, Council for Europe Publishing, 2005, p. 65.

70 *Brogan v. United Kingdom* 145 ECtHR, 1998.

71 *Douiyeb v. The Netherlands*, Application No. 31464/96, 4 August 1999.

72 1996-V, European Court of Human Rights, 1831.

73 Farrell Brian R., 2018, *Habeas Corpus in International Law*, Cambridge: Cambridge University Press, p. 77.

74 The current institutional mechanisms within the Organization of American States (OAS) for the protection of human rights in the Americas are three: (1) Supervision

not so developed when compared to the European system and compliance with the Court's ruling is also very low.[75] The original charter of the Organization of American States (OAS) did not create any human rights institution. The Inter-American Commission on Human Rights was established in 1959 and a limited petition system was available under it in 1966. In 1970, the Commission became a charter organ and the charter based rights system applies to all OAS members regardless of whether they have ratified the American Convention or not. The Inter-American System for Human Rights (IAS) of the Organization of American States (OAS) has a broad mandate to monitor human rights in all 35 independent states of the Americas, including the United States.

The right to *habeas corpus* is guaranteed in both the American Declaration of the Rights and Duties of Man and the American Convention on Human Rights. Article XXV of the American Declaration provides that every individual who has been deprived of his liberty has the right to have the legality of his detention ascertained without delay by a court. Article 7(6) of the American Convention provides:

> Anyone who is deprived of his liberty shall be entitled to recourse to a competent court, in order that the court may decide without delay on the lawfulness of his arrest or detention and order his release if the arrest or detention is unlawful. In States Parties whose laws provide that anyone who believes himself to be threatened with deprivation of his liberty is entitled to recourse to a competent court in order that it may decide on the lawfulness of such threat, this remedy may not be restricted or abolished. The interested party or another person in his behalf is entitled to seek these remedies.

The Inter-American Court of Human Rights in its advisory opinion on '*Habeas Corpus* in Emergency Situation' has described *habeas corpus* as: "In its classical form, the writ of *habeas corpus*, as it is incorporated

---

of compliance with a state's treaty obligations under the American Convention on Human Rights by the Inter-American Commission on Human Rights. (2) Supervision of compliance with a state's obligation under the American Declaration of the Rights and Duties of Man (for those states that have not yet ratified the American Convention) by the Inter-American Court of Human Rights. (3) Supervision of compliance with a state's treaty obligation under the American Convention on Human Rights by the Inter-American Court of Human Rights. Cerna Chrisitna M, International Law and the Protection of Human Rights in the Inter-American System: Rethinking National Sovereignty in an Age of Regional Integration, p. 210.

75 Hawkins Darren and Wade Jacoby, Partial Compliance: A Comparison of the European and Inter-American American Courts for Human Rights, 18 August 2008.

in various legal systems of the Americas, a judicial remedy designed to protect person freedom of physical integrity against arbitrary detentions by means of a judicial decree ordering the appropriate authorities to bring the detained person before a judge so that the lawfulness of the detention may be determined and, if appropriate, the release of the detainee be ordered." Further, "In order for *habeas corpus* to achieve its purpose, which is to obtain a judicial determination of the lawfulness of a detention, it is necessary that the detained person be brought before a competent judge or tribunal with jurisdiction over him. Here *habeas corpus* performs a vital role in ensuring that a person's life and physical integrity are respected, in preventing his disappearance or the keeping of his whereabouts secret and in protecting him against torture or other cruel, inhumane, or degrading punishment or treatment."[76]The Inter-American Court has maintained that a primary obligation of the state is to ensure that detained person has access to the remedy of *habeas corpus*.[77]

The African Charter on Human and Peoples' Rights does not contain any express provision relating to guarantee to *habeas corpus*. The Charter came into existence with its independent Commission, known as the "African Commission on Human and Peoples Rights." The African Charter guarantees the right to personal liberty in Article 6 and a general right to recourse in Article 7.[78] The African Commission has expressed the view that a detained person should have recourse to national courts. In Guidelines on Police Custody and Pre-Trial Detention issued by the Commission, it has been impressed upon that a person under arrest should be afforded the right to challenge promptly the lawfulness of their arrest before a competent judicial body.[79]

---

76 Advisory Opinion OC-8/87 by The Inter-American Court of Human Rights, dated 30 January 1987; Requested by the Inter-American Commission on Human Rights.

77 The Inter-American Court, *Juan Humberto Sanches Case*, No. 99, dated 7 June 2003.

78 African Charter: Article 6:- Every individual shall have the right to liberty and to the security of his person. No one may be deprived of his freedom except for reasons and conditions previously laid down by law. In particular, no one may be arbitrarily arrested or detained. Article 7(1):- Every individual shall have the right to have his cause heard. This comprises: (a) the right to an appeal to competent national organs against acts of violating his fundamental rights as recognized and guaranteed by conventions, laws, regulations and customs in force; (b) the right to be presumed innocent until proved guilty by a competent court or tribunal; (c) the right to defense, including the right to be defended by counsel of his choice; (d) the right to be tried within a reasonable time by an impartial court or tribunal.

79 See Article 4(j): The Guidelines on the Conditions of Arrest, Police Custody and Pre-Trial Detention in Africa (the Luanda Guidelines) were adopted by the African

In addition, the Arab Charter on Human Rights adopted by the League of Arab States in 2004 also contains the following *habeas corpus* provision under Article 14(6): "Anyone who is deprived of his liberty by arrest or detention shall be entitled to petition a competent court in order that it may decide without delay on the lawfulness of his arrest or detention and order his release if the arrest or detention is unlawful."

Derogations: Human Rights Treaty Regime

Human Rights law provides for the suspension of certain rights during time of national crises. In case a state is facing serious threat to its security or survival, it may adopt emergency measures including suspension of civil and political liberties that the state has pledged to uphold. The three human rights treaties, the ICCPR, and the European and American Conventions on Human Rights recognize that under crisis situations, the governments need to enhance their powers to repress the threats to its security and existence.[80] Article 4(1) of the ICCPR provides that during public emergency that "threatens the life of the nation," a treaty party may derogate from certain civil and political liberties, but only "to the extent strictly required by the exigencies of the situation." Article 4(2) however, contains a limitation that a derogating state may not lawfully suspend fundamental rights designated as non-derogable, including the prohibitions of murder, torture, slavery, and discrimination.[81] Further, under Article 4(3) the derogating country must inform the UN Secretary General of the rights and freedoms suspended, the reasons for the suspension, and the date when emergency measures will end. The Secretary General is to publicize this information and circulate it to other treaty parties, who may challenge the derogation before an international monitoring body. However, in none of the human rights treaties, a right to *habeas corpus* is explicitly listed as

Commission on Human and Peoples' Rights (the Commission) during its 55th Ordinary Session in Luanda, Angola, from 28 April to 12 May 2014.

80 Each human rights treaty contains a derogation provision under which a state party may derogate certain obligations under the treaty in defined circumstances. A state must proclaim emergency and provide notice of its derogation to other state parties. See: ICCPR, Article 4 (1), European Convention Article 15(1), American Convention Article 27(1).

81 The International Covenant on Civil and Political Rights (ICCPR), Article 4(2) explicitly prescribes that no derogation may be made concerning the right to life, the prohibition of torture or cruel, inhuman or degrading punishment, or of medical or scientific experimentation without consent, the prohibition of slavery, slave trade and servitude, the prohibition of imprisonment because of the inability to fulfill a contractual obligation, the recognition of everyone as a person before the law, and the freedom of thought, conscience and religion.

non-derogable right.[82] The ECHR has not expressly held till date that the right to *habeas corpus* to be non-derogable.[83]

There is no doubt that sovereign nations have a legitimate right to defend their constitutional and democratic orders during times of crisis. During the past six decades, 33 states have invoked the emergency clauses in the three treaties. These countries which include France, Russia, the UK, Argentina, Colombia, Israel, Turkey, and Sri Lanka are responsible for nearly 600 instances of derogations. The UK has filed derogations on more than 50 occasions, whereas Peru has filed derogations on more than 260 occasions in the last six decades.[84]

War on Terror and *Habeas Corpus*

Today India is facing serious threats from terrorism. A large number of plots alleged to have been inspired by the Islamic States have been discovered in Delhi, Uttar Pradesh, Rajasthan, Maharashtra, Andhra Pradesh, Kerala and elsewhere.[85] This raises few questions, whether it will be possible for India to fight terrorism in accordance with basic requirements that follow from a broad conception of the rule of law? Can a state commit lesser evils when it believes it faces the greater evil of its own destruction? Whether the suspension of civil liberties and the prolonged detention of terrorist be allowed as a last resort, if the life of the state were in danger. Since 'terrorism' is very difficult to define, the state may have serious problems in fighting these enemies--labeled as 'terrorists', 'extremists', 'religious fanatics', 'insurgents', etc.-- without compromising certain principles of the rule of law. India may have to relook at principles of freedom of speech, liberty, basic rights of suspects, etc. It may have to take harsh measures to deprive certain civil rights to terrorists.

In an unconventional armed conflict, where terrorists launch deadly attacks against the innocent civilians and the state resources, the executive

---

82 See: ICCPR, Article 4 (2), European Convention Article 15(2), American Convention Article 27(2).

83 Farrell Brian R., 2018, *Habeas Corpus in International Law*, Cambridge: Cambridge University Press, p. 144.

84 Hafner-Burton Emilie M., Laurence R. Helfer, and Christopher J. Fariss, Emergency and Escape: Explaining Derogations from Human Rights Treaties, *International Organization*, Vol. 65, Fall 2011, pp. 673–707.

85 Swami Praveen, "Invisible Jihad: Challenges for India and Asia", In Pandalai Shruti (ed.), 2019, *Combating Terrorism: Evolving Asian Perspectives*, New Delhi: Pentagon Press, p.27.

must be given greater latitude to deal with the unconventional nature of the threat. The lethal capabilities of terrorists have fundamentally changed the political and legal landscape. In the recent past, the domestic counterterrorism roles of the armed forces have expanded greatly across the world. The State is empowered to adopt all lawful and constitutional means and create a vigilante force to counter violence. The underlying rationale of self-defence, resting on the concept of necessity, is often expressed in the maxim *salus populi suprema lex esto* (the safety of the people is the highest law). The concept of 'reason of State' also advocates the exercise of unrestricted penology of measures by the State when faced with existential challenges. Every State has the right to defend itself; the right needed is inherent in the necessity of the State. The State is entitled to protection against those who seek to destroy it. We need to give the executive this latitude in the face of threats to national security. The question which comes up is that whether there a possibility that in future, if martial law in proclaimed in India, can military commander make an order denying the right to *habeas corpus*. Parker (1861) writes, "Magna Charta and the general principles of the common law, while they recognize and protect private rights, such as the right to be secure from searches and seizures, the right to the *habeas corpus,* and the like, recognize at the same time the necessities of war; and, in case of actual war, make those rights subservient to the martial law, wherever that exists."[86]

In case war on terror becomes intensified to a terrifying degree in India, only time will tell us whether the higher judiciary will insist on upholding the freedom of those trying to disintegrate the country or interpret it otherwise. The Supreme Court must have the jurisdiction to review the acts of military authorities and set aside unlawful military detentions.[87] It is necessary that the government must create a mechanism so that

86 Parker Joel, 1861, *Habeas Corpus and Martial Law: A Review of the Opinion of Chief Justice Taney in the Case of John Merryman*, Cambridge: Welch, Bigelow, and Company, p. 57.

87 In the case of United States, Article I, Section 9, Clause 2 of the Constitution allows for the suspension of "The Privilege of the Writ of *Habeas Corpus*" when in "Cases of Rebellion or Invasion the public Safety may require it." It is believed by few experts that that suspension of *habeas corpus* eliminates the constitutional due process rights of the detained. The Suspension Clause is one of the more extreme forms of war power in the US Constitution, because due process has been the cornerstone of the Anglo-American legal system for a long time. Congress has not explicitly suspended the privilege of the writ of *habeas corpus* in its fight against terrorism, and individual detainees have filed petitions for *habeas corpus* in the federal courts. A number of such petitions contain arguments that the President has violated the Suspension Clause by denying detainees review of the legality of their detentions.

the detained terrorists in such situations are charged and tried promptly according to established procedures in specialized courts. These, however, must not be done in undue haste, in particular where the accused is likely to be awarded life imprisonment or death sentence. The mechanism for trial should satisfy minimum procedural justice standards of fair trial as being followed by various democracies across the world. The trial must be conducted by impartial judges and an experienced counsel must be appointed to defend the accused, if he is not represented.[88]

A state has a solemn duty to ensure and respect the right to life of all persons. Persons deprived of their liberty are at heightened risk of ill-treatment and torture, including through legally sanctioned violence, such as penalties or disciplinary measures prohibited under international human rights law. There could be situations of armed conflict where state institutions, including the judicial system, become dysfunctional. International human rights law, and the rights related to liberty and security of the person in particular, apply everywhere and at all times, both in peace and in armed conflict. There is a general agreement that the norms of international human rights instruments and customary international law protecting individuals against arbitrary detention should be complied with by the governments during armed conflict.[89]

The right to *habeas corpus* has gained widespread acceptance in international constitutional law. Nearly 120 constitutions in the world provide for a remedy in the nature of *habeas corpus*.[90] India has ratified the Geneva Conventions of 1949 and is bound by the provisions of Common Article 3 (CA3). Under CA3, the prohibited acts include the violence to life and person, in particular murder of all kinds, mutilation, cruel treatment and torture; humiliating and degrading treatment; the passing of sentences and the carrying out of executions without previous judgment pronounced by a regularly constituted court affording all the judicial guarantees which are recognized as indispensable by civilized peoples. During detention, as a minimum, the fundamental 'laws of humanity' in the sense of the Martens

88 In all cases where there is a possibility of life sentence or death sentence, advocates who have put in minimum of 10 years practice at the Bar alone be considered to be appointed as *Amicus Curiae* or through legal services to represent an accused. The Supreme Court in *Anokhilal v. State of Madhya Pradesh* (Criminal Appeal Nos. 62-63 of 2014) decided on 18 December 2019.

89 UN General Assembly Doc. A/HRC/16/47 of 19 January 2011, paragraph 51.

90 Farrell Brian, From Westminster to the World: The Right to *Habeas Corpus* in International Constitutional Law, *Mich. St. U. Coll. L. J. Int'l L.*, Vol. 17, No. 3, 2009, p. 551-565.

Clause and Common Article 3 of the Geneva Conventions are applicable. This includes judicial guarantees which are recognized as indispensable by civilized peoples. Even if one accepts the concept of unlawful combatants, the fair trial protection of the GC cannot be suspended. In times of peace, the right to a fair trial is guaranteed by international human rights instruments.[91] Therefore, India has an international obligation to provide adequate procedural guarantees to every detained person, including judicial guarantees, in particular the right to *habeas corpus*, i.e., the right to challenge before a court the lawfulness of any detention. The Human Rights Committee has rightly viewed that "during armed conflict, whether international or non-international, the rules of international humanitarian law become applicable and help, in addition to the provisions in article 4 and article 5, paragraph 1, of the ICCPR, to prevent the abuse of a State's emergency powers".[92]

91 Kai Ambos and Annika Maleen Poschadel, Terrorists and Fair Trial: The Right to a Fair Trial for Alleged Terrorists Detained in Guantánamo Bay, *Utrecht Law Review*, Volume 9, Issue 4, September 2013, pp. 109-126.

92 General comment No. 29 (2001), para. 3.

Chapter V

Martial Law and AFSPA

Introduction

Recent anti-government protests have rocked Hong Kong for the last few months and the situation shows no sign of dying down.[1] Escalating violence in Hong Kong has led the city's leader to invoke Emergency Regulation Ordinance (ERO) on 4 October 2019—introduced by the British in 1922—to quell months of unrest with a ban on face masks. It has been claimed by a few commentators that the powers under the ERO are akin to martial law.[2] It affords the chief executive (Hong Kong's post-colonial

1 Hong Kong is a former British colony handed back to China in 1997. It has its own judiciary and a separate legal system from mainland China. Those rights include freedom of assembly and freedom of speech. The extradition bill which triggered the first protest was introduced in April 2019. It would have allowed for criminal suspects to be extradited to mainland China under certain circumstances. Opponents said this risked exposing the citizens of Hong Kong to unfair trials and violent treatment. They also argued the bill would give China greater influence over Hong Kong and could be used to target activists and journalists. The bill was withdrawn in September but demonstrations continue. Clashes between police and activists have become increasingly violent, with police firing live bullets and protesters attacking officers and throwing petrol bombs. The government then banned protesters wearing face masks, which was turned unconstitutional by the court. In many cases, people supporting the demonstrators were confronted by pro-Beijing rallies and in early November 2019 a pro-Beijing lawmaker was stabbed in the street by a man pretending to be a supporter. There were many reports of sexual violence against female protesters. Chinese president Xi Jinping has warned against separatism, saying any attempt to divide China would end in bodies smashed and bones ground to powder. Protests supporting the Hong Kong movement have spread across the globe, with rallies taking place in the UK, France, US, Canada and Australia. For more details see: https://www.bbc.com/news/world-asia-china-49317695.

2 Shelly Banjo, How Far Hong Kong's Emergency Law Can Go (Online Too), 3 October 2019, available at:https://www.bloomberg.com/news/articles/2019-10-03/how-far-hong kong-s-emergency-law-can-go-online-too-quicktake; Hong Kong's Emergency

leader) the power to make "any regulations whatsoever which he may consider desirable in the public interest." Its provisions include arrests, property seizures, deportation, control of the ports and transportation and censorship.

Similar concerns have been raised by few researchers claiming that in India the Armed Forces (Special Powers) Act (AFSPA) confers sweeping powers on the armed forces and areas where the AFSPA is applicable remains under de facto martial law.[3] In addition, a number of inter-governmental organizations, such as the United Nations Human Rights Office of the High Commissioner, international non-governmental organizations (including International Commission of Jurists and Amnesty International), and academics have a broad consensus that provisions of AFSPA challenge various international human rights norms and fundamental rights enshrined in the Indian Constitution.[4] In view of this

---

Ordinance Effectively a Declaration of Martial Law, *Japan Forward*, 10 October 2019, available at: https://japan-forward.com/editorial-hong-kongs-emergency-ordinance-effectively-a-declaration-of-martial-law/;James Palmer, Hong Kong's Violence Will Get Worse, *Foreign Policy*, 11 November 2019, available at: https://foreignpolicy.com/2019/11/11/police-killing-protests-beijing-lam-xi-hong-kong-violence-will-get-worse/; Hong Kong Martial Law Is the Latest Risk Worrying Investors, *Bloomberg*, 4 September 2019, available at: https://www.bloomberg.com/news/articles/2019-09-04/hong-kong-martial-law-is-the-latest-tail-risk-worrying-investors.

3 Gautam Khagesh, Martial Law in India: The Deployment of Military under the Armed Forces Special Powers Act, 1958, *Southwestern Jour of International law*, Vol. 24, 2018, pp. 117-146; Rajput Parvesh Kumar, Undeclared Martial Law in India: An Analysis of Article 34 vis-à-vis Armed Forces (Special Powers) Act, 1958, *IRJMSH*, Vol. 7, No. 10, 2016, pp. 33-42.

4 Report on the Situation of Human Rights in Kashmir, Office of the United Nations High Commissioner for Human Rights, 14 June 2018, pp. 49; No More "Missing Persons": The Criminalization of Enforced Disappearance in South Asia, International Commission of Jurists, Geneva, August 2017, pp. 58; The Myth of Normalcy: Impunity and the Judiciary in Kashmir, Allard K. Lowenstein International Human Rights Clinic Yale Law School, April 2009, pp. 55; Sen Arijit, Marginal on the Map, Hidden Wars and Hidden Media in Northeast India, Reuters Institute Fellowship Paper, University of Oxford, 2011, pp. 61; Ghosh Shrimoyee Nandini, Kashmir: Let's Call a War by its Rightful Name, 13 August 20016, available at:https://thewire.in/law/kashmir-lets-call-war-rightful-name; Baruah Sanjib, AFSPA: the darker side of Indian democracy, available at: https://www.india-seminar.com/2017/693/693_sanjib_baruah.html; Kazi Seema, Law, Governance and Gender in Indian-Administered Kashmir, Working Paper Series, Centre for the Study of Law and Governance, Jawaharlal Nehru University, New Delhi, 2012, pp. 36; and Denied: Failures in Accountability for Human Rights Violations by security force personnel in Jammu and Kashmir, Amnesty International, 2015, pp. 72; Nath Himanshu R. and Askari F., The Armed Forces Special Powers Act, 1958, and Federal Conflicts, *ILI Review*, Vol. II, Winter 2017, pp. 47-63.

perception, it is important to examine in depth the true nature of AFSPA, the scope and extent of power that is entrusted in the hands of the army under AFSPA and the operation of AFSPA in various areas in India. So, this chapter briefly discusses the power and functioning of the armed forces under of AFSPA and compares the same with that under martial law. Since post-Independence, martial law has not been proclaimed in India, therefore situations prevailing in a few other States where martial law has been witnessed in the last two or three decades will be examined.

Role of the Armed Forces

The primary role of the armed forces is to defend the State from external threats by using lethal force offensively. However, in the last two decades, terrorist attacks all over the world has changed the security situation and blurred the lines between internal security and external threat. The threat posed to internal security by terrorists has changed the role played by the military and their professionalism is now being utilized to deal with internal security matters. The governments of Australia, Belgium, Canada, Germany, India, Italy, Japan, the UK, the USA among others have employed the armed forces for internal security duties. The internal security or police duties of the military, according to Major General Charles W. Gwynn (1939), may be grouped into three non-rigid interchangeable categories:[5]

> (i) **Riot Control**: This category pertains to those occasions when the civil power continues to exercise undivided control, but finds the police forces on which it normally relies insufficient. In such cases, the military is employed "in aid of the civil power" and its responsibility goes little further than for the methods the troops adopt to give effect to the directions of the executive magistrate. In this situation, the military is bound to exercise the minimum force required to attain its objective. The provisions for such situations, for example, are contained in sections 129 to 132 of the Criminal Procedure Code (Cr PC), 1973.[6]

5 Gwynn Charles W, Major General, 1939, *Imperial Policing*, London: Macmillan and Co. Limited, pp. 3-4.

6 Sections 129 to 132 of the Cr PC, dealing with maintenance of public order and tranquility, empower an executive magistrate or the officer in-charge of a police station to command any unlawful assembly to disperse. If the unlawful assembly shows no disposition to disperse quietly, the executive magistrate may use the armed forces to disperse it. In practice, such requests are made by the executive magistrate to the commanding officer of the nearest military station, who in turn details an officer of suitable rank with the required number of troops. The officer and persons under his command must use as little force and cause as little injury to persons and property as

(ii) **The Small Wars:**[7] deliberate campaigns with a definite military objective, but undertaken with the ultimate object of establishing civil control. The conduct of such wars differs in no respect from defensive or punitive wars undertaken to check external aggression. No limitations are placed on the amount of force which can legitimately be exercised, and the military is free to employ all the weapons that the nature of the threat permits. Such campaigns are clearly a purely military responsibility. Special Forces may be called in certain circumstances during such wars. This is mostly a short term measure, but may extend for longer duration. International law not only permits but requires States to protect their citizens, without discrimination, by responding effectively to security threats. Thus, States can use their armed forces to deal with threats to their integrity and to the lives of their citizens. Special legislation (such as AFSPA), must give additional powers to the security forces to deal with situations in small wars.

(iii) **Martial Law**: This includes cases when the normal civil control does not exist, or has broken down to such an extent that the Army becomes the main agent for the maintenance of or for the restoration of order. The military in such cases is then vested with the responsibility for the action to be taken. In certain cases, as when martial law is proclaimed, the civil authority abdicates its position temporarily and is superseded by military government in the area proclaimed. Special powers which they do not ordinarily possess may be given to military officers; but in any case they are required to take such action on their own responsibility as the situation demands. Certain responsibilities may be shared between the civil and military authorities in giving effect to measures required to restore control.[8]

---

may be necessary for dispersing the assembly. The law also empowers a commissioned officer to use force when public security is manifestly endangered by such an assembly and no executive magistrate can be communicated with. Sanction of the Central Government is necessary for prosecution of a military person and an act done in good faith is not an offence.

7 Several terms, low intensity operations, counter-revolutionary war, low intensity conflict, military operations other than war, sub-conventional operations, asymmetrical war, war against terror and small wars are part of current military vocabulary worldwide. They are similar in meaning and are used interchangeably. Nanavatty, Rostum K., 2013, *Internal Armed Conflict in India: Forging a Joint Civil-Military Approach*, New Delhi: Pentagon Press, p. xv.

8 Even when martial law is in force the task of restoring order does not rest on the military alone. The machinery and forces of the civil power are then at the disposal of

Riot Control

So long as the disturbances amount to no more than a riot, the measures contemplated in the Cr PC under sections 129 to 131 may be expected to suffice to restore order. Since the unlawful assembly is not acting in general defiance of the Government, the danger is, as a rule local and disappears with the dispersal of the rioters and the arrest of the ringleaders. The military when called in the aid of civil authority under such provisions, must use minimum force (lethal) to bring the situation under control. In India, suitable guidelines in the form of "Do's and Don'ts" have been issued to the military on the use of force during aid to civil authorities.[9] But where the disturbances are recurrent, widespread, concerted and directed against the constituted authorities, it becomes duty of the executive, in exercise of common law of repelling force by force, to assume such exceptional powers and to take such exceptional measures as may be necessary for the purpose of restoring order".[10]

---

the military authority and should be used to the utmost, not only to increase its power but in order to initiate, at an early stage, the process of re-establishing civil control and respect for it. When unity of control, which is perhaps the most important result of proclaiming martial law, is not provided, the necessity of close co-operation and of mutual understanding is all the more important. Anything in the nature of jealousy or competition to secure credit is certain to lead to lack of co-ordination in courses of action. Gwynn Charles W, Major General, 1939, *Imperial Policing*, London: Macmillan and Co. Limited, p. 16.

9 The following instructions [**List of "Do's and Don'ts"**] must be followed while providing aid to the civil authority. List of Do's and Don'ts while providing Aid to Civil Authority: **Do's**: 1. Act in closest possible communication with civil authorities throughout. 2. Maintain inter-communication if possible by telephone/radio. 3. Get permission/requisition from the magistrate when present. 4. Use as little force and do as little injury to person and property as may be consistent with the attainment of objective in view. 5. In case you decide to open fire: (a) Give warning in local language that fire will be effective; (b) Attract attention before firing by bugle or other means; (c) Distribute your men in fire units with specified commanders; (d) Control fire by issuing personal orders; (e) Note number of rounds fired; (f) Aim at the front of crowd actually rioting or inciting to riot or at conspicuous ring leaders, i.e., do not fire into the thick of the crowd at the back; (g) Aim low and shoot for effect; (h) Keep light machine gun and medium gun in reserve; (i) Cease firing immediately once the object has been attained; and (j) Take immediate steps to secure wounded. 6. Maintain cordial relations with civilian authorities and paramilitary forces. 7. Ensure high standard of discipline. **Don'ts** are: 1. Do not use excessive force. 2. Do not get involved in hand-to-hand struggle with the mob. 3. Do not ill-treat any one, in particular, women and children. 4. No harassment of civilians. 5. No torture. 6. No meddling in civilian administration affairs. 6. No military disgrace by loss/surrender of weapons. 7. Do not accept presents, donations and rewards. 8. Avoid indiscriminate firing.

10 Manual of Indian Military Law, 1937, Government of India: Defence Department,

Small Wars

The use of lethal force in counterinsurgency operation poses significant challenges for the military, particularly in relation to balancing necessity against the right to life. The core issue is whether a State can deploy its armed forces in internal conflicts, and if so, whether and to what extent they should be given the power to shoot to kill.[11] Military forces, particularly the ground forces, have often provided key support in a number of democracies. The US and Canada, have created separate military commands, specifically tasked with internal security. In many democracies, due to the traditional involvement of the military in law enforcement missions, when violence breaks out the government and the civil society consider it appropriate that the military should be brought in. Once the armed forces are deployed they have sweeping powers, which includes the authority to use lethal force, shoot down civilian aircraft, issue orders to civilians, raid premises and seize documents. The rules of engagement (ROE) issued by the military to authorize and specify the level of force to be used by its members during domestic deployment remains highly classified. There is an international trend towards establishing greater executive powers to deploy the armed forces for domestic and political purposes. In India, a special legislation, the AFSPA gives power to the members of the security forces to deal with such contingencies.

AFSPA--Background: In order to deal with the disorder in certain parts of India on account of partition of the country, the Government of India issued four ordinances in 1947.[12]These ordinances were based on the Armed Forces (Special Powers) Ordinance, 1942 (Ordinance No. XLI of 1942).[13]

Delhi: Manager of Publication, p. 126.

11 All armed forces have both domestic and international responsibilities. As a general rule, the less democratically and economically developed a State is, the more these responsibilities and capabilities focus on domestic control and the greater the political role and share of defense budgets that go to armies rather than navies and air forces. As countries mature both economically and politically, maintaining domestic order through the use or threat of force usually declines, while concern over the preservation of one's territory, borders, and trade routes increases. Sheldon W. Simon, Asian Armed Forces: Internal and External Tasks and Capabilities, *The NBR Analysis Series*, Vol. 11, No. 1, May 2000, p. 1-28.

12 The Bengal Disturbed Areas (Special Powers of Armed Forces) Ordinance, 1947 (Act 11 of 1947); the Assam Disturbed Areas (Special Powers of Armed Forces) Ordinance, 1947 (Act 14 of 1947); the East Punjab and Delhi Disturbed Areas (Special Powers of Armed Forces) Ordinance, 1947 (Act 17 of 1947); and the United Provinces Disturbed Areas (Special Powers of Armed Forces) Ordinance, 1947 (Act 22 of 1947).

13 The Armed Forces (Special Powers) Ordinance was promulgated by the British on

The four Ordinances of 1947 were replaced by the Armed Forces (Special Powers) Act, 1948 (Act 3 of 1948). Act 3 was a temporary statute, enacted for a period of one year, though it continued till it was repealed by Act 36 of 1957, only to be resurrected a year later in 1958. The reason for the introduction of the Act of 1958 was the deteriorating situation with respect to internal security in the 'unified Assam'.[14] The Nagas, who inhabited the Naga Hills of Assam and Manipur, had opposed the merger of their area with the rest of India on the ground that they were racially and socio-politically different from the Indians.[15] They voted in favour of a referendum declaring independence in 1951, boycotted the first general election of 1952, demonstrating their non-acceptance of the Indian Constitution.[16] In order to deal with the difficult situation, the Assam Government imposed the Assam Maintenance of Public Order (Autonomous District) Act in

---

15 August 1942 to suppress the Quit India movement. It bestowed 'special powers' on officers not below the rank of Captain or equivalent ranks in the Air Force and the Navy to deal with an 'emergency'. The said officer or the personnel under his command were empowered to arrest and take into custody any person who did not stop when challenged by a sentry or attempted to damage or was engaged in damaging property. The said officer or personnel under his command were empowered to use such force as may be necessary, even if it caused death. The arrested person was required to be handed over to the appropriate authority for further action. Section 4 of the Ordinance dealing with the protection to persons provided: "No prosecution, suit or other legal proceedings for any order purporting to be made under this ordinance or for any act purporting to be done in obedience to any such order shall be instituted in any Court except with the previous sanction of the Central Government, and notwithstanding anything contained in any other law for the time being in force, no person purporting in good faith to make such an order or to do any act in obedience thereto shall, whatever consequences ensure, be liable therefor."

14 Before Independence, the Naga and Mizo Hills were not properly administered by the British, so the independent Indian government inherited little authority in those areas. Prior to the outbreak of armed violence, the degree of governance in both the Naga and Mizo Hills was insignificant. Governance in the state of Assam was marked by corruption, economic weakness and administrative neglect. The insurgency movements in these areas were also rife with internal tensions. There were competing sources of power, and disagreements about strategy and tactics. For more details see: Walter C Ladwig III, 'Insights from the Northeast: Counterinsurgency in Nagaland and Mizoram', in Ganguly Sumit and David P. Fidler (ed.). 2009. *India and Counterinsurgency: Lessons Learned*, London: Routledge, p. 45-62.

15 The Naga movement for an independent unified homeland for Naga inhabitants has a long history. Its roots can be traced back to the British colonial period. For more details see: Goswami Namrata, The Naga Narrative of Conflict: Envisioning a Resolution Roadmap, *Strategic Analysis*, Vol. 31, No. 2, March 2007, p. 287-313.

16 Das Pushpita, 'The History of Armed Forces Special Powers Act', in Chadha Vivek (ed.), *Armed Forces Special Powers Act: The Debate*, IDSA Monograph Series No. 7, 2012, New Delhi: IDSA, p.12.

the Naga Hills in 1953 and intensified police action against the rebels. When the situation worsened, the state government deployed the Assam Rifles in the Naga Hills and enacted the Assam Disturbed Areas Act, 1955 (ADAA), to provide a legal framework for the paramilitary forces as well as the armed state police to contain insurgency.[17] However, the Assam Rifles and the state armed police were not successful in containing the Naga rebellion and the rebel Naga Nationalists Council (NNC) formed a parallel government 'The Federal Government of Nagaland', on 22 March 1956. This intensified the widespread violence in the Naga Hills. The state administration could not handle the situation effectively and it asked for Central assistance. In response, the Central government sent the army to quell the rebellion and restore normalcy in the region. The President of India promulgated the Armed Forces (Assam and Manipur) Special Powers Ordinance on 22 May 1958 to confer 'special powers' on the armed forces, as well as provide them with a legal framework to function within the 'disturbed areas' of Assam and the Union Territory of Manipur. This Ordinance was reincarnated in the name of the Armed Forces (Special Powers) Act, 1958, or AFSPA.[18] The Parliament has enacted the AFSPA which draws legitimacy from a combined reading of Article 246(1), Entry 2A of List I and Article 355 of the Constitution.[19]

---

17 The ADAA was a copy of the Armed Forces Special Powers Ordinance of 1942. It gave 'special powers' to the armed forces engaged in counterinsurgency operations. For more details see: Kotwal Dinesh, The Naga Insurgency: the Past and the Future, *Strategic Analysis*, Volume 24, No 4, July 2000, p 751.

18 A Bill seeking to replace the ordinance was subsequently introduced in the monsoon session of Parliament on 18 August 1958. While introducing the Bill, the Union Home Minister, G B Pant, said: "This is a very simple measure. It only seeks to protect the steps the armed forces might have to take in the disturbed areas... It will be applied only to such parts as have been declared by the administrations concerned as being disturbed.... After such a declaration has been made, then alone the provisions of this Bill will be applicable to that particular area. I do not think it is necessary for me to say more in this connection. It is a simple measure." Several members of Parliament, however, argued that giving such sweeping powers to the armed forces would lead to the violation of the fundamental rights of the people. They felt that it would allow the government to circumvent the Constitution to impose an emergency, without actually declaring it and the armed forces would usurp all the powers of the civilian government. Further, they feared that it would allow the armed forces to commit excesses with impunity. After a brief discussion, the Bill was passed by both the houses of the Parliament with retrospective effect from 22 May 1958.

19 In the Indian Constitution, the Central legislative authority vide entry 2A, list I (Seventh Schedule) reads: "Deployment of any armed force of the Union or any other force subject to control of the Union or any contingent or unit thereof in any State in aid of the civil power, powers, jurisdiction, privileges and liabilities of the members of such forces while on such deployment." The Central Government may, in order to

In the decade that followed, the northeast was divided into separate states to accommodate the ethnic claims of various tribal and other ethnic groups. In 1972, the AFSPA was amended to cover the states of Assam, Manipur, Meghalaya, Nagaland and Tripura and the Union Territory of Arunachal Pradesh. In 1986, the Act was further amended to additionally cover Arunachal Pradesh and Mizoram. The AFSPA now extends to certain parts of the State of Arunachal Pradesh, Assam, Manipur, Meghalaya, Mizoram, Nagaland and Tripura.[20]

The Armed Forces (Special Powers) Act, 1958:[21] It is a small Act having only six sections. The AFSPA defines the 'armed forces' as 'the military forces and the air forces of the Union so operating'.[22] Under the Act, the term 'disturbed area' means an area which has for the time being been declared by notification to be a disturbed area. The Delhi High Court has held that the lack of precision in the definition is not an issue since the government and the people of India understand its meaning. According to the Court, "The term 'disturbed area' defies any definition—it has to be adjudged according to the location, situation and circumstances of a particular case."[23] The Act provides that all the words and expressions

ensure the maintenance of public order, may deploy its armed forces or any other force under its control "in aid of the civil power." Article 355 provides, "It shall be the duty of the Union to protect every State against external aggression and internal disturbance and to ensure that the government of every State is carried out in accordance with the provisions of this Constitution."

20 See: The Armed Forces (Special Powers) Act, 1958, section 1. The AFSPA is not applicable in the entire northeastern part of India. For example, in Arunachal Pradesh the Act is applicable only to the two eastern districts of Tirap and Changlang, which have been declared as 'disturbed areas'. In Meghalaya, the Act is applicable only in a 20-Kilometer belt along the Assam border. Similar is the case with other States.

21 There were two other related legislations, (i) The Armed Forces (Punjab and Chandigarh) Special Powers Act, 1983; and The Armed Forces (Jammu and Kashmir) Special Powers Act, 1990. The Act of 1983 was allowed to lapse in Punjab once violence ended in 1997. Both these Acts were broadly the same as that of the Armed Forces (Assam and Manipur) Special Powers Act of 1972 except for two provisions which provided additional powers to the armed forces. The additional provisions provided that any vehicle could be stopped, searched and seized forcibly if it was suspected of carrying proclaimed offenders or ammunition or explosive substance; and that a soldier had the power to break open lock of any door, almirah, safe, box, cupboard, drawer, package or other thing, if the key thereof is withheld.

22 The Armed Forces (Jammu and Kashmir) Special Powers Act, 1990, defines the term 'armed forces', as 'the military forces and the air forces operating as land forces and includes any other armed forces of the Union so operating.'

23 *Indrajit Barua v State of Assam* AIR 1983 Del 54.

used in the AFSPA, but not defined in it shall have meanings assigned to them in the Air Force Act 1950, or the Army Act 1950.[24]

It is necessary to explain the term "enemy," which under the Army Act, 1950, "includes all armed mutineers, armed rebels, armed rioters, pirates and any person in arms against whom it is the duty of any person subject to military law to act."[25] The Regulations for the Army, in paragraph 348 further amplify that the term "enemy" would include a soldier 'running amok'.

Power to Declare Areas as Disturbed Areas: The AFSPA provides that if the Governor of a state or the Central Government is of the opinion that the whole or any part of the state is in such a disturbed or dangerous condition that the use of the armed forces in aid of the civil powers is necessary, the said Governor or the Central Government may, by notification in the Official Gazette, declare the whole or such part of the state or Union territory to be a disturbed area.[26] The expression 'in aid of civil power' implies that the deployment of the armed forces of the Union shall be for the purposes of enabling the civil power in the state to deal with the situation (affecting the maintenance of public order)[27] which has necessitated the deployment of the armed forces in the state. The word 'aid' implies the continued existence of the authority to be aided, i.e., the

24 The Armed Forces (Special Powers) Act 1958 section 2(c).

25 The Army Act, 1950, section 3 (x).

26 The Armed Forces (Special Powers) Act 1958 (AFSPA) section 3. AFSPA becomes enforceable only when an area is declared as 'disturbed area.' An explanation that what constitutes 'disturbed area' is therefore necessary. AFSPA as enacted in 1958 allowed only Governors of the States and the Administrators of the Union Territories to declare an area as 'disturbed'. However, the amendment of 1972 enabled the Central Government, too, make such a declaration. This is because keeping in view the duty of the Union under Article 355 of the Constitution, to protect every state against internal disturbance, it is considered desirable that the Central Government should also have power to declare areas as 'disturbed', to enable its armed forces to exercise the special powers. In *Naga People's Movement of Human Rights case*, it was held that there is no requirement that it Central Government shall consult the State Government before making the declaration.

27 The Supreme Court has explained the term "public order" in *Madhu Limaye v. S.D.M. Monghyr* 1971 AIR 2486: 1971 SCR (2) 711 as: 'Public order' no doubt requires absence of disturbance, of a state of serenity in society, but it goes further. It means what the French designate '*ordre publique*', defined as an absence of insurrection, riot, turbulence, or crimes of violence. The expression 'public order' includes absence of all acts which are a danger to the security of the State and also acts which are comprehended by the expression '*ordre publique*' explained above but not acts which disturb only the serenity of others.

civil authority will continue to function even after the deployment of the armed forces.[28]

Section 3 of the Armed Forces (Jammu and Kashmir) Special Powers Act, 1990 dealing with the power to declare areas to be disturbed areas provides:

If, in relation to the state of Jammu and Kashmir, the Governor of that state or the Central Government, is of opinion that the whole or any part of the state is in such a disturbed and dangerous condition that the use of armed forces in aid of the civil power is necessary to prevent:

> (1) activities involving terrorist acts directed towards overawing the Government as by law established or striking terror in the people or any section of the people or alienating any section of the people or adversely affecting the harmony amongst different sections of the people;
>
> (2) activities directed towards disclaiming, questioning or disrupting the sovereignty and territorial integrity of India or bringing about cession of a part of the territory of India or secession of a part of the territory of India from the Union or causing insult to the Indian National Flag, the Indian National Anthem and the Constitution of India;
>
> the Governor of the state or the Central Government, may, by notification in the Official Gazette, declare the whole or any part of the state to be a disturbed area. Under this provision, 'terrorist act' has the same meaning as in explanation to Article 248 of the Constitution of India as applicable to the state of Jammu and Kashmir.[29]

The power to declare an area as "disturbed area" has been used by the Union Government in a state troubled by insurgency or violent public disturbances. Because of its responsibility to protect a state against such internal disturbance, the Union Government is competent to assess the situation and decide what special measures, including powers for its armed forces, are necessary for dealing with it. While the Union Government, under Article 355 has all the powers that it may need to deal with an internal disturbance, it cannot assume the sole responsibility for dealing with an internal disturbance by superseding or excluding the state police

28 *Naga People's Movement of Human Rights v Union of India* (1998) 2 SCC 109; AIR 1998 SC 431, para 24 and 74.

29 The Armed Forces (Jammu and Kashmir) Special Powers Act 1990 section 3.

and other authorities responsible for maintaining public order. Neither can the Union Government deploy, in contravention of the wishes of a State Government, its armed forces to deal with a relatively less serious public order problem which is unlikely to escalate and which the State Government is confident of tackling. The power to declare an area as a disturbed area cannot be construed as conferring the power to issue such a declaration without any time limit. There should be a periodic review of the declaration before the expiry of six months. Although a declaration under this provision can be made by the Central Government *suo moto* without consulting the concerned state government, it is desirable that the state government be consulted. The conferment of the power to make such a declaration on the Central Government is not violative of the federal scheme as envisaged by the Constitution.[30]

Power to Use Force: Section 4 of the AFSPA confers special powers on commissioned officers, warrant officers and non-commissioned officers (NCOs) or any other persons of equivalent rank in the armed forces.[31] Under section 4(a), these officers, acting in a disturbed area, for the maintenance of public order, may after giving due warning, fire upon or otherwise use force against, even to cause the death of, any person who acts in contravention of any law in the disturbed area or carries weapons or things capable of being used as weapons or ammunition or explosive substances.

The designated members of the armed forces are also empowered to destroy any arms dump or fortified position or shelter from which armed attacks are made or are likely to be made or any structure used as a training camp for armed volunteers or utilized as a hide-out by armed gangs or absconders wanted for any offence. They can arrest, without warrant, any person who has committed a cognizable offence or against whom a reasonable suspicion exists that he has committed or is about to commit a cognizable offence and may use such force as may be necessary to effect the arrest.[32] They are also empowered to enter and search, without warrant,

30 *Naga People's Movement of Human Rights v Union of India* (1998) 2 SCC 109; AIR 1998 SC 431.

31 The term "armed forces" includes "other armed forces of the Union"; see AFSPA section 2(a). The term "other armed forces of the Union so operating" refers to both armed and paramilitary forces operating in 'disturbed areas', such as the Border Security Force (BSF), Assam Rifles, Rashtriya Rifles (RR), National Security Guards (NSG), and the Central Reserve Police Force (CRPF). Each of these forces is governed by their own Acts.

32 Section 4 (c), the Armed Forces (Special Powers) Act 1958. The power conferred under

any premises to make any arrest or to recover any person believed to be wrongfully restrained or any arms, ammunition or explosive substances believed to be unlawfully kept in such premises and may for that purpose use necessary force.[33]

The power to enter and search must be exercised in accordance with the provisions relating to search and seizure contained in the Cr PC 1973 and the property or the arms, ammunitions, etc., that is seized during the course of the search must be handed over to the officer in charge of the nearest police station with the least possible delay, together with a report of the circumstances occasioning the search and seizure.

Interpretation of section 4 (a) of the AFSPA by different bodies suggests that the special power to use force to the extent of causing death is not absolute or unguided. The armed forces personnel under the power conferred by section 4(a), cannot kill a person without any reason. The pre-conditions are: (i) there has to be a declaration of 'disturbed area' by the designated authority as mentioned in the Act; (ii) the concerned officer has to be of the opinion that it is necessary to do for the maintenance of public order; (iii) he has to give such due warning as he may consider necessary; (iv) the person against whom action is being taken by armed forces must be "acting in contravention of any law or order for the time being in force in the disturbed area." Further, the said powers under the AFSPA are conditional upon the existence of a prohibitory order issued under a law, e.g. Cr PC or the Arms Act, 1959. Such law or order must relate to prohibiting the assembly of five or more persons or the carrying of weapons or of things capable of being used as weapons or of fire-arms, ammunition or explosive substances. Such prohibitory orders can be issued only by the civil authorities of the State. In the absence of such a prohibitory order, the power conferred under section 4 (a) of the AFSPA cannot be exercised.

---

this provision read with the Section 5 of the AFSPA has to be exercised in consonance with the overriding requirements of Article 22 clauses (1) and (2) of the Constitution which means that the person who is arrested by an officer has to be made over to the officer in charge of the nearest police station together with a report of the circumstances occasioning the arrest with the least possible delay so that the person arrested can be produced before the nearest magistrate within a period of 24 hours of such arrest excluding the time necessary for the journey from the place of arrest to the court of the magistrate and no such person can be detained in custody beyond the said period without the authority of a magistrate. *Naga People's Movement of Human Rights v Union of India* (1998) 2 SCC 109.

33 The Armed Forces (Special Powers) Act, 1958, section 4.

Justice Jeevan Reddy Committee[34] has also observed that according section 4(a), the power to fire upon the persons is not unregulated or absolute. Such a power comes into play only where the two ingredients are satisfied[35] and furthermore, where such officer of the armed forces is of the opinion that it is necessary to fire upon such person(s) or to otherwise use force against such person(s) for the purpose of maintaining public order. It goes without saying that the 'opinion' must be formed honestly and fairly. The Second Administrative Reforms Commission in its Fifth Report (2007) on 'Public Order' supported the views expressed by the Jeevan Reddy Committee and recommended the repeal of AFSPA.[36]

The Supreme Court in *Naga People's Movement of Human Rights* observed that 'the power conferred under clauses 4(a) to (d) of section 4 and 5 of the AFSPA on the officers of the armed forces, including a non-commissioned officer, are not arbitrary and unreasonable and are not violative of the provisions of Article 14,19, 21 of the Constitution and while exercising the powers conferred under section 4 (a) of the AFSPA, the officer in the armed forces shall use minimal force under a prohibitory order.' Thus, the provisions of section 4(a), as claimed by various human rights organizations, are not violative of right to life guaranteed under

34 There was an intense agitation in Manipur following the death of Ms Manorama Devi on 11 July 2004 while in the custody of the Assam Rifles. On 19 November 2004, the Government of India set up the Jeevan Reddy Committee with the following terms of reference: "Keeping in view the legitimate concerns of the people of the North Eastern Region, the need to foster human rights, keeping in perspective the imperatives of security and maintenance of public order to review the provisions of the Armed Forces (Special Powers) Act, 1958 as amended in 1972 and to advise the Government of India whether: (a) To amend the provisions of the Act to bring them in consonance with the obligations of the government towards protection of human rights; or (b) To replace the Act by a more humane Act." The Committee had specifically asked the people who appeared before it whether they wanted both the AFSPA and the Army to go, or whether they want only the Act to go but the Army to remain. The overwhelming response to this question was that while the AFSPA should be repealed, the Army should remain to fight the militants and guard the borders. The Committee submitted its report to the government in June 2005. Though the report was not made public, some media persons managed to access it.

35 These ingredients are: (i) where there is in force, in the disturbed area, a law or an order prohibiting the assembly of five or more persons or the carrying of weapons or of things capable of being used as weapons or of fire arms, ammunition or explosive substances; and (ii) any officer of the armed forces of the above named rank, may, if he is of the opinion that it is necessary so to do for the maintenance of public order, after giving such due warnings as he may consider necessary, fire upon or otherwise use force even to the causing of death of such person.'

36 Second Administrative Reforms Commission, Fifth Report (2007), p. 130.

article 21 of the Indian Constitution. In addition to it, the orders issued by the military in the form of 'Do's and Don'ts' while operating under AFSPA removes any arbitrariness in the use of lethal force by the military.

List of Do's and Don'ts while acting Under AFSPA (1978)[37]

Do's

1. Action before Operation

   (a) Act only in the area declared "Disturbed Area" under Section 3 of the Act.

   (b) Power to open fire using force or arrest is to be exercised under the AFSPA only by an officer/JCO/WO and NCO.

   (c) Before launching any raid/search, definite information about the activity to be obtained from the local civil authorities.

   (d) As far as possible co-opt representative of local civil administration during the raid.

2. Action during Operation

   (a) In case of necessity of opening fire and using any force against the suspect or any person acting in contravention to law and order, ascertain first that it is essential for maintenance of public order. Open fire only after due warning.

   (b) Arrest only those who have committed cognizable offence or who are about to commit cognizable offence or against whom a reasonable ground exists to prove that they have committed or are about to commit cognizable offence.

   (c) Ensure that troops under command do not harass innocent people, destroy property of the public or unnecessarily enter into the house/ dwelling of people not connected with any unlawful activities.

   (d) Ensure that women are not searched / arrested without the presence of female police. In fact, women should be searched by female police only.

37 These instructions provide an effective check against any misuse or abuse of the powers conferred under the AFSPA on an officer in the Army inasmuch as contravention of these instructions is punishable under sections 41, 42(e), 63 and 64(f) of the Army Act, 1950; see *Naga People's Movement of Human Rights v Union of India*, 1998 AIR SC 459.

3. Action after operation

(a) After arrest prepare a list of the persons so arrested.

(b) Hand over the arrested persons to the nearest police station with least possible delay.

(c) While handing over to the police a report should accompany with detailed circumstances occasioning the arrest.

(d) Every delay in handing over the suspects to the police must be justified and should be reasonable depending upon the place, time of arrest and the terrain in which such person has been arrested. Least possible delay may be 2-3 hours extendable to 24 hours or so depending upon particular case.

(e) After raid make out a list of all arms, ammunition or any other incriminating material/document taken into possession.

(f) All such arms, ammunition, stores, etc. should be handed over to the police State along with the seizure memo.

(g) Obtain receipt of persons, arms/ammunition, stores etc. so handed over to the police.

(h) Make record of the area where operation is launched having the date and time and the persons participating in such raid.

(i) Make a record of the commander and other officers/JCOs/NCOs forming part of such force.

(j) Ensure medical relief to any person injured during the encounter, if any person dies in the encounter his dead body to be handed over immediately to the police along with the details leading to such death.

4. Dealing with civil court

(a) Directions of the High Court/Supreme Court should be promptly attended to.

(b) Whenever summoned by the courts, decorum of the court must be maintained and proper respect paid.

(c) Answer questions of the court politely and with dignity.

(d) Maintain detailed record of the entire operation correctly and explicitly.

Don'ts

1. Do not keep a person under custody for any period longer than the bare necessity for handing over to the nearest police station.
2. Do not use any force after having arrested a person except when he is trying to escape.
3. Do not use third degree methods to extract information or to extract confession or other involvement in unlawful activities.
4. After the arrest of a person by a member of the armed forces, he shall not be interrogated by the member of the armed forces.
5. Do not release a person directly after apprehending on your own. If any person is to be released, he must be released through civil authorities.
6. Do not tamper with official records.
7. The armed forces shall not take back person after he is handed over to civil police.

Unlike the US, UK, Australia, Germany and Canada, in India, there are no written manual on the laws of war.[38] The military's Standard Operating Procedures (SPOs) or the Rules of Engagement (ROE) remain restricted documents. Therefore, applicable principles, legal system and practices which are to be followed by the armed forces during small wars or internal conflict are not available in the public domain. It leaves a lot of uncertainty in the mind of the members of the civil society.

---

38 The necessity of such a manual is envisaged in Article 1 of the 1899 Hague Convention II, with respect to the laws and customs of war on land makes it obligatory on a State Party to issue "instructions ... which shall be in conformity with the "regulations ... attached to the present Convention". Use of the term "instructions" manifested a direct commitment by the State Parties to issue instructions consistent with treaty obligations providing elaboration and explanation. The provision does not obligate the Governments merely to reprint the texts of treaties it has ratified. The 1949 Geneva Conventions, to which India is State Party, necessitates preparation of a law of war manual. According to the terms of Articles 48, 49, 128 and 145, which are common to the four Geneva Conventions of 1949, the state parties must communicate to one another the official translations of the treaties and the laws and regulations they have adopted to ensure implementation. The term "laws and regulations" is to be understood here in the broadest sense. It covers all legal instruments issued by both the executives and the legislative powers that have any bearing on the implementation of the treaties in question. The term "implementation" covers all measures that must be taken—both wartime and peacetime---to ensure the rules of law of war are fully respected.

A number of human rights activists, both in India and abroad, have claimed that the powers to military persons under Section 4 of the AFSPA are draconian and excessive. In fact, these powers are similar to that available to a police officer under the Cr PC, 1973. Any police officer may, without an order from a magistrate and without a warrant, arrest any person against whom a reasonable complaint has been made or a reasonable suspicion exists that he has committed a cognizable offence punishable with imprisonment for a term which may be less than seven years.[39] The provisions under the Arms Act and Explosives Act also confer such powers on police officers. The Cr PC gives every private person the power to arrest a person who in his presence commits a non-bailable and cognizable offence or is a proclaimed offender.[40] In making an arrest, a police officer or a private person may use the necessary force and if the person being arrested forcibly resists the endeavour to arrest him, or attempts to evade arrest, the police officer or private person may use all means necessary to effect the arrest.[41] If an offender has taken shelter in a place to which a police officer is not allowed free ingress, it is lawful for the officer to enter such place and search. He can break open any outer or inner door or window to enter or exit from a house or place where the alleged offender is thought to be present. The only condition is that if such place is in the actual occupancy of a female, the police officer shall, before entry, give notice to the female to withdraw.[42] The civil police are also empowered to search an arrested person in order to seize any weapon.[43] If a person in lawful custody escapes or is rescued, the person in whose custody he was, may pursue and arrest him in any place in India. The person pursuing may enter any place to search and may break open any outer or inner door for ingress or egress.[44]

The power to open fire in a disturbed area is necessary for the functioning of the armed forces against actions of militants/ terrorists that could be described as perfidy.[45] Militants posing as civilians have attacked

39 See section 41 of the Cr PC, 1973. Incidentally any police officer may arrest without warrant any person reasonably believed to subject to the Army, Navy or Air Force Acts and to be a deserter or to be travelling without authority. The Army Act 1950 section 105 (2) and the Cr PC, 1973 section 41 (f).

40 The Criminal Procedure Code, 1973 section 43.

41 The Criminal Procedure Code, 1973 section 46 (2).

42 The Criminal Procedure Code, 1973 section 47.

43 The Criminal Procedure Code, 1973 section 51 and 52.

44 The Criminal Procedure Code, 1973 section 60.

45 Perfidy has been prohibited under international law. Article 37 of the 1977 Additional

the military convoys, tossed grenades on military personnel and fired at them. They have taken refuge in houses occupied by civilians or in places of worship. They have also employed or forced women and children to carry arms for them and act as shields. The armed forces deployed in disturbed areas, therefore, have to use force to eliminate those who violate the general principles of laws of armed conflict.

The 'special powers' conferred upon the armed forces to open fire, even causing death, is not unfettered. It may be used in a disturbed area, where the assembly of five or more persons or the carrying of weapons is forbidden, only if a person is seen as violating such a law. In keeping with this, the armed forces deployed in disturbed areas do not open fire unless it becomes absolutely necessary to do so for self-defence or for the defence of comrades or the civilian population. The Supreme Court has held that the powers conferred on the officers of the armed forces, including a NCO under the AFSPA are not arbitrary and unreasonable and are not violative of the provisions of Articles 14, 19 or 21 of the Constitution.[46] However, there are views contrary to this.[47]

The power to make arrest without warrant under section 4(c) of the AFSPA on the suspicion that the accused 'has committed or is about to commit a cognizable offence' is similar to one available to a police officer. The issue of arrest warrant by a magistrate is not possible in such situations. However, it has been alleged that often arrests without warrant lead to torture and other human rights violations including extrajudicial killings. The isolated incidents of such violations including that of

---

Protocol I states: It is prohibited to kill, injure or capture an adversary by resort to perfidy. Acts inviting the confidence of an adversary to lead him to believe that he is entitled to, or is obliged to accord, protection under the rules of international law applicable in armed conflict, with intent to betray that confidence, shall constitute perfidy. Killing or wounding treacherously a combatant adversary in non-international armed conflicts amounts to war crime under the Rome Statute Article 8 (2)(e)(ix). For more details see: Jackson, Richard B., Perfidy in Non-International Armed Conflicts, in Watkin Kenneth and Andrew J. Norris (eds.). 2011. *Non-International Armed Conflict in the Twenty-first Century*, International Law Series, Vol. 88, the US Naval War College, p. 237-259.

46 Conferment of power on non-commissioned officer like a havildar cannot be said to be bad and unjustified. *Indrajit Barua v State of Assam* AIR 1983 Del 54; *Naga People's Movement of Human Rights v Union of India* (1998) 2 SCC 109; *Luithukia v Rishang Keishing* (1988) 2 Gau LR 159.

47 The AFSPA can be held to be actually in violation of Article 21 of the Constitution, the right to life, basic to the Fundamental Rights. Habibullah Wajahat, 'Armed Forces Special Powers Act, Jammu & Kashmir' in Chadha Vivek (ed.), *Armed Forces Special Powers Act: The Debate*, IDSA Monograph No. 7, 2012, New Delhi: IDSA, p. 25.

custodial torture have been reported and military has taken strict actions against the involved persons.

Arrested persons to be made over to the police: Section 5 of the AFSPA stipulates that any person arrested and taken into custody under the AFSPA shall be made over to the officer-in-charge of the nearest police station with the least possible delay, together with a report of the circumstances occasioning the arrest. It has been held that the words 'least possible delay' means 'within the shortest possible time' though no arbitrary time limit can be set down as it may not be possible in many cases to precisely quantify the period of time by reference to hours, days or months. Therefore, whenever the question of 'least possible delay' arises for decision in computing the period of time, the court has to have regard to the particular circumstances of the case, for example, physical impossibility or otherwise to make over the arrested person to the nearest police station, and how, where and in what circumstances the arrest was effected.[48] Justice Jeevan Reddy Committee observed that the person arrested under Section 4 (c) has to be produced before a Magistrate within 24 hours of his arrest (excluding the time taken for journey) and it is within this period that the officer of the armed forces who made the arrest shall hand over the person to the police and the police shall produce the person before the Magistrate. The provision does not permit the arresting personnel of the armed force to keep the arrested person in custody for the purpose of interrogation, or to be fully satisfied whether the concerned person was really involved in the matter which led to his (her) arrest. This satisfaction has to precede the arrest, and not to follow it.[49]

---

48 *Bacha Bora v. State of Assam* (1991) 2 GLR 119. In *Pumima Baruah v. Union of India* 1991 Cri LJ 2675, although the nearest police station was within 1km, the army authority had taken the victim to 300 km away and took two more days to handover him to the police. The Gauhati High Court held it as violation of Article 22 of the Constitution and section 5 of AFSPA and awarded compensation.

49 In *Kinjinbou Liangnei v. Union of India* (1998) 4 GLT, 139, it was held by Gauhati High Court that 'the law is quite clear that if any person is arrested and taken into custody under the AFSPA, he shall be made over to the officer in charge of the nearest police station with the least possible delay'. In this case Assam Rifle took 4 days to hand over the detenu to nearest police station which was only half km away and the Court observed that that it 'is completely in violation of the established principle of law'. The Court observed, 'under sections 4 and 5 of AFSPA there are procedure for arrest and production of person or persons and the armed personnel or the paramilitary authority or police officers who are the custodians of law and order, should have greatest respect for the personal liberty of the citizens and should not flout the laws by stopping to such bizarre acts of lawlessness'.

Protection of persons acting under AFSPA: Section 6 of the AFSPA provides limited immunity to the members of the armed forces operating in disturbed areas.[50] This provision prevents the filing of frivolous claims[51] and protects armed forces personnel engaged in a difficult task and risking their lives to prevent destruction of life and property. The Supreme Court has recently held that the words 'no' and 'shall' in Section 6 denotes the mandatory requirement of obtaining the sanction of the Central Government before the institution of prosecution, suit or legal proceedings.[52] Since the order of the Central Government refusing or granting the sanction under Section 6 of the AFSPA is subject to judicial review, the Central Government must pass a speaking order.

Incidentally, the protection from unnecessary and unwarranted prosecution is not exclusive to the armed forces. The civil police also enjoy similar protection under Section 197 of the Cr PC. The following case amply illustrates this. In a complaint before the Deputy Commissioner of Police, a lady had claimed that her husband, a social worker, was beaten to death by few members of the Calcutta police. On 28 May 2001, she filed a complaint in the court of the Chief Judicial Magistrate, Alipore, in respect of offences, punishable according to her, under Sections 302, 201, 109 read with Section 120-B of the Indian Penal Code. In the complaint, she stated that her husband, a law-abiding citizen with no criminal background was severely assaulted by the police staff, instigated by the officer-in-charge of Police Station; and later succumbed to his injuries. She demanded stern punishment for the murderer of her husband.

The Chief Judicial Magistrate took cognizance of the offence and issued a warrant for the arrest of Assistant Commissioner of Police (ACP) and his application for anticipatory bail was rejected by the Calcutta High Court. The ACP, meanwhile, filed a Petition under Section 482 of the Cr PC before the High Court for quashing of the complaint on the ground that the Chief Judicial Magistrate had no jurisdiction to entertain the complaint since the condition precedent for entertaining the complaint, i.e. a sanction under section 197(1) of the Cr PC had not been obtained. The High Court

50 The Armed Forces (Special Powers) Act 1958 s. 6 states: "No prosecution, suit or other legal proceeding shall be instituted, except with the previous sanction of the Central Government against any person in respect of anything done or purported to be done in exercise of the powers conferred by the Armed Forces (Special Powers) Act 1958.

51 *Naga People's Movement of Human Rights v Union of India* (1998) 2 SCC 109; *Indrajit Barua v State of Assam* AIR 1983 Del 54.

52 *General Officer Commanding v Central Bureau of Investigation* AIR 2012 SC 1890.

(by an order dated 11 July 2003) dismissed the application. It overruled the contention of the accused and held: "In its considered view section 197 CrPC has got no manner of application in the present case. Under section 197, sanction is required only if the public servant was, at the time of commission of offence, 'employed in connection with the affairs of the Union or of a state' and he was 'not removable from his office save by or with the sanction of the Government'. The bar under section 197 Cr PC cannot be raised by a public servant if he is removable by some authority without the sanction of the Government." The High Court further held: "Committing an offence can never be a part of an official duty. Where there is no necessary connection between the act and the performance of the duties of a public servant, section 197 Cr PC will not be attracted. Beating a person to death by a police officer cannot be regarded as having been committed by a public servant within the scope of his official duties."

On appeal, the Supreme Court referred to the Constitution Bench decision on the scope of Section 197 of the Cr PC in *Matajog Dobey v HC Bhari*[53] wherein it was held that section 197 of the Cr PC was not violative of the fundamental rights conferred on a citizen under Article 14 of the Constitution of India. The Supreme Court had observed: "Public servants have to be protected from harassment in the discharge of official duties while ordinary citizens not so engaged do not require this safeguard." The Court also referred to its earlier decision in the case of *Bakhshish Singh Brar v Gurmej Kaur*[54], wherein it was held that it was necessary to protect public servants in the discharge of their duties. They must be made immune from being harassed in criminal proceedings and prosecution, and that is the rationale behind Sections 196 and 197 of the CrPC. The Supreme Court set aside the order of the Calcutta High Court holding that for the prosecution of a public servant, sanction under Section 197(1) of the Cr PC was necessary.[55] The Jammu and Kashmir Public Safety Act (PSA), enacted in 1978 and amended in 1987 and 1990, also allows for immunity from prosecution, stating: "No suit, prosecution or any other legal proceeding shall lie against any person for anything done or intended to be done in good faith in pursuance of the provisions of this Act."

53 1955 (2) SCR 925.

54 (1987) 4 SCC 663.

55 *Sankaran Moitra v. Sadhna Das* (2006) 4 SCC 584: (2006) 2 SCC (Cri) 358: AIR 2006 SC 1599. Also see: *Om Prakash v State of Jharkhand*, Criminal Appeal No. 1491 of 2012, decided by the Supreme Court on 26 September 2012.

Various human rights organizations in the country and abroad and the foreign and local media have questioned the effectiveness of Indian laws in dealing with the violation of human rights by armed forces personnel. They have also criticized the AFSPA, which gives enhanced powers to the armed forces for dealing effectively with disruptive activities in specific areas. The United Nations Human Rights Committee, in 1991, found Section 4 of the AFSPA to be incompatible with Articles 6, 9 and 14 of the International Covenant on Civil and Political Rights (ICCPR), 1966, which was ratified by India on 10 April 1979. In reality, there are safeguards related to imposition of AFSPA to prevent the possibility of arbitrariness in the exercise of power under the Act. The provisions of the AFSPA can be applied only in the following special cases.

- The central government is satisfied that the normal law and order situation has deteriorated to the extent that it has created a disturbed or dangerous situation.
- The state police force is not in a position to stop infiltration or undesirable forces.
- The power conferred by the statute can be exercised only in the specified area and in no other state.
- The law has to be followed even in a disturbed area, for example, an order under Section 144 of the Cr P C must be in force before the powers under Section 4 of the Act can be exercised.
- The powers under the Act can be exercised only in respect of those who are violating law and order.
- Before exercising such power, a warning is required to be given to those who are violating the law in force.
- The military person exercising the power is answerable to the organization for any breach in the policy directives issued by the organization.

The AFSPA also contemplates that in the event of the deployment of armed forces, the said forces will operate in the state concerned in cooperation with the civil administration[56] so that the situation that has

56 The responsibility of maintaining law and order is primarily that of the State Governments. State Governments have adequate machinery at their disposal for the dispersal of unlawful assemblies, suppression of disturbances and riots and the maintenance of law and order generally, by arrest and punishment of offenders. Civil

necessitated the deployment of the armed forces is effectively dealt with and normalcy is restored. Thus there are ample safeguards to prevent the wanton abuse of the power conferred by the AFSPA.

> In the armed forces, when troops are assigned the task of "aid to civil power", they follow pertain principles which govern the use of force: (a) Necessity: (i) There must be justification for each separate act; (ii) Action should not be taken in one place with the object of creating effect in another place; (iii) There should be no reprisals; (iv) Action should be preventive and not punitive. (b) Minimum force: No more force is to be used than is necessary to achieve the immediate object. This refers to the actual amount of force used and not to the number of troops employed. (c) Impartiality: Officers and other persons must be impartial in communal disturbances or labour strikes. They should not accept gifts or show favours. (d) Good faith: Officers and other persons must act in good faith.[57]

The method of dispersal of unlawful assembly, as explained in the Manual of Military Law, clearly state that the troops employed will not use police methods or be armed with police weapons like lathies and truncheons. While central police forces deployed in the aid to civil power may be equipped with non-lethal weapons, the armed forces, being a last resort, are always armed with lethal weapons.[58]They use their own weapons and military tactics to deal with the situation. According to Military Manual, when fire is to be opened on a mob, the procedure should be as follows:

---

authorities are first required to utilise the civil forces at their disposal for restoring law and order, and seek the aid of the Army only when the civil forces are inadequate to deal with the situation (of this the civil authority is the judge). The causes for civil unrest and disturbances may be many but primarily they are due to labour dissatisfaction and industrial disputes, strikes organised by labour for redress of real or imaginary grievances, and disputes among religious sections and rival political parties.

57 Manual of Military Law, 2013, Vol, I, Chapter VII. Paragraph 8.

58 It is sometimes advocated that troops called out in aid of the civil power should be specially armed with non-lethal weapons, such as batons. The use of non-lethal weapons by the armed forces is prohibited to avoid the troops becoming engaged in hand-to-hand conflicts of a nature for which they are not specially trained nor physically specially fitted. The moral effect of the appearance of troops depends largely on the fact that they carry lethal weapons. It is a warning to spectators that it is time to get away and it awakens the more moderate element to the seriousness of the situation. Gwynn Charles W, Major General, 1939, *Imperial Policing*, London: Macmillan and Co. Limited, p. 32.

(a) Before firing: If possible the crowd should be warned that unless the unlawful assembly disperses, fire is to be opened and that it will be effective. The magistrate present should give this warning in vernacular, if he is able to do so. Attention of the crowd can be attracted by sounding a bugle or whistle. A warning notice in appropriate vernacular, where possible, should be carried and exposed to the mob at the required moment. The police force present at the spot does not come under the command of the officer commanding the body of troops. Troops should be kept out of sight of the mob, until they are to be actively used.

(b) During firing: Firing will be controlled strictly. If officer commanding the body of troops considers that firing by a single or a few individuals is likely to prove sufficient, he will issue orders to one person of a few specified individuals. If more fire is required, he will issue orders to specified section commanders. While giving fire orders, he will indicate definite targets and state the number of rounds to be fired. The most effective targets are usually the ring leaders. Troops should shoot for effect. They should normally direct their fire low in order to injure and incapacitate rather than to kill. Firing with blank ammunition or over the heads of the crowd is strictly forbidden. Rapid fire should never be necessary except in self-defence. Pauses in firing will give the crowd an opportunity to disperse. Firing should be stopped immediately the crowd begins to disperse. It should be ensured that the mob does not get too close, to the troops, so as to hamper their tactical handling of weapons or to get involved into hand to hand fighting.

(c) After firing: Immediate steps should be taken to succour the injured. Arrangements should be made for first-aid, medical attention, and evacuation of injured rioters to the hospital. All empty cases should be recovered and the number of rounds fired counted and recorded in a diary. Important witnesses to the incident should be detained with the help of the executive magistrate. All arrested rioters should be handed over to the civil authority for being dealt with in accordance with the law. It is absolutely essential that a minute to minute and item by item diary of events is maintained by the officer commanding the body of troops. Importance of this record cannot be over-emphasized, since in case of an inquiry about the firing, such a diary would be most useful.

The Regulations for the Army further amplify on the use of lethal force in aid to civil power. It states that, "If it becomes necessary to fire, officers and soldiers have a serious duty, which they must perform with coolness and steadiness and in such a manner as to be able to ceasefire the instant it is no longer necessary. Care will be taken to fire only on those persons who can be seen to be implicated in the disturbance. To fire over the heads of a crowd has the effect of favouring the most daring and guilty, and sacrificing the less daring, and even the innocent."[59]

There is a contention that drastic powers have been conferred on low-ranking officials like NCOs, without understanding that an NCO holds a responsible position. When troops are deployed, the sections/patrols which go for search and patrolling operations, are commanded by the NCO. In isolated places/ remote areas, while encountering insurgents, the NCO is expected to take a decision as regards the suitable use of force in the particular situation, for which he is trained. It is strange that we question his capability in such situations when we never do so in a war or natural calamity. The Cr PC section 130 provides that when the executive magistrate is unable to disperse an unlawful assembly with the help of police force under his command, he may ask any "officer" in command of troops to disperse the assembly with the help of the troops under his command. Such officer is mandated to arrest and confine person forming part of unlawful assembly. The term "officer" as explained in section 132 of the Cr PC includes an NCO.

During contemporary small wars in which the members of the armed forces takes part, the opponent or "enemy" may also be criminals under domestic law. Under international humanitarian law (IHL), fighters are legitimate targets and can be targeted according to the conduct of hostilities paradigm. Under IHL, the legality of an attack does not depend on a determination of the existence of an imminent risk to life but rather on the qualification of a person/object as a military objective – which could in turn constitute a danger for military operations only remotely. However, in certain cases, the law enforcement paradigm may also be relevant and force may be used against such enemies in order to maintain or restore public security, law and order. In contemporary conflicts, military operations are increasingly conducted amongst the population. Adversaries intermingle with the civilian population and at times it may become extremely difficult

59 The Regulations for the Army, 1987, Volume I, Para 306.

to distinguish an "enemy" combatant from the civilian population. In such situations it may be very difficult to regulate the use of force and law does not always provide clear and straightforward answers to these challenges.[60]

The military personnel, while performing their task under the second category (i.e. Small Wars) must be allowed to engage in the proxy war and insurgency with their military training and standard operating procedures, and must not confuse with the restraints of minimum force required while operating under the first category. When armed rebellion is encountered, the only limitations to the use of weapons are those imposed by the nature of the terrain and the characteristics of the enemy.

The responsibility of officers engaged in police duties is of a very different order from their responsibility in military operations. In the latter case, it is mainly for the method with which they give effect to definite orders; for producing the maximum effect with the force at their disposal; and for the extent of the demands they make on their men. In the former, they are often confronted with an unforeseen situation and must rely on their own judgment to reconcile military action with the political conditions. They must be guided in most cases by certain general principles rather than by definite orders. In fact, the reality is the other way round.

There is a general misconception amongst the members of civil society and human rights defenders that the members of the armed forces 'enjoy' the rights conferred on them by the AFSPA, that they are trigger-happy and enjoy terrorizing the civilian population. Further, the military officers will lose their importance, if the AFSPA is removed altogether by the government. In reality, most distasteful duty which falls on the members of the security forces, in particular the army, is the duty in aid of civil power. If his measures adopted by the military are too mild, the commander fails in his duty and could face displeasure of his superiors. If the measures are deemed to be excessive, the commander is liable to be attacked as brutal and human rights violator by a large section of the civil society.[61] So, a fine balance has to be struck between the two so that the quantum of force used is just right to meet the objective. However, this is easier said than done.

---

60 Gloria Gaggioli (ed), 2103, *The Use of Force in Armed Conflict: Interplay between the Conduct of Hostilities and Law Enforcement Paradigm*, Geneva: ICRC, p. iii.

61 Shoul Simeon, Soldiers, Riot Control and Aid to the Civil Power in Indian Egypt and Palestine, 1919-1939, *Journal of the Society for Army Historical Research*, Vol. 86, 2008, pp. 120-129.

Does this mean that the protest for removal of AFSPA for gross violations of human rights by human rights activists is completely baseless? It may be observed that there have been instances where excess force has been used by the security forces where AFSPA is in operation.[62] However, the fact that punishment have been meted out to members of the security force committing grave violations shows that they are not above the rule of law. On the other hand, it pertinent to note that in spite of the territorial integration of India, the emotional integration is yet to complete and therefore, the secessionist forces do continue to work and hence the inevitability to continue operation of AFSPA.

In reality, most so-called human rights defenders, activists and their organizations would lose their importance if the law and order situation remains normal in the country.[63] A case in point is of Irom Sharmila, who ended her 16 years of protest against AFSPA in Manipur in July 2016. A good number of human rights activists, and columnists lost their prominence and gains when Sharmila returned to her normal life.[64]

---

62 For e.g. Thangjam Manorama case of Manipur, the Malom massacre in Manipur, the remarks of the Committee set up by the court, which is available at: https://main.sci.gov.in/jonew/bosir/orderpdfold/1704536.pdf.

63 Non-governmental organizations (NGOs) have helped spread the movement for the protection of human rights the world over. The emergence of NGOs represents an organized response by the civil society in areas in which the State has either failed to act or done so inadequately. However, this may not be true in the case of India, as the existence and functioning of a large number of NGOs is dubious. In January 2017, the Supreme Court directed the Centre and state governments to scrutinize the accounts of NGOs and voluntary organizations. These organizations were accused of misusing grants and donations as only 10 per cent of the 32.97 lakh registered NGOs had their accounts audited. Besides, a few activists portray themselves as human rights crusaders and make irresponsible statements about the functioning of the state forces in the process. The judiciary, unaware of the ground reality, often gets influenced by these activists and places unjustified restrictions on the forces' functioning. The Central Government doles out nearly Rs 1,000 crore annually to NGOs and voluntary organizations. In contrast, *ex gratia* payment to the families of the forces' personnel is restricted to Rs 45 lakh. The Delhi government has been paying an *ex gratia* of Rs 1 crore to the families of police personnel who die on duty. It is not known whether any NGO or activists has taken up the matter of enhancing *ex gratia* payments for the forces with the judiciary or government.

64 Irom Sharmila, a twenty-eight-old lady was working as an intern with a Manipur based human rights group. She decided to fast until AFSPA was abolished from the state of Manipur. The first time Sharmila was force-fed was around 10 November 2000, about six days after her last voluntary meal, and soon after she had been arrested and charged with the crime of attempting suicide. Over the 5,574 days Sharmila fasted to demand that the AFSPA be abolished, she was allegedly fed through a nasal tube and kept in government hospital. Sharmila became the face of the struggle against AFSPA. She

Martial Law:

Martial law is distinct from merely using force to suppress internal disturbances because it extends to fulfilling some functions of civilian government, even legislative and judicial functions.[65] Martial law is the imposition of direct military control of normal civilian functions by a government, especially in response to a temporary emergency in a state. In the recent past, during the state of emergency, martial law has been imposed by the governments to enforce the military rule over the public in a number of countries.[66] When martial law is proclaimed, the civil authority abdicates its position temporarily and is superseded by military government in the area proclaimed. More commonly, responsibility is shared between the two authorities in giving effect to measures required to restore control. Special powers which they do not ordinarily possess may be given to military officers to take responsible actions as the situation demands.[67]

The imposition of martial law is essentiality based upon necessity and is an act of self-preservation and self-defence of the State. Since

was lavished with international prizes, awarded thousands of dollars and declared a prisoner of conscience by Amnesty International. Apparently a large sum of money was collected in her name. Her poster adorned homes across the state. The Human Rights group which launched her, claimed, "We thought if things went well she could be the first Nobel laureate from Manipur. She has created a big joke out of herself, which not only destroyed her as a persona, but destroyed our movement, and it has taken us a long time to recover." Now Sharmila, 46, has become an outcast in her home state. Sharmila says, "I was isolated and idolised, living on a pedestal, without voice, without feeling." The same activists who praised her as a goddess now call her a prostitute, she says. She has accused them of "acting like the Taliban". Safi Michael, How love and a taste of honey brought one Indian woman's 16-year hunger strike to an end, *The Guardian*, 11 November 2018, available at: https://www.theguardian.com/world/2018/nov/11/irom-sharmila-love-story-worlds-longest-hunger-strike.

65 Moore Cameron, 2017, *Crown and Sword: Executive power and the use of force by the Australian Defence Force*, ANU Press, pp. 129.

66 The list includes: Philippines (since May 2017 to 31 December 2019, 2009, from 1972 to 1981), Ukraine (in 2018), Turkey (in 2016 after a coup which eventually failed and in 1980s),Thailand (in 2014 and 2006 after a coup), Egypt (in 2011 during Egyptian revolution), Syria (after 2011), Iran (in 2009 after Iranian Green Movement that led to the takeover by Revolutionary Guards, earlier in 1978, 1953-57), Pakistan (in 2007, 1977, 1971, 1962 and 1958), Indonesia (in 2003 during a military activity in Aceh),China (in 1989 during Tiananmen Square protest), Poland (in 1981 to suppress political opposition; Canada (in 1970 to stabilize insurrections or perceived insurrections—October crisis).

67 Gwynn Charles W, Major General, 1939, *Imperial Policing*, London: Macmillan & Co. Ltd., pp. 3-4

independence, the Indian courts have not dealt the issue of martial law. The US Supreme Court had held that "martial law is founded on necessity and is inherent in government ... Unless the right and power exist, peace and good order, security ...government, itself ...may be destroyed and obliterated ... when the domination of the mob becomes so powerful that it cannot be stayed by the civil authorities."[68] The state practices show that in the event of terrorist attacks, invasion, insurrection or rebellion, martial law has not been proclaimed on a matter of routine. The state may give considerations to a number of issues before declaring martial law. It is a measure of preserving the government when the usual or normal methods prove inadequate. The military, during the rule of martial law, is viewed as an instrument of the civil government with the end of controlling disorder, disturbance or lawlessness among the civilian population and thereby restore peace and order. Martial Law is the exercise of the State's right of private defence by repelling force by force, for a temporary period till restoration of peace and order.

The Indian Manual of Military Law states, "Conditions of extreme disorder times arise when the civil authorities, even with the help of the armed forces, are unable to bring the situation under control, martial law may be imposed in the disturbed area by a military commander." Also, "Martial law may also be imposed by a military commander when there is a complete breakdown of civil administration e.g., during an insurrection against the Government."[69] The Manual further provides:

> Being an extreme step, the decision to declare Martial Law has to be taken at the highest level possible. Before imposing Martial Law, as far as practicable, the military commander should obtain the approval of the Central Government. Where the situation is grave, and the circumstances are such that it is not possible to obtain the prior approval of the Central Government, the military commander may, on his own, assume supreme authority for the maintenance of law and order. He should, however, inform the Central Government as soon as possible after Martial Law is proclaimed. He should also issue proclamation for the information of the inhabitants that Martial Law has been declared.[70]

68 The Constitutuion of the United States, Article VII, section 10(2).

69 The Manual of Military Law, 2010, Vol. I, Chapter VII, para 15.

70 The Manual of Military Law, 2010, Vol. I, Chapter VII, para 16.

The military commander is empowered to supersede all laws by his own authority and carry out the orders of the government fearlessly and justly. Since the main object of imposition of martial law is to restore law and order and the functioning of essential services vital to the community, the military commander issues Martial Law Regulations, specifying therein the martial law offences, punishments for such offences, and constitute military courts for the trial of offenders against martial law. One civil member having judicial experience, if possible, may be appointed to each military court. The martial law administrator may, by general or special order, also empower any military or naval or air force officer to hold a summary military court in his area of administration for the trial of any offence committed in that area.

In order to remove any ambiguity over the power and jurisdiction of military commander during martial law, few states have included martial law in the Constitution itself or other security related legislations. The legislations of Ukraine and China relating to martial law are discussed in detail.

Ukraine

Ukraine has defined the term martial law as, "a special legal regime that is introduced in Ukraine in case of an armed aggression or a threat of an attack, a threat to state sovereignty and territorial indivisibility of Ukraine. This rule involves granting the relevant State Executive, Local Self Government organs, the Military Command and military administrations, necessary powers to prevent threats, repel armed aggression and to guarantee national security, remove the threat of danger to national security of Ukraine and its territorial integrity. It also involves temporary (threat determined) restrictions of human constitutional rights and freedoms[71] as well as the rights and legitimate interests of all legal persons with an indication of the period of effectiveness for these restrictions."[72]Article 2

71 Article 64 of the Constitution stipulates that during martial law the human and civil rights and freedoms stipulated in Articles 24, 25, 27, 28, 29, 40, 47, 51, 52, 55, 56, 57, 58, 59, 60, 61, 62 and 63 of the Constitution shall not be restricted. Under the conditions of martial law or a state of emergency, specific restrictions on rights and freedoms may be established with the indication of the period of effect for such restriction only as provided in the Constitution of Ukraine.

72 Article 1, Law of Ukraine "On the Legal Regime of Martial Law," Bulletin of the Verkhovna Rada, 2015, No. 28; see: Oleksandr Lytvynenko, Philipp Fluri, Valentyn Badrack, 2017, The Security Sector Legislation of Ukraine, Geneva Centre for Security Governance, Geneva: Kyiv, pp. 76-87, available at: https://www.dcaf.ch/security-sector-legislation-ukraine-2017.

further provides that the legal basis for the introduction of Martial Law is the Constitution of Ukraine, the present Law and other laws of Ukraine as well as Presidential Decrees approved by the Verkhovna Rada (the Parliament) of Ukraine. In Ukraine, law gives the Military Command together with the State Executive, military administrations, the Council of Ministers of the Republic and Local Self Government organs the right to introduce and undertake legal measures under Martial Law.[73] The decision to create a military administration is made by the President of Ukraine, by proposal of regional state administration or the military command.

Article 4 provides the procedure for the introduction of martial law. The National Security and Defence Council of Ukraine submits proposals to introduce martial law to the President of Ukraine. If martial law is to be introduced expediently in Ukraine, the President issues Decree introducing martial law in Ukraine or separate territories of the country and immediately submits it to the Verkhovna Rada of Ukraine request for its approval. A Decree by the President of Ukraine on the introduction of Martial Law shall specify: (i) A substantiation of the necessity for the introduction of Martial Law; (ii) A territorial boundary where Martial Law is introduced, a time of its introduction and its period of effectiveness; (iii) The responsibilities of the Military Command, military administrations, State Executive and Local Self Government organs regarding the introduction and execution of measures relating to Martial Law; (iv) The tasks to subjects of ensuring civil protection on transfer of unified state system of civil protection, its functional and territorial subsystems in readiness for accomplishment of their missions for the special period; and (v) An exhaustive list of human and constitutional rights and freedoms that are to be provisionally restricted through the introduction of Martial Law. The Presidential Decree for martial law is subject to approval of the Verkhovna Rada within two days from an address made by the President. After approval by the Verkhovna Rada, the Decree is made public through the mass media.

---

73 The Military Command consists of the following components: (i) The General Staff of the Armed Forces of Ukraine, the Joint Operational Headquarters of the Armed Forces of Ukraine, the command of the services of the Armed Forces of Ukraine, the Special Operations Command of the Armed Forces of Ukraine, Command of the High-mobile Airborne troops of the Armed Forces of Ukraine, headquarters of operational commands, commands of joint units and units of the Armed Forces; and (ii) Headquarters of other military formations, created in accordance with the Laws of Ukraine. Article 3, Law of Ukraine "On the Legal Regime of Martial Law".

Martial law in Ukraine is to be terminated after expiry of the duration announced. The President of Ukraine may also withdraw the Decree introducing martial law prior to the end of the period of its effectiveness after the elimination of the threat, and this termination must be made public without delay through the mass media.[74]

Some of the measures, which the military commander in Ukraine are empowered to introduce during martial law, are as follows:[75]

(1) Place guards at installations vitally important to the national economy and objects providing for the vital needs of the population, as well as establish a special regime for their operation.

(2) Introduce civilian duty provided by capable citizens, not involved in contemporaneous defence activities, defence support activities and not reserved for enterprises, institutions and organizations during a mobilization period of Martial Law.

(3) Use the capacities and manpower resources of enterprises, institutions and organizations (both publicly and privately owned) for defence needs to change the system of their work, and to introduce other changes within production activity and working conditions in accordance with the labour legislation;

(4) Forcefully alienate private and community property, expropriate the property and assets of state enterprises and state commercial organizations for the needs of the state under Martial law.[76]

(5) Impose a curfew (a prohibition to be out on the streets during a designated time of the day without special passes or identity cards) and a special screening regime;

(6) Introduce a special entry-departure procedure, to restrict the freedom of movement of citizens, foreigners, stateless persons as well as their vehicles;

---

74 Articles 5-7, Law of Ukraine "On the Legal Regime of Martial Law".

75 Article 8; Measures of the legal regime of Martial Law, Law of Ukraine "On the Legal Regime of Martial Law".

76 Article 41 of the Constitution of Ukraine guarantees the right to own, use, or dispose of property as well as intellectual or creative activities. It further provides that no one shall be unlawfully deprived of the right for property and the right for private property shall be inviolable. However, the expropriation of private property objects with subsequent complete compensation of their value shall be permitted under conditions of martial law or a state of emergency.

(7) Examine an individual's documents and, in case of necessity, their belongings, vehicles, luggage, cargo, office premises, dwellings, except within the limitations pre-determined by the Constitution of Ukraine;

(8) Prohibit peaceful rallies, meetings, marches and demonstrations and other mass gatherings;

(9) Raise an issue, in accordance with procedures pre-determined by the Constitution and Laws of Ukraine, on the prohibition of the activity of political parties, public organizations, if it threatens the sovereignty, national security, independence, forceful change of Constitutional order, territorial indivisibility of the state, undermining its security, unlawful seizure of state power, propaganda of war, violence, instigation of interethnic, race and religious animosity, as well as threat to rights and freedoms and the health of the citizens of Ukraine;

(10) Set the prohibition or restrictions on the choice of the place of stay or the residence for persons on the territories under martial law;

(11) Exercise control over the activity of TV-radio enterprises, print media, publishing houses and other cultural and media enterprises, institutions and organizations; and use these facilities for military needs and the carrying out of educational work among the military and the population. In case of any violation of the measures prescribed by a legal regime of martial law, seize telecommunication equipment, TV, video, audio equipment, computers, etc. from publicly and privately owned establishments as well as from private citizens;

(12) Prohibit the trade in arms, strong chemical and poisonous substances as well as alcoholic drinks and other substances produced with alcohol;

(13) Establish the special regime in the sphere of production and sale of medicines that contain drugs, psychotropic substances and precursors, other strong substances according to the list determined by the Cabinet of Ministers of Ukraine;

(14) Seize firearms, ammunition, and cold steel arms from citizens; to seize military and military-training equipment, explosive, radioactive substances and materials, strong chemical and poisonous substances from enterprises, organizations and institutions;

(15) Establish procedures for the use of shelters and other installations for the protection of the civilian population and other defence needs;

(16) Evacuate civilian population as well as material assets of national and cultural importance from high risk areas in accordance with the list approved by the Cabinet of Ministers of Ukraine;

(17) Provide in case of necessity the civilian population with basic food, non-food goods and medicines;

(18) Dismiss the heads of the enterprises, organizations and institutions for their failure to fulfill their duties stipulated by present Law and appoint acting heads for the above mentioned enterprises, organizations and institutions.

(19) Take additional measures for strengthening the protection of state secrets;Intern citizens of the foreign state that threatens security of Ukraine;

(20) Perform compulsory evacuation of the detained persons held in temporary detention centres; the suspects and accused persons concerning whom the measure of restraint; the transfer of convicted persons serving such punishments as arrest, imprisonment on the definite term and the life imprisonment from jails and places of detention located in districts, close to areas of combat operations to the relevant organizations located in the safe areas.

In the event of introduction of Martial Law in Ukraine, the Verkhovna works in a session mode. The authorities of the Verkhovna Rada of Ukraine determined by the Constitution of Ukraine cannot be restricted under martial law. The introduction of martial law cannot be used as a justification for torture, cruel, inhumane or degrading treatment that violates a person's dignity. Any attempt to use martial law for the seizure of power entails legal liability.[77] Under martial law, the following are prohibited:[78]

- Any amendments to the Constitution of Ukraine or of Crimea;
- The conducting of presidential elections;

77 Article 22, Law of Ukraine "On the Legal Regime of Martial Law".

78 Article 19, Law of Ukraine "On the Legal Regime of Martial Law".

- The conducting of elections for the Verkhovna Rada of Ukraine, the Verkhovna Rada of the Autonomous Republic of Crimea and Local-Self-Government organs;
- The organising of strikes and mass gatherings.

An introduction of Martial Law in Ukraine is immediately conveyed to the States and parties through the UN Secretary General, highlighting any restrictions on human rights and freedoms that are a departure from the responsibilities undertaken in the International Covenant on Civil and Political Rights, as well as on the limits of these restrictions and the reasons for their introduction. Any person guilty of a violation of the requirements or a failure to carry out the measures prescribed by Martial Law are to be brought to account in accordance with law. When martial law is in effect, the courts still exclusively administer justice in Ukraine. Courts created in accordance with the Constitution of Ukraine continue to function. The shortening or acceleration of judicial proceedings is strictly prohibited. In case of impossibility to function for the courts in the territory where martial law is introduced, the territorial cognizance of the legal cases considered in these courts can be changed by the laws of Ukraine, or in the procedure established by the law, the location of courts is changed. The control over the activities of Military Command of the State Executive and the State Local Government under martial law is carried out by the National Security and Defence Council of Ukraine.[79]

China

After 1989 declarations of martial law during Tiananmen Square protests which prompted condemnation abroad and criticism at home, China adopted a Law on Martial Law in 1996 in accordance with the Constitution of the People's Republic of China.[80] Article 2 of the statue provides that

79 Article 24-27, Law of Ukraine "On the Legal Regime of Martial Law".

80 China has adopted a variety of legal means to address the diverse security threats. Legal means fall primarily into three categories: ordinary criminal and quasi-criminal laws that apply both to dire or ostensibly dire threats to national security and domestic order and to more ordinary criminal behaviour; more focused provisions that target the specific types of non-traditional security threats that truly or purportedly have been alarming to the regime, such as terrorist acts, separatism, and sedition; and laws that authorize, under conditions of especially serious threats, a more wholesale departure from the usual legal rules, including those that protect citizens' rights and restrict the state's powers. This last category includes rarely used but high profile laws that authorize martial law, states of emergency, or other legal states of exception. There is no simple relationship between the legal mechanisms that Chinese authorities have employed and the categories of threats they identify to justify them. The responses

the State may decide to apply martial law when such state of emergency as unrest, rebellion or grave riot occurs which seriously endangers unification and security of the State or public security and under which public order cannot be maintained and safety of people's lives and property cannot be ensured unless extraordinary measures are taken. Article 3 further states, "When it is necessary to impose martial law in the country as a whole or in an individual province or region directly under the Central Government, the matter shall be submitted by the State Council to the Standing Committee of the National People's Congress for decision. The President of the People's Republic of China, in accordance with the decision made by the Standing Committee, proclaim the order of martial law. When it is necessary to impose martial law in part(s) of a province or region directly under the Central Government, the matter shall be decided by the State Council, and the Premier of the State Council shall proclaim the order of martial law.

In order to guarantee execution of martial law and preserve public security and public order during the period of martial law, the State may, lay down special rules and regulations regarding the citizens' exercising of their rights and freedom as stipulated by the Constitution and laws in the area under martial law. The people's government of the area under martial law shall adopt measures necessary for bringing public order to normal as soon as possible and ensuring safety of people's lives and property and supply of their daily necessities. All organizations and individuals in the area under martial law are to strictly observe the order of martial law and the rules and regulations for executing the order of martial law and actively assist the people's government in bringing public order to normal.[81]

---

to the Tiananmen Square and Tibet protests and their aftermath in 1989 ranged from non-criminal administrative punishments to prosecutions for ordinary crimes to the only declaration of martial law in the history of the People's Republic. In 1996, China adopted a Law on Martial Law. Martial Law of the People's Republic of China, 1996; adopted at the 18th Meeting of the Standing Committee of the Eighth National People's Congress on March 1, 1996 and promulgated by Order No. 61 of the President of the People's Republic of China on March 1, 1996. That law articulated substantive preconditions for declaring martial law, including "turmoil, riot or disturbance" where "emergency measures" are necessary to "preserve social order and protect people's lives and property." The law also set forth special powers and departures from ordinary law, including use of force, displacement of ordinary civil and criminal laws, and limits to citizens' constitutional and other legal rights. Jacques deLisle, Security First? Patterns and Lessons from China's Use of Law to Address National Security Threats, *Journal of National Security Law & Policy*, Vol. 4, 2010, p. 397-436. A copy of the 1996 Law on Martial Law is at Appendix F to the book.

81 Articles 4-6, Martial Law of the People's Republic of China; adopted at the 18th Meeting

Martial law duties in China are be performed by the People's Police and the People's Armed police (PAP).[82] When necessary, the State Council may make a suggestion to the Central Military Commission that it decide to dispatch troops of the People's Liberation Army to help perform the martial law tasks. The martial-law-executing organ set up a martial law command, which coordinates actions taken by the units concerned to fulfill martial law tasks and works out unified plans and measures for enforcing martial law. The units of the People's Liberation Army assigned with martial law tasks, while executing the unified plans of the martial law command, are directed by a military organ designated by the Central Military Commission. As soon as the state of emergency, for which martial law is enforced, is eliminated, the martial law is lifted.[83]

During the period of martial law, the martial-law-executing organ may decide to take the following measures in the area under martial law and may also adopt specific execution methods: (i) to ban or restrict assembly, procession, demonstration, street speeches, and other mass activities; (ii) to ban strikes of workers, shop assistants and students; (iii) to impose press

of the Standing Committee of the Eighth National People's Congress on March 1, 1996 and promulgated by Order No. 61 of the President of the People's Republic of China on March 1, 1996.

82 The People's Armed Police (PAP) is China's premier paramilitary force. PAP is undergoing its most profound restructuring since its establishment in 1982. Previously under dual civilian and military command, the PAP has been placed firmly under China's military. As chairman of the Central Military Commission, Xi Jinping now has direct control over all of China's primary instruments of coercive power. This represents the highest degree of centralized control over China's paramilitary forces since the Cultural Revolution. Local and provincial officials have lost the ability to unilaterally deploy PAP units in the event of civil unrest or natural disasters, but can still request support through a new coordination system. The China Coast Guard, which previously reported to civilian agencies, has been placed within the PAP and is thus now part of the military command structure. New PAP operational commands, known as "mobile contingents," have been established with a diverse mix of capabilities. They will play a key role in protecting the capital and could be deployed in a Taiwan contingency, among other missions. PAP internal security forces remain focused on domestic security missions, including maintaining stability in western China, guarding government compounds, and disaster relief. PAP units would also be on the frontlines in responding to a major threat to the regime. The PAP has also been encouraged to play a stronger role in supporting People's Liberation Army (PLA) combat operations. Key roles could include guarding critical infrastructure and supply lines during wartime. Wuthnow Joel, China's Other Army: The People's Armed Police in an Era of Reform, Centre for the Study of Chinese Military Affairs, Institute for National Strategic Studies, China Strategic Perspectives, No. 14, National Defense University Press, Washington, D.C., April 2019, pp. 44.

83 Articles 8-12, Martial Law of the People's Republic of China, 1996.

embargo; (iv) to enforce control over communications, postal services and telecommunications; (v) to enforce control over entry into and exit from the country; and (vi) to ban any activities against the martial law. During the period of martial law, curfew may be imposed in the area under martial law. During the curfew, people passing through the streets or other public places in the area under curfew must carry their identification papers and special passes issued by the martial-law-executing organ. In addition, restrictive measure may be adopted in traffic control, restricting entry and exit of the area under traffic control and checking the documents, vehicles, etc., of people entering or leaving such an area. During the period of martial law, the martial law command may adopt special measures to control (i) weapons and ammunition; (ii) knives; (iii) inflammable or explosive goods; and (iv) hazardous chemicals, radioactive, deadly poisons, etc. in the area under martial law.

In case of necessity for fulfilling tasks of martial law, the government may temporarily requisition houses, places, facilities, means of transport, engineering machinery, etc. of State organs, enterprises, institutions, public organizations and individual citizens. Under conditions of unusual emergencies, the commanders of the People's Police, the People's Armed-police and the PLA may make immediate decisions on temporary requisition of things.[84] During the period of martial law, measures shall be taken to mount rigid guard over the headquarters, military organs and key military facilities and installations; foreign embassies and consulates in China, representative agencies of international organizations in China and guest houses for leaders of foreign countries; important mass media such as broadcasting stations, television stations and national news agencies, public utility enterprises and public facilities that have a vital bearing on the national economy and the people's livelihood; airfields, railway stations and ports; prisons, places of reforms and houses of detention. In order to guarantee supply of the basic daily necessities of the people in the area under martial law, the martial-law-executing organ may take special measures to control the production, transport, supply and pricing of such necessities.

Martial-law-enforcing officers are members of the People's Police, the People's Armed-police and the PLA, who are assigned with tasks of

84 A receipt of the things requisitioned is to be made out. The property temporarily requisitioned, is to be returned to the owner immediately after their use or after the martial law is lifted. The things that are damaged shall be compensated, as appropriate, by the people's government at or above the county level in accordance with relevant regulations of the State.

enforcing the martial law, shall use uniform insignias as required by the martial-law-executing organ. They will have the right to check the papers, vehicles and other things of people in the streets or other public places in the area under martial law. They will have the right to detain people who violate the regulations on curfew, the right to search the person of the detainees and check the things they carry. The martial-law-enforcing officers have the right to detain the persons (i) who are committing an offence that endangers State security or disrupts public order or those who are strongly suspected of such an offense; (ii) who obstruct or resist performance of martial law tasks by martial-law-enforcing officers; (iii) who defy traffic control or regulations on curfew; and (iv) who engage in the activities against the order of martial law. The martial-law-enforcing officers also have the right to search the detainees and the houses of criminal suspects and the places where criminal offenders, criminal suspects or weapons, ammunition and other dangerous articles are suspected of being concealed.

The martial-law-enforcing officers are also empowered to use police implements to stop or disperse persons engaging in mass activities in the area under martial law. The persons who engage in unlawful assembly, procession, demonstration or other mass activities; who occupy public places illegally; who attack State organs or other important units and places; who disrupt traffic order or deliberately create traffic jams; and plunder or destroy the property of State organs, public organizations, enterprises, institutions or individual citizens may be arrested and detained. The detained persons may be interrogated, and those found innocent shall be released. During the period of martial law, the procedures and time limit for detention and arrest may be free from the restrictions of the relevant provisions of the Criminal Procedure Law of the China, except that an arrest shall be subject to approval or decision of a People's Procuratorate.

The martial-law-enforcing officers may, under any of the following unusual emergencies in the area under martial law, use guns or other weapons when they cannot stop violence with police implements: (i) when the safety of the lives of citizens or martial-law-enforcing officers are endangered by violence; (ii) when persons subject to detention or arrest or offenders under escort resort to violence in resistance, commit physical assault or try to escape; (iii) when persons use violence to seize weapons and ammunition; (iv) when important objects under guard are assaulted by violence or are in imminent danger of being assaulted by violence; (v) when, in the course of fighting a fire, rushing to deal with an emergency, rescuing people or performing other major urgent tasks, they are obstructed by extreme violence; or (vi) other circumstances under which guns and other weapons may be used in accordance with the provisions of laws and administrative rules and regulations. While using guns and other weapons, the martial-law-enforcing officers must strictly observe the regulations on the use of guns and other weapons. The martial-law-enforcing officers are protected for performing their tasks during martial law. The officers, who act in violation of the provisions of the Martial Law, abuse their powers and infringe upon the lawful rights and interests of citizens, are to face investigation and further action in accordance with law.

AFSPA v. Martial Law

AFSPA is the legislative measure used to counter small wars[85] and its provisions cannot be equated with martial law. The functioning of the security forces under the special powers vested by AFSPA does not amount to *de facto* proclamation of Martial Law. The powers granted by the AFSPA to military officers (to use force, arrest, detain, enter and search) are the powers available to police officers in normal circumstances under the provisions of Criminal Procedure Code, 1973. In order to use deadly force, the members of the armed forces are restrained by a number of orders and instructions, which they are bound to follow. The application of the AFSPA in a few states in India does not affect the citizens' basic human rights and fundamental freedoms, such as the right to life, the right to be free from torture, cruel, inhuman or degrading treatment, and the right to personal freedom and security. While certain restrictions on the freedom of movement may be temporarily imposed, by and large, law abiding citizen enjoy all basic human rights guaranteed under the Indian Constitution or the international human rights laws.[86] The civilian

85 Presently, AFSPA is operational in entire States of Assam, Nagaland, Manipur (except Imphal Municipal area), three districts namely Tirap, Changlang and Longding of Arunachal Pradesh and the areas falling within the jurisdiction of the eight police stations in the districts of Arunachal Pradesh, bordering the State of Assam. The notifications declaring Manipur and Assam as "Disturbed Areas" have been issued by the State Governments. In December 2019, the Centre declared the whole of Nagaland as a "disturbed" area under the AFSPA for a further period of six months with effect from 30 December 2019.The Minister of State for Home Affairs, Shri Kiren Rijiju in written reply to a question in the Lok Sabha on 8 January 2019 stated that there was no proposal to repeal the AFSPA. Press Information Bureau, Government of India, Ministry of Home Affairs, available at: https://pib.gov.in/newsite/PrintRelease.aspx?relid=187330.

86 Article 19 (1) (b) of the Indian Constitution of India provides that "*all citizens have the right to assemble peaceably and without arms.*" This right includes the right to

authorities and courts continue their functions in disturbed areas affected by AFSPA; those arrested by military are handed over to the civilian authorities for further penal action, if any. It has incorrectly concluded by a commentator that, "When the AFSPA starts operating in an area, the military 'virtually replaces' the civilian administration."[87] There have been few isolated incidents where security personnel have crossed the legal limits and the military has taken strict action against the violator.[88] In two such recent cases, the military court has imposed life imprisonment on senior officer allegedly involved in the incident.[89] The Supreme Court of India has upheld the constitutionality of the AFSPA. Responding to the UN Human Rights Committee in March 1991 in regard to the Second Periodic Report under the ICCPR, the then Attorney General emphasized that given secessionist activities in the Northeast of India, the AFSPA was necessary. The AFSPA does not provide legal immunity to military personnel for their actions. It only puts a condition that the prosecution cannot be initiated without the prior permission of the central government.

India has submitted its National Report to the Human Rights Council on 21 May 2012 justifying the continuance of AFSPA in J&K and the Northeastern states. According to para 25 of the report:

---

hold meetings and take out processions, subject to the condition that the assembly is peaceful and unarmed. However, the individual's right and liberty is preceded by public order. Article 19 (3) provides that "*nothing in sub-clause (b) (Article 19 (1) of the Constitution) shall effect the operation of any existing law in so far as it imposes or prevents the State from making any law imposing, in the interest of the sovereignty and integrity of India or public order, reasonable restrictions on the exercise of the right conferred by the said sub-clause.*" The Government is, therefore, empowered to impose reasonable restrictions on the right to take out processions, or hold meetings, which are likely to lead to a disturbance of public tranquility.

87 Gautam Navlakha, On Ending the War against Our Own People, *Economic & Political Weekly*, Vol. 46, Issue No. 8, 19 February 2011.

88 However, in the case of Manorama Devi, her family is still waiting for justice and her killers need to be identified and punished. Jha U.C., 2017, *Indian Military Domestic Deployment: AFSPA and Human Rights*, New Delhi: Vij Books India Pvt Ltd, p. 146.

89 A military unit in J&K had claimed that they had killed three infiltrators in the Machil sector along the Line of Control. The three victims were allegedly shot dead in a staged gun-battle near the Line of Control. Eleven persons including nine army officials and two civilians were charged under Sections 302 (murder), 364 (abduction), 120-B (criminal conspiracy) and 34 (common intent) of the Ranbir Penal Code (RPC). Six officers were sentenced to life for fake killing in 2014. In the second incident, five members of the ULFA were allegedly killed in a fake encounter because they were setting up a militant camp at the Dibru-Saikhowa National Park in Assam. After the CBI completed the investigation, 7 army officers were tried by summary general court martial and sentenced to life imprisonment in 2018.

> "This Act (AFSPA) is considered necessary to deal with serious terrorist and insurgency/ militancy situation arising in certain parts of the country and uphold the duty of the state to protect and secure its citizens. It provides necessary powers, legal support and protection to the Armed Forces for carrying out proactive operation against the terrorists in a highly hostile environment. An analysis of the ground realities shows that the violence levels and the fighting ability of terrorists have reduced over the years. Nevertheless, they still possess sophisticated weapons and modern communication equipment and the terrorist infrastructure across the borders is still active. The terrorists continue to intimidate the public. In such a challenging environment, where the very lives of its citizens and the unity and integrity of India is at stake, as long as deployment of armed forces is required to maintain peace and normalcy, AFSPA powers are required."[90]

In the last National Report submitted to the Human Rights Council in 2017, the Government of India has clarified that, "AFSPA is applied only to disturbed areas where the ordinary law and order machinery is deemed insufficient to deal with exigent circumstances like insurgency. Whether or not AFSPA should be repealed or the provision for sanctions should continue, is a matter of on-going and vibrant political debate in the country." The Report also quoted the Supreme Court verdict in the case of *EEVFAM v. Union of India*,[91] where the Court has held that use of excessive force or retaliatory force by the armed forces of the Union is not permissible in the course of the discharge of their duty under the Act, and that AFSPA does not allow blanket immunity to perpetrators of unjustified deaths or offences."[92] In this case, the Supreme Court also analyzed the provisions of the Army Act, 1950, containing the offences in relation to the 'enemy' which are punishable with death, offences not punishable with death and offences that are more severely punishable while on active service. According to Court, while functioning under the AFSPA, the armed forces are entitled while maintaining public order in a disturbed area to cause the death of an enemy, that is a militant, terrorist, insurgent, underground element or secessionist who belongs to or is associated with a terrorist

90 Para 25, India's National report submitted to Human Rights Council, Working Group on the Universal Periodic Review, Thirteenth session, Geneva, (21 May–4 June 2012).

91 *EEVFAM v. Union of India*, WP (Criminal) No. 129 of 2012, judgment dates 8 July 2016.

92 Para 29 and 30, India's National report submitted to Human Rights Council, Working Group on the Universal Periodic Review, Twenty-seven session, Geneva, (1-12 May 2017).

organization or terrorist gang or unlawful association and is threatening or is likely to threaten the unity, integrity, security or sovereignty of India.

There are increasing international trend towards domestic deployment of the military in aid to civil powers. The states have empowered the military with additional special powers during their engagement in internal security duties. The citizens of a democracy hold the armed forces in high esteem for their well defined command structure, standard of professionalism and integrity. For many decades, the Northeast is known to be a haven of militants where engineers and government officers are abducted for extortion of money. This prompted a full bench of the Meghalaya High Court to issued a *suo moto* order in November 2015, directing the Government of India to consider promulgation of the AFSPA in the Garo Hills region of the State. The High Court cited various recent instances of widespread lawlessness in the region including extortions and kidnappings by Garo National Liberation Army (GNLA) insurgents. The court said even the police and civil administrative stealthily fulfill the illegal demands of the insurgents.[93]

The terms and conditions on which a force of the Union is deployed in a state in aid of the civil power have to be determined by the Union. The superintendence, control and administration of a force (whether armed or otherwise) of the Union have necessarily to vest in the Union Government. While on deployment in a State in aid of the civil power, the force is subject to the command, supervision, control and direction of such authorities and officers as may be appointed by the Union Government. As such, the powers, jurisdiction, privileges and liabilities of the members of the force while on such deployment can be prescribed by the Union alone. The State police continue to be responsible for maintaining public order and there can be no question of the military encroaching either on the jurisdiction and powers of the State Government or in the public order.

93 The Court Order particularly cited the abduction of 25 civilians, 27 businessmen, 25 private sector employees, five government engineers, five teachers and a Block Development Officer between January and October 2015. An assistant central intelligence officer was also abducted and killed in the last week of September 2015. The Court Order also mentioned that the judges have also received veiled threats. The Bench reminded the Union Government of its constitutional obligation to protect the State against internal disturbance under Article 355 and the fundamental rights of the citizens under Article 21. However, the officials of the Central Government were of the view that situation in Garo Hills was not serious enough to warrant deployment of the army and the local government was competent to manage the situation with the help of central police forces. Sen Gautam, Meghalaya High Court Calls for Invoking Armed Forces Special Powers Act in Garo Hills, IDSA Comment, 17 November 2015.

Maintenance of public order involves a whole range of functions starting with cognizance of offences, search, seizure and arrest, and followed by registration of reports of offences (FIRs), investigation, prosecution, trial and, in the event of conviction, execution of sentences. The armed forces, where their members have been invested with powers under the Cr PC, are responsible broadly for only the first four operations. The remaining have to be attended to by the State Criminal justice machinery, *viz.* the police, the magistrates, the prosecuting agency, the courts, the jails etc.

Today it has become fashion to write about AFSPA, calling it 'draconian,' giving the 'low ranking military personnel,' power to 'shoot to kill,' and providing them total 'immunity from prosecution'. The human rights defenders must understand few nuances of military operations in small wars. A soldier deployed in such situations always faces a dilemma about the use of force. The legal classification of a particular situation determines the law which governs the actions, rights, and obligations of those involved. While military analysts have tried to define low-intensity conflict, insurgency, militancy, and operations other than war, these are really one and the same thing for a soldier who faces the situation on the ground. No military can draft rules of engagement for different situations. Understanding how the various terms used translate into practice on the ground is a challenging task for a man in the midst of the situation. He has to decide on whether to 'kill' an intruder or risk the lives of comrades and civilians in a fraction of a second. There have been a few instances in India in which the military have used lethal force against individuals who failed to respond to a warning.

On 2 November 2014, a suicide bomber targeted visitors returning after the flag-lowering ceremony at Wagha on the Indo-Pakistan border. The blast occurred a few hundred metres on the Pakistani side of the border, killing nearly 70 and injuring another 200 civilians. A few Pakistan-based terrorist outfits claimed responsibility for the attack and an alert was issued in India too. The very next day, two civilians were killed and two others critically injured in the Chattargam area in Budgam, Jammu & Kashmir (J&K), when army men opened fire on the vehicle in which they were travelling. The army regretted the loss of innocent lives, but added that the vehicle did not stop at two checkpoints and kept speeding. The National Human Rights Commission issued a notice to the defence ministry and the Superintendent of Police, seeking reports on the matter. While investigating the matter they may ask the army men why they did not aim at the tyres to stop the vehicle. Before jumping to conclusions, our enlightened judicial authorities must remember that a vehicle with flat tyres can travel a couple of hundred metres, and if laden with explosives, could create havoc.

In Ganowpora village in South Kashmir, on 27 January 2018, around 150-200 stone-pelters had attacked a military convoy and were trying to lynch a junior commissioned officer. Three stone-pelters were killed when the troops fired in self-defence.[94] The local police was prompt in lodging of FIR against Major Aditya and other members of 10 Grarhwal under sections 302, 307 and 336 of the Ranbir Penal Code (RPC) at the behest of the Chief Minister of J&K. The Supreme Court later restrained the J&K Government from initiating any investigation against Major Aditya who was named in the FIR. It is not known whether the J&K government has initiated any action against the stone-pelters who had attacked military convoy.

In another incident, a stone-pelter was arrested in J&K on 9 April 2018 and was tied to the bonnet of a military vehicle and was used as a "human-shield" to rescue over a dozen security personnel and election officials from an angry stone-pelting mob. The said man was later released. This action was in response to an SOS from the trapped security personnel and election staff at a polling booth in Budgam. Human rights organisations, a few politicians, and activists have termed the incident outrageous, and raised a hue and cry, forcing the government to conduct an inquiry and punish the wrongdoer. The use of a human-shield by the military in Budgam to avoid casualty was, perhaps, one method to deal with the extraordinary situation. The tactics are not new; Israeli military has used such measures in the past to protect civilians and others from Palestinian stone-pelting. More innovative tactics could be used by the military personnel in the future. The emerging security environment is radically different from what it was even two decades ago. Geneva Conventions, drafted in 1949, could never envisage such situations. Who could have imagined that few terrorists would hijack a passenger-laden airliner and use it to destroy the World Trade Centre in the US?

94 The right of private defence is a very valuable right recognized in all democratic and civilized societies. It says that every person has a right to defend himself and his property against any threat, danger or violence. The law does not expect a person to behave like a coward when confronted with dangerous situations. Law requires people to rise to the occasion in such situations. It is perfectly justifiable to use force, if it is needed, to protect oneself or others from an unlawful attack. While it is true that law does not expect from the person, whose life is placed in danger, to weigh, with nice precision, the extent and the degrees of the force which he employs in his defence. The Indian Penal Code in section 100 justifies the killing of an assailant in the case of apprehension of death or grievous hurt as consequence of assault.

It is a fallacy to think that India's Constitution confers only rights and imposes no duties. The citizens have certain constitutional duties towards the state.[95] They are to defend the country and are bound to uphold its sovereignty, unity, and integrity. They are also to safeguard public property and abjure violence. So when there is a high alert in a certain area and the forces have been tasked to protect their rights against violators, all citizens have a corresponding duty to help the security forces in their mission. A soldier on the ground cannot take a chance, particularly when the enemy remains faceless and fiercely lethal. While the death of every civilian is regrettable, the civil society has to understand its duty towards the country.

Recent judgments in Britain's highest courts have extended the human rights of soldiers in the battlefield and military camps abroad. In order to arrest and detain non-state actors in a conflict zone, a soldier should not be expected to comply with peace-time standards such as those exercised by a civilian police force. Many legal luminaries, human rights organisations and activists grant rights to an insurgent or to a fleeing bank robber than to soldiers who are trying to do their assigned task. With the terrorist camps operating across the line of control and attempting to destabilize our country, it has become all the more necessary for the civil society to support the security forces.

In a disturbed area, conditions of extreme disorder may arise when the civil authorities, even with the help of the armed forces, are unable to bring the situation under control. In such scenario, the government may authorize the military commander to bring the normalcy in the disturbed area. For this, an enabling proclamation is issued by the government declaring a state of national emergency on account of violence in the affected area. This is called 'Martial Law'. It means the suppression of the civil authority, by military authority, whose sole object is to restore conditions, as expeditiously as possible to enable the civil authority to resume charge. During the British regime, there were many instances of martial law in various parts of India. It has been invoked number of times in Pakistan and on a few occasions in Bangladesh.

95 The Fundamental Duties are defined as the moral obligations of all citizens to help promote a spirit of patriotism and to uphold the unity of India. These duties, set out in Part IV–A of the Constitution of India concern individuals and the nation. Citizens are morally obligated by the Constitution to perform these duties. The Fundamental Rights in Part III, the Directive Principles of State Policy in Part IV and the Fundamental Duties in Part IVA forms a compendium and have to be read together. Though there is no legal sanction provided for violation or non-performance of Fundamental Duties, the Fundamental Duties have an inherent element of compulsion regarding compliance.

Martial law is not a written or codified law in India as there is no express provision in the Indian Constitution for declaration of martial law. However, the statutory provisions of Ukraine and China as discussed above provide details of power and responsibilities of military during such emergencies. They provide sweeping powers to the military commanders to bring back normalcy. In the disturbed areas where AFSPA has been applicable for a long duration, the military does not enjoy any additional power, other than what is contained in section 4 of AFSPA. Martial law is the answer of the common law to situations of grave disorder and rests on legal maxim *Salus populi suprema est lex* (safety of the people is the supreme law). It is based on the proposition that when the civil power in an area becomes incapable of maintaining law and order, it is lawful for all loyal citizens, including the military to use necessary force for the restoration of order.

By imposing Martial Law a military commander assumes the appointment of Martial Law Administrator (MLA) and takes control of the affected area. The MLA also issues a proclamation for the information of the inhabitants that Martial Law has been declared. Since the main object of imposition of martial Law is to restore law and order and the functioning of essential services vital to the community, the military commander also issues Martial Law Regulations (MLR), specifying therein the Martial Law offences and punishments for such offences. The functions of all civil tribunals may be suspended temporarily except in so far as the military commander might require their assistance.

The authority to appoint martial law courts and approve their sentences rests only with the MLA. Following the analogies of ordinary criminal courts, it has been held by the American as well British courts that martial law tribunals can take cognizance of cases arising within the particular martial law district where the tribunal sits. The rules of procedure and of evidence of martial law tribunals may not be of international standard.

When law and order has been restored, and civil authority resumes charge, civil courts may inquire into the legality of acts of military authorities while Martial Law was in force. For this reason, it is necessary to protect persons who have been administering Martial Law from actions and prosecutions. This is done by an Act of Indemnity passed by the Parliament to disarm the courts by preventing enquiry into the justification for the acts done in executing martial law. Such an Act would free the individuals concerned from legal liability and make the judgment of military courts valid. The protection afforded under the Act of Indemnity is only for those acts which were bonafide and performed in the honest belief that they were part of their duty.

There may be an apprehension in the mind of the members of the civil society that military men are anxious to exercise martial law powers over the civil community. With few exceptions, military authorities would like to support the civil authorities rather than act alone and independently of them in civil affairs. There have been examples in the history that military officers had assumed the responsibilities of martial law but reluctantly, after the civil authorities failed to meet the ends of government, and it becomes necessary to have an authoritative substitute to maintain order in the distracted district.

The sole justification of martial law as seen in two cases above is "necessity". The military commander becomes the sole responsible agent for carrying out the policy of the Government. The powers of military authorities are much more extensive under martial law, when compared to the power available under security legislation like AFSPA. Other advantages of martial law are that actions not normally offences can be made criminal, or the scale of punishment for crimes can be raised at the discretion of military commander. Violators and martial law can be tried by special military courts, whereas in the case of AFSPA, the civil courts continue to function. The military courts may pass any sentence authorised by law or by the martial law regulations. Further, during martial law, the judicial procedure can be speeded up to ensure that a maximum deterrent and moral effect will be produced by punishment. The establishment of martial law also facilitates the establishment of an efficient intelligent service. It places the police intelligence establishments under direct control of the military and also enables pressure in many forms to be exercised which will elicit information or check information reaching the hostile elements. There may not be any limit on the use of authorized means and methods of warfare during martial law. For instance, during martial law in Punjab in 1919, the military authorities justified their firing on civilians from armoured cars, using machine guns and dropping bombs from aircraft over people gathered in villages.[96] When martial law is proclaimed or is in force, the civil machinery is placed at the disposal of the military commander; however, the task of restoring order does not

96 See: Report of the Disorder Inquiry Committee 1919-1920, Calcutta: Government Printing Press, 1920, pp. 362.

rest on the Army alone.[97] The military authorities can also acquire civilian and other government properties for effective functioning during martial law. Once martial law has achieved its purpose, the Government issues Indemnity Act under the Constitution.

Article 355 of the Constitution casts a duty upon the government of India to protect every state not only from external aggression but also from internal disorder. The power to legislate with regard to martial law falls within Entry I, List I, which provides for the defence of the whole or part of the territory of India. Although problems affecting public order are to be dealt with by the state police forces, on a few occasions the State have sought assistance from the Centre, and the Central Para-military Force/ Army has been deployed in aid of civil power. So far as proclamation of martial law in India is concerned, the Committee of the Group of Minister on National Security constituted in 2000, succinctly sums up the Governments' view (on martial law): "The Union Government and the State Governments have the constitutional responsibility for running the administration, in accordance with the Constitution. Although problems affecting public order are to be dealt with by the state police forces, the State may sometimes seek assistance from the Centre, and the Central Para-military Force/Army may be deployed in aid of civil power.[98] ...The reins of Government must, of course, never be handed over to the Armed Forces. The civil face of governance must remain visible at all levels, even in situations of militancy and terrorism. The Armed Forces of the Union can be used only in aid of civil power and not in supersession of it."[99]

97 Gwynn Charles W, Major General, 1939, *Imperial Policing*, London: Macmillan and Co. Limited, p. 15.

98 The Standard Operating Procedures (SOPs) for doing this are laid down in the Instructions on Aid to the Civil Authorities by the Armed Forces, 1970/SOP of CPMFs.

99 Report of the Committee of the Group of Minister on National Security, 2000, Chapter I, para 4.17 and 4.18, Available at: https://www.vifindia.org/sites/default/files/GoM%20Report%20on%20National%20Security.pdf.

Chapter VI

Conclusion

During British rule, martial law was proclaimed in India on various occasions. After gaining territorial possessions in India, the East India Company proclaimed martial law under the Bengal State Offences Act of 1804 and later, under the ordinances issued by the Governor-General in India. The ordinances empowered the military authorities to issue regulations and orders and to set up special courts, and laid down the procedure to be followed by these courts. In 1942, martial law was imposed under the common law rule in Sindh. During martial law in Sindh, a military court was constituted for the trial of the main rebel, Soreh Badshah, who was sentenced to death. The implementation of martial law in Punjab and Sindh was characterized by the use of excessive force, and the infliction of avoidable suffering, torture and inhuman treatment and punishments on citizens. In most instances, special courts awarded harsh punishments to the natives. During martial law in Punjab in 1919 and Sindh in 1942, aircraft were used to machine gun unarmed civilians, bomb villages and drop incendiary bombs to destroy huts and localities.[1]

The framing of the Indian Constitution began soon after martial law was lifted in Sindh. The Constituent Assembly, which met for the first time on 9 December 1946, took almost three years to finish drafting the Constitution. Though the execution of martial law is not expressly mentioned anywhere in the Indian Constitution, the framers were aware of

1 During military operations, the force retaliated by destroying most of the wells left intact by the rebels, thus causing considerable hardship to the people in the area and their cattle, as they were left with no sources of water to drink. The air reconnaissance was stepped up, huts and hamlets were destroyed by incendiary bombs and the Hurs were machine gunned from the air. Wisal M. Khan (retd Major General), Hur Operation in Sindh, Published in *Sindh Quarterly* in Five Parts in 1980 and 1981, p. 2, available at: http://www.sanipanhwar.com/HUR%20OPERATIONS%20IN%20SINDH.pdf.

the concept of martial law. Article 34 was one of the few provisions that were not part of the Draft Constitution, but was introduced and debated in the Assembly towards the end of the constitution-making process on 14 and 16 November 1949. It appears that Dr. Ambedkar, who proposed Article 34, had in mind the proclamation of martial law by the British in Sindh.[2] Two substantive amendments were moved to oppose Article 34. The first was in favour of deleting the draft Article as it was felt that it would give military officers the power to indulge in excesses during martial law.[3] The second was in favour of removing the words 'any person' from the text, arguing that there was no need to extend the immunity provided in the Article to individuals who were not military officers of the state.[4]

Both amendments were countered. First, it was clarified that a military officer, to successfully engage with a situation of 'insurrection or

2 India was partitioned amidst unprecedented carnage and destruction. Some of the erstwhile primary rulers of the Indian States wanted to remain outside the union; in neighbouring Burma, political leaders were assassinated; and finally, there was an armed revolt by communists in one of the States. All these events influenced the decision of the framers of the Constitution to make the Union strong and endow it with ample emergency powers. States of Emergency: Their Impact on Human Rights, International Commission of Jurists, Geneva, 1983, p. 171.

3 During the Constituent Assembly debates on the revised draft of the Constitution, Prof. Shibban Lal Saksena stated: "Yes Sir, this Article 34 is a new article. It says that when martial law is declared, then Parliament will have the power to indemnify the officers. I think that this new article should be ruled out of order. It was never passed by the Assembly before. Secondly, I think the provision of this article will encourage officers working in the martial law area to commit excesses and hope for indemnification by an Act of Parliament. Therefore, I say it is not proper. Martial law, whenever proclaimed, should be proclaimed according to the law about it. It should not be permitted to go beyond the law. So I think this article is not necessary and it should be removed from the Constitution, and also as I said, it is out of order. I move 'that article 34 be deleted'."

4 During the Constituent Assembly debates on the revised draft of the Constitution, H. V. Kamath moved three amendments: "That in Article 34, the words 'or any other person' be deleted"; "That in Article 34, for the word 'order' the words 'public order' be substituted"; and "That in Article 34, for the words 'done under martial law' the words 'done by such person under martial law' be substituted". While stressing the need for Article 34, Kamath clarified, "There are sufficient provisions in the Constitution for the maintenance of public order and peace and tranquility in the country. We have also adopted Chapter I dealing with emergency provisions in the Constitution. But once we accept or assume that a situation may arise when martial law will have to be proclaimed, then certain consequences follow. There are certain acts done during the administration of martial law. We are all very well aware of the operation of marital law, and there are acts done by persons in charge, or in authority, which strictly under the law of the Constitution may be illegal, and so those persons may have to be indemnified later on so as to safeguard their position against any undue penalty or punishment for acts done by them. It is with a view to this that I submit these amendments to the House."

rebellion or the overthrow of the state', required the ability to pass orders and prescribe procedures for cases in which his/her orders were violated. These powers were barred by Articles 20 and 21, as the military officer was not a law-making person and the procedures that he/she prescribed would not come under 'procedures according to law'. The draft article, therefore, was indispensable for the military or any officer of the state to discharge his/her duties effectively during martial law. It was also clarified that in some cases, the onus to act in ways to deal with a martial law situation might shift on a civilian who might not be an officer of the state. In these cases, the civilian's actions must come under the ambit of the draft article. At the end of the debate, the Assembly adopted Article 34 without any amendment. It reads:

> Restriction on rights conferred by this Part (Part III) while martial law is in force in any area notwithstanding anything in the foregoing provisions of this Part, Parliament may by law indemnify any person in the service of the Union or of a State or any other person in respect of any act done by him in connection with the maintenance or restoration of order in any area within the territory of India where martial law was in force or validate any sentence passed, punishment inflicted, forfeiture ordered or other act done under martial law in such area.

The Constitution is silent about the circumstances in which martial law may be proclaimed in India. There is no certainty that martial law will never be proclaimed in India. In case it is to be imposed in future in any part of India, it may be proclaimed by the executive without reference to the legislature. The proclamation of martial law depends upon necessity,[5] when less drastic measures have failed. Necessity would justify its proclamation by the government and necessity would limit its duration. The Manual of Military Law contains a few provisions relating to the imposition of

5 According to Sir James Mackintosh, "The only principle on which the law of England tolerates what is called Martial Law is necessity; its introduction can be justified only by necessity; its continuance requires precisely the same justification of necessity; and if it survives the necessity on which alone it rests for a single minute, it becomes instantly a mere exercise of lawless violence. When foreign invasion or civil war renders it impossible for courts of law to sit, or to enforce the execution of their judgments, it becomes necessary to find some rude substitute for them, and to employ for that purpose the military, which is the only remaining Force in the community. While the laws are silenced by the noise of arms, the rulers of the armed force must punish, as equitably as they can, those crimes which threaten their own safety and that of society; but no longer." Quoted in Clode Charles M., 1869, *Military Forces of the Crown: Their Administration and Government*, Vol. II, London: John Murray, p. 486.

martial law, but these are old and have not been revised earnestly after India gained Independence. Moreover, these provisions are not supported by legislation or governmental policy. The extent of the military force to be used, sentences passed, punishments inflicted, forfeitures ordered or other actions taken under martial law would depend upon the actual threat to order and public safety at that point of time. While the decision to impose martial law may be made by the local military commander, if the circumstances demand immediate action, the final decision to impose martial law can be made by the chief executive or the Prime Minister. However, the view of the Committee of the Group of Ministers on National Security on the imposition of martial law is conflicting.[6] It states that the reins of government must never be handed over to the armed forces. The civil face of governance must remain visible at all levels, even in situations of militancy and terrorism. Further, the armed forces of the Union can be used only in aid of civil power and not in supersession of it.[7] Therefore, the government may like to avoid imposing martial law at all costs as it would threaten civil liberties and the values of democracy in the country.

In spite of such strong objections to the proclamation of martial law and the use of the armed forces for governing a territory in the country, the future remains uncertain. The fact is that Article 34 could be used by Parliament to pass an Act of Indemnity in respect of actions committed under martial law.[8] Moreover, the common law power of proclaiming martial law as part of the law of India was recognized by the courts during British rule.[9] It has been usual for all governments to proclaim martial law

6 Following the submission of the Kargil Review Committee (KRC) Report, the Prime Minister had set up a Group of Ministers (GoM), vide Cabinet Secretariat OM No.141/1/2000/TS dated 17 April 2000, to review the national security system in its entirety and in particular, to consider the recommendations of the KRC and formulate specific proposals for implementation. The composition of the GoM was as follows: L.K. Advani, Minister of Home Affairs; George Fernandes, Minister of Defence; Jaswant Singh, Minister of External Affairs; and Yashwant Sinha, Minister of Finance. The National Security Adviser, Brajesh Mishra, was designated as a special invitee to the meetings of the GoM and the Cabinet Secretariat (National Security Council Secretariat) was tasked to service it.

7 Report of the Committee of the Group of Ministers on National Security, 2000, Chapter I, para 4.17 and 4.18, available at: https://www.vifindia.org/sites/default/files/GoM%20Report%20on%20National%20Security.pdf.

8 Article 34 of the Indian Constitution (in Part III – Fundamental Rights) empowers the Union Parliament to pass an Act of Indemnity after martial law is in force, notwithstanding the Fundamental Rights.

9 *Channappav. Emperor*, A.I.R. (1931) Bombay, 57.

during a crisis or actual rebellion. The common law position in England has been that when there is an insurrection or rebellion amounting to war, the government may use the amount of force necessary in the circumstances to restore order. This use of force is sometimes termed "martial law". The imposition of martial law does not require a formal proclamation. The right to use force against force in a martial law regime does not actually depend upon the proclamation of martial law at all. A proclamation of martial law is merely a notification to all concerned that the right in question is about to be exercised and the lines along which it will be exercised. The subsequent passing of the indemnity legislation tantamount to a declaration that martial law is in force.

The concluding part of this book has been written at a time when the world is facing the COVID-19 pandemic, which has touched each and every country. Most of those seeking medical attention for COVID-19 cannot be tested for it because of the shortage of testing kits and other medical facilities. As I write this, about 13,876,500 people have been infected and nearly 593,100 have died worldwide, and that number is growing daily.[10] A large number of countries have mobilized their armed forces to help the civil authorities tackle the disaster.[11]

Let us consider a hypothetical situation. In a certain state of India, while the government is busy fighting COVID - 19 pandemic, terrorists have been able to infiltrate and have launched lethal attacks against its citizens.[12] Certain factions of the local population support the terrorists

10 The World Health Organization response as on 16 July 2020.

11 In May 2020, the Chinese city of Shulan has imposed martial law after 11 fresh cases of coronavirus were reported in the city. The city borders North Korea and fears a second wave of the killer virus. As reported, the secretary of the Jilin Provincial Committee of the Communist Party of China, Bayin Chaolu called for the imposition of martial law while stressing on the need to ensure highest-risk level prevention and control. Border Chinese city imposes martial law after 11 new cases of coronavirus, WION, 11 May 2020, available at:https://www.wionews.com/world/border-chinese-city-imposes-martial-law-after-11-new-cases-of-coronavirus-297903.

12 In November 2008, the Taj Mahal hotel was one of the five targets selected by the 10 heavily-armed Pakistani terrorists from Lashkar e-Toiba (LET–a jihadi group originally set up by the Pakistani Army to fight as insurgents in Kashmir), who conducted a sea-borne assault on Mumbai. Over the course of three days, the LET terrorists killed over 170 people in a series of grenade and gun attacks at these locations, overwhelming the inadequately-armed and poorly-trained police and causing pandemonium. The civil authorities in Mumbai were unable to cope with the terrorist atrocity, which was unprecedented in scale and scope. The Indian Army and Special Forces were summoned to quell the LET attackers. In another deadly terror attack on the security forces, 40 Central Reserve Police Force personnel were killed on 14 February 2019, when a Jaish-

and have been instigating people to flout the safety precautions aimed at controlling the spread of COVID-19. This has created serious disorder. The civil administration is unable to contain them with the police forces available[13] and in due course of time, there are violent uprisings against the state. In such a situation, the Central government has no choice but to involve the armed forces in the defence of the state and authorize a military commander to tackle the situation by proclaiming martial law in the affected territory.

Over the past century, governments throughout the world have declared states of emergency in response to a variety of real and perceived crises, including not only threats of insurrection, but also political unrest, general civil unrest, criminal or terrorist violence, labour strikes, economic crises, the collapse of public institutions, the spread of infectious diseases, and natural disasters.[14] In modern times, besides the use of the term martial law, States may use various other terms for special legal orders introduced in crisis situations. These include 'state of exception', 'state of emergency', 'state of alarm' and 'state of siege'.[15] In these exceptional situations, the State may introduce special powers of arrest and detention, enact criminal laws that can be applied retroactively and permit trial by special military courts. In addition, the right to have recourse to remedies such as the writ of *habeas corpus* may be suspended. Martial rule can never exist where the courts are open, and are exercising their jurisdiction in a proper and unobstructed manner. In emergency situations, the rights to freedom of expression, association and assembly may also be restricted.

The Governor of California has recently stated that he may implement martial law if necessary to curb COVID-19. The precedent for martial

e-Mohammad terrorist drove a suicide vehicle-borne improvised explosive device into a convoy of vehicles carrying paramilitary troops on the Srinagar–Jammu national highway in south Kashmir's Pulwama district.

13 The two instruments of force available to the State are the police and the army. Due to increasing political interference in the functioning of the police at all levels, the police has become both politicized and demoralized. Often one sees a nexus between the politician, the criminal and the policeman. It is no wonder that the police is now not a very effective instrument for maintaining order, and that the administration has to seek Army assistance frequently to combat internal disorder. Sinha S.K., Civil Power and the Army, *Indian Defence Review*, Vol. 2, Jan–Mar 1887, September 2015.

14 Criddle, Evan J. and Fox-Decent, Evan, Human Rights, Emergencies, and the Rule of Law, *Human Rights Quarterly*, Vol. 43, 2012, pp. 39-87.

15 Special Rapporteur for States of Emergency, The Administration of Justice and the Human Rights of Detainees: Question of Human Rights and States of Emergency: Tenth Annual Rep., UN Doc. E/CN.4/Sub.2/1997/19 dated 23 June1997.

law in the US provides for the suspension of certain civil liberties, such as the rights not to be subjected to unreasonable searches and seizures, freedom of association and freedom of movement. If enacted, "it would temporarily replace civil rule with military authority and the writ of *habeas corpus* may be suspended".[16] Any government facing an invasion, a domestic insurrection, an emergency or a war has the right to determine how it will respond. How much power will the executive be given? What will be the role of the other branches of government? How long will the response last? How will the government administer justice during this period? Which, if any, fundamental rights will be sacrificed in order to protect the nation? The way in which a nation responds to such questions will undoubtedly determine how successful it will be in responding to the crisis faced by it.

In its Departmental Instructions to Military Authorities in 1942, the Government of India stated in very clear terms the duties of a military commander when dealing with insurrection or rebellion. The Instructions read in part:[17]

> In case of open rebellion, when the military force available may, unless the military commander assumes exceptional powers, prove inadequate to meet the emergency, he should enforce Martial Law… supplementing the ordinary law as may be necessary, but no more than is necessary, by military tribunals. In general, he should confine the exercise of his exceptional powers to taking such measures as can, on the restoration of order, be shown to have been necessary for ensuring the safety of his troops and suppressing the rebellion. Any exceptional measure taken must not only be clearly directed to the attainment of these objects, but be reasonably likely to achieve them. Martial law means the suppression of ordinary law in any part of the country by military authority, whose sole duty is to restore such condition of things as will enable the civil authority to resume charge. In order to attain that object, the military officer may issue such orders, and enforce them in such manner as may be necessary for that purpose only. His authority is, for the time being, supreme, but in practice the amount of his interference with the civil administration and the ordinary courts is measured by military necessity. He should not interfere beyond what is necessary for the restoration of order,

16 Danielle Zoellner, Coronavirus: California prepared to enact martial law if it's a 'necessity', Governor says, *Independent*, 18 March 2020.

17 Quoted in *Muhammad Umar Khan* v. *Crown*, PLR 1953 Lah 828.

and should, whenever possible, act in consultation with the local civil authorities. Offenders should be handed over to the ordinary courts for trial whenever this is possible; but persons charged with offences which are not offences against the civil law cannot be so handed over. The military officer has power to try an offender and punish him under martial law, but he should not exercise this power except where it is necessary for him to do so for the purpose of restoring order or when it is not possible to keep an accused person in arrest until he can be handed over for trial by the ordinary courts. Such occasion may arise if communications are interrupted during a considerable period, but even then the military officer can generally arrange for the attendance of a civil magistrate to whom prisoners can be handed over for trial, and this should be done when possible. If the military officer has to try an offender, though this should only be necessary in very exceptional circumstances, the trial should follow the forms of military law; and a record must be kept of every trial so held, and of every punishment inflicted under martial law. Any punishment so inflicted must not be excessive.

When deployed in martial law area, the armed forces may use lethal force against the 'enemy'.[18] The use of force is purely a tactical matter and the military commander must not be asked to prove that he weighed with scrupulous accuracy the amount of force apparently necessary to suppress the rioters. The exercise of reasonable and honest discretion is all that is required to protect those who are suddenly called upon to save the community from the mob from being put on trial and forced to justify the actions they have taken in good faith. While the law should allow wide discretion, it must remain supreme and enforce some sense of responsibility among those in the military force and in authority to act with humanity and justice, as well as firmness. Verbal abuse by a mob does not in itself justify the use of severe measures of repression by a military officer.[19] The military may arrest without a warrant and merely on suspicion, and may hold and detain prisoners so arrested and hand them over to the magistrate/police for further action. If military personnel take the life of or injure a person or damage property, they must remain immune from civil suits and criminal prosecutions.

18 The term 'enemy', as defined under section 3(x) of the Army Act, 1950, includes all armed mutineers, armed rebels, armed rioters, pirates and any person in arms against whom it is the duty of any person subject to military law to act.

19 Ballantine Henry Winthrop, Qualified Martial Law, a Legislative Proposal, *Michigan Law Review*, Vol. 14, No. 2, December 1915, pp. 102–118.

Paragraph 305(c) of the Regulations for the Army provides that when troops called into action against an unlawful assembly or rioters are to apply military tactics, "the strength and composition of the force, the amount of ammunition to be taken and the manner of carrying out the task are matters for the decision of the military authorities alone". The manner in which the troops shall use their weapons –whether fire of musketry and artillery, or bayonets and sabres, or both – is purely a tactical question. The same goes for the stage of the operations at which each or either mode of attack shall be employed. It is further provided in paragraph 306(a) that "all orders to the troops will be given by their commander. They will on no account fire except by his word of command. If it becomes necessary to order them to fire, he will exercise a humane discretion in deciding both the number of rounds and the object to be aimed at. If the commander is of the opinion that a slight effort will attain the object, he will give the command to one or more selected soldiers to fire. If a greater effort be required, he will give the command to one of the sections to fire; the fire of each of the other sections, if required, will only be given on the regular word of command of the commander. If it is necessary for more sections than one to fire at a time, the commander will clearly indicate to the troops which subordinate commander is to order any of the sections to fire. The order to any one or more selected soldiers or to a particular section to fire will be given only by the commander indicated." Paragraph 306(d) clarifies that firing with blank ammunition is forbidden.

The use of lethal force during martial law is justified on the grounds of an 'honest belief', perceived for good reasons, to be valid at the time. Reference to objectively established facts is not required to show that the honest belief is reasonable. An honest belief is said to be held for good reasons even if, objectively, another person might consider it to be irrational or based on either a flawed premise or faulty perceptions. The European Court for Human Rights (Grand Chamber), in the case of *Armani Da Silva v. the United Kingdom,* had applied the concept of 'honest belief' with respect to the fatal shooting of Jean Charles de Menezes, a Brazilian national, who was mistakenly identified by the police as a suicide bomber. The incident occurred on 22 July 2015 at a station in the London underground. The following is an interesting case relating to the duty of a soldier while dispersing an unlawful assembly and is of relevance here.

Duty of soldiers when called upon to disperse an unlawful assembly

During the late 1890s, the British coal industry faced a serious decline as the price of coal fell drastically. The employers were determined to reduce the wage rates, but this was vociferously opposed by the miners. Initially, the dispute was relatively peaceful, though several miners were brought before the courts for obstructing footpaths, assaulting the police and various offences under the Conspiracy and Protection of Property Act of 1875.

On 7 September 1893, Captain Barker and a small number of soldiers were placed in the Ackton Hall colliery to defend it from an attack by a mob. When the troops arrived at the colliery, there was no crowd or disorder, except that there were about 20 men who stood jeering derisively at the troops. News of the arrival of the troops spread rapidly and created a sense of excitement in the local community. Crowds of people, some armed with cudgels, began to assemble in the streets and the concourse gradually increased in size.

A body of rioters armed with sticks and cudgels entered the colliery yard and issuing threats, demanded the withdrawal of the soldiers. The colliery was surrounded, the engine house was stoned, all the windows in the building were broken and the crowd taunted the frightened soldiers. The mob gradually grew in size and broke the windows of the building in which the troops were stationed and threw stones at them. One rioter tried, unsuccessfully, to ignite the engine house in order to flush out the troops, and timber was actually set on fire. The soldiers retreated, but were eventually surrounded by a mob of 2000 persons. The crowd was called upon to disperse and the Riot Act read out. More stones were hurled at the troops, and it was necessary to protect the colliery.

The troops had sustained several injuries and Barker was of the opinion that his men should tolerate no more. He ordered his men to advance towards the crowd with fixed bayonets. The mob of people retreated temporarily, but proceeded to spread themselves out and slowly surround the soldiers. The magistrate then gave Barker written permission to open fire and added verbally that blank cartridges should be used, if possible. However, Captain Barker informed him that the troops had not been supplied with blanks as it was against army regulations to use anything but live ammunition in the prevailing circumstances. At last, before an hour since the reading of the Riot Act and on the crowd's refusal to disperse, Captain Barker, officer-in-charge of the troops, gave orders to fire. The mob dispersed, but one or two bystanders who were not taking an active part in the riot were killed. Commissioners, including Lord Justice Bowen, afterwards Lord Bowen, were appointed to report on the conduct of the troops.[20]

The following passage from the report of the Committee appointed to look into the matter is an almost judicial statement of the law as to the duty of soldiers when called upon to disperse a mob:[21]

> We pass next to the consideration of the all-important question whether the conduct of the troops in firing on the crowd was justifiable. By the law of this country everyone is bound to aid in the suppression of riotous assemblages. The degree of force, however, which may lawfully be used in their suppression depends on the nature of each riot, for the force used must always be moderated and proportioned to the circumstances of the case and to the end to be attained.
>
> The taking of life can only be justified by the necessity for protecting persons or property against various forms of violent crime, or by the necessity of dispersing a riotous crowd which is dangerous unless dispersed, or in the case of persons whose conduct has become felonious through disobedience to the provisions of the Riot Act, and who resist the attempt to disperse or apprehend them. The riotous crowd at the Ackton Hall colliery was one whose danger consisted in its manifest design violently to set fire and do serious damage to the colliery property and in pursuit of that object to assault those upon

20 Two soldiers fired at the "ground line" with the intention of injuring as many people as possible by the ricochets of the bullets. After a momentary silence the crowd, under the misapprehension that only blanks had been fired, advanced towards the soldiers and swept into the pit premises throwing volleys of stones. Five minutes passed and then the second order to fire was given. This time eight soldiers fired sixteen rounds of ammunition in sectioned volleys, and the noise and stone-throwing stopped instantly, for it was apparent that people had been hit. Two men, James Gibbs, a miner from Loscoe, and James A. Duggan, an Ackton Hall Colliery employee, were severely wounded and later died as a result of their injuries, and approximately a dozen other people received wounds of varying severity. One man standing on the footpath, outside Featherstone Main Colliery, almost a quarter of a mile away, was injured by a bullet in the thigh. The deaths of the two men, and the injuries received by other people, generated bitter tension and anger amongst the Yorkshire miners. Neville Robert G., The Yorkshire Miners and the 1893 Lockout: The Featherstone "Massacre", pp. 337–357, available at: https://www.cambridge.org/core.

21 Report of the committee appointed to inquire into the circumstances connected with the disturbances at Featherstone on 7 September 1893 [C-7234].

the colliery premises. It was a crowd accordingly which threatened serious outrage, amounting to felony, to property and persons, and it became the duty of all peaceable subjects to assist in preventing this. The necessary prevention of such outrage on person and property justifies the guardians of peace in the employment against a riotous crowd of even deadly weapons.

Officers and soldiers are under no special privileges and subject to no special responsibilities as regards this principle of law. A soldier for the purpose of establishing civil order is only a citizen armed in a particular manner. He cannot, because he is a soldier, excuse himself if without necessity he takes human life. The duty of magistrates and peace officers to summon or to abstain from summoning the assistance of the military depends in like manner on the necessities of the case. A soldier can only act by using his arms. The weapons he carries are deadly. They cannot be employed at all without danger to life and limb, and in these days of improved rifles and perfected ammunition, without some risk of injuring distant and possibly innocent bystanders. To call for assistance against rioters from those who can only interpose under such grave conditions ought, of course, to be the last expedient of the civil authorities. But when the call for help is made, and a necessity for assistance from the military has arisen, to refuse such assistance is in law a misdemeanour.

The whole action of the military when once called in ought, from first to last, to be based on the principle of doing, and doing without fear, that which is absolutely necessary to prevent serious crime, and of exercising all care and skill with regard to what is done. No set of rules exists which governs every instance or defines beforehand every contingency that may arise. The military may come from a distance. They know nothing, probably, of the locality, or of the special circumstances. They find themselves introduced suddenly on a field of action. No officer is justified by English law in standing by and allowing felonious outrage to be committed merely because of a magistrate's absence.

The question whether, on any occasion, the moment has come for firing upon a mob of rioters, depends, as we have said, on the necessities of the case. Such firing, to be lawful, must, in the case of a riot like the present, be necessary to stop or prevent such serious and violent crime as we have alluded to; and it must be conducted without recklessness or negligence.

When the need is dear, the soldier's duty is to fire with all reasonable caution, so as to produce no further injury than what is absolutely wanted for the purpose of protecting person and property. An order from the magistrate who is present is required by military regulations, and wisdom and discretion are entirely in favour of the observance of such a practice. But the order of the magistrate has at law no legal effect. Its presence does not justify the firing if the magistrate is wrong. Its absence does not excuse the officer for declining to fire when the necessity exists.

With the above doctrines of English law, the Riot Act does not interfere. Its effect is only to make the failure of a crowd to disperse for a whole hour after the proclamation has been read a felony; and on this ground to afford a statutory justification for dispersing a felonious assemblage, even at the risk of taking life. In the case of the Ackton Hall colliery, an hour had not elapsed after what is popularly called the reading of the Riot Act, before the military fired. No justification for their firing can therefore be rested on the provisions of the Riot Act itself, the further consideration of which may indeed be here dismissed from the case. But the fact that an hour had not expired since its reading, did not incapacitate the troops from acting when outrage had to be prevented. All their common law duty as citizens and soldiers remained in full force. The justification of Captain Barker and his men must stand or fall entirely by the common law. Was what they did necessary, and no more than was necessary, to put a stop to or prevent felonious crime? In doing it, did they exercise all ordinary skill and caution, so as to do no more harm than could be reasonably avoided?

If these two conditions are made out, the fact that innocent people have suffered does not involve the troops in legal responsibility. A guilty ringleader, who under such conditions is shot dead, dies by justifiable homicide. An innocent person killed under such conditions, where no negligence has occurred, dies by an accidental death. The legal reason is not that the innocent person has to thank himself for what has happened, for it is conceivable (though not often likely) that he may have been unconscious of any danger and innocent of all imprudence. The reason is that the soldier who fired has done nothing except what was his strict legal duty.

Assaulted by missiles on all sides, we think that, in the events which had happened, Captain Barker and his troops had no alternative left

> but to fire, and it seems to us that Mr. Hartley was bound to require them to do so.
>
> We feel it right to express our sense of the steadiness and discipline of the soldiers in the circumstances. We can find no ground for any suggestion that the firing, if it was in fact necessary, was conducted with other than reasonable skill and care. The darkness rendered it impossible to take more precaution than had been already employed to discriminate between the lawless and the peaceable, and it is to be observed that even the first shots fired produced little or no effect upon the crowd in inducing them to withdraw. If our confusions on these points be, as we believe them to be, correct, it follows that the action of the troops was justified in law.

The US Supreme Court has also held[22] that during martial law, any person may be arrested by the military authorities on suspicion of participating in, or aiding and abetting insurrection. He may be imprisoned without hearing or bail, and the legality of the arrest and detention cannot be inquired into or reviewed by the courts. The arrested person held by the military may not be guilty of crime and may not have rendered himself or herself in any way amenable to the laws of the state, but if, in the opinion of the military authorities, he is a suspect or dangerous character, an agitator, whose presence is deemed "prejudicial to public order" or "incompatible with public tranquility", he may be arrested without warrant, may be imprisoned for weeks and months, and may then be removed by force to any other place. He may or may not be informed of the reason for this summary proceeding. But in either case, he is perfectly helpless. He cannot examine witnesses or summon his friends. He has no right to demand a trial or even a hearing. He cannot sue out a writ of *habeas corpus*, or if he does, it is denied, as matter of course. His communications with the world are severed so suddenly that even his own relatives may not know what has happened to him. He is literally and absolutely without any remedy or means of self-defence. This doctrine leads to absolute martial law.

Since the Governor is at all times bound to take care that peace be preserved and the laws be faithfully executed, it would logically follow that he has at all times an executive discretion as to the measures to be taken with which neither the legislature nor courts may interfere, and it would not matter whether the military had been called out or not.

22 *In re Moyer*, 35 Colo. 159, 12 LRA (NS) 979, 117 Am. St. Rep. 189.

Today, the security forces in India confront irregular adversaries that conceal themselves within a civilian population. It is necessary to employ force with precision and minimize casualties among the wider populace. Members of the armed forces are also required to be accountable for their actions and to ensure that their operations are coordinated with those of the local government. When deployed under martial law, the armed forces must ensure that the norms of international human rights are not violated. The military commander must see to it that, at all levels, the troops are not involved in "torture", "enforced or involuntary disappearances" and extra-judicial killings of dissenters, not only because these are unethical, but also because they undermine the legal foundations upon which a government's legitimacy and credibility with its citizens are founded.

Action against soldiers engaged in civil disorder: The Army Act, 1950 regulates the relationship between soldier and soldier during peace and war. It does not dwell much on the relationship between soldiers and civilians. Its reference to civilians is confined to matters in which civilians may be involved. Some examples are 'mutiny' or 'procuring and assisting desertion', and when the military is operating outside the jurisdiction of civil courts, say, during United Nations peacekeeping missions.

In India, a soldier is liable to be tried by the ordinary civilian courts for any offence against the laws that apply to civilians in general. A civil court cannot try him for military offences against the Army Act. A military court can try him for all the civil offences under Section 69 of the Army Act. It provides: "Any person subject to the Army Act who at any place in or beyond India commits any civil offence shall be deemed to be guilty of an offence against this Act and, if charged therewith under this section, shall be liable to be tried by a court martial." It, therefore, follows that if a person is subject to the Army Act, while stationed in any country other than India, commits an act or omission which is an offence under the civil law of that country, but which if committed in India would not amount to a 'civil offence', he cannot be charged under Section 69 of the Act. However, a charge may properly be framed under Section 63 (violation of good order and military discipline), if the facts so warrant. In case of any dispute between the military and the civilian court on the trial of the military personnel, Section 125 of the Army Act provides that the decision of the military commander shall be final.[23] In case of any dispute between the civil

23 Section 125 of the Army Act, which deals with the choice between criminal court and court martial provides: "When a criminal court and a court martial have each jurisdiction in respect of an offence, it shall be in the discretion of the officer commanding the army, army corps, division or independent brigade in which the accused person is serving or

court and court martial, the decision of the Central Government is final.[24] A military offender is normally handed over to the civil authorities for trial, where he is alleged to have committed an offence in collaboration with other persons who are not subject to military law. Under Section 70 of the Army Act, military courts may not try him for certain serious civil offences (murder, culpable homicide not amounting to murder, and rape) inside the country, although they may try him on active service, at a frontier post specified by the Central Government by notification, or overseas.[25] The Armed Forces (Special Powers) Act (AFSPA) as well as the Criminal Procedure Code, 1973 specifically offers protection to military persons acting in good faith in their official capacity; prosecution in civil courts is possible only if sanctioned by the Central Government.[26]

Indian military personnel have been deployed to aid the civil power under the AFSPA since the last four decades. While functioning under the AFSPA, many soldiers have been charged, and a few have been convicted with civil offences ranging from murder to minor assault. In two recent cases, military persons were charged with murder and awarded life imprisonment by court martial.[27] There have been allegations and demands

---

such other officer as may be prescribed to decide before which court the proceedings shall be instituted, and if that officer decides that they should be instituted before a court martial, to direct that the accused person shall be detained in military custody."

24 See: The Criminal Courts and Court Martial (Adjustment of Jurisdiction) Rules, 1978.

25 Section 70 of the Army Act prohibits trial by court martial for three civil offences, viz. murder, culpable homicide not amounting to the murder of a person not subject to military law, and rape in relation for such a person, unless the said offence was committed: (a) while on active service, (b) at any place outside India, or (c) at a frontier post specified by the Central Government, by notification in this behalf.

26 The Manual of Military Law (2011), Vol. I, Chapter VII, para 11, dealing with the 'protection of officers and men acting in aid to civil power', provides: "No commissioned officer acting in good faith (for the dispersal of unlawful assembly, etc.), no officer acting at the request of an executive magistrate, no Junior Commissioned Officer (JCO), Warrant Officer (WO), or other rank (OR--non-commissioned officers and persons placed below them) acting in obedience to any order of his superior officer which he was bound to obey by law, is deemed to have committed any offence and no prosecution can be instituted in any civil (criminal) court against any such officer, JCO, WO or OR except with the sanction of the Central Government."

27 In 2018, a summary general court martial (SGCM) sentenced a former major general, two colonels and four soldiers to life imprisonment for killing five persons. The proceedings of the SGCM after confirmation by the General Officer Commanding, Northern Command has been sent to the Chief of the Army Staff for confirmation. The accused have the right to file appeals against the verdict of the SGCM in the armed forces tribunal and then in the Supreme Court. Earlier, in 2015, a SGCM awarded life imprisonment to six army personnel, including a colonel, for faking an encounter

from the civil society that military persons are not punished suitably by court martial and they should instead be tried in a civil court. There are a few problems associated with this. First, the system for ensuring military discipline can be nullified by a civilian legal system, thus weakening discipline in the military. Second, the judicial system in our country can be used to implicate military personnel of any rank before the civil courts. Third, the soldier can be legally harassed and convicted on the evidence of the very people who he has been ordered to suppress for disorder or insurrection. And fourth, a soldier is placed by the processes of military law in a worse position as an individual before the civil law than other citizens, or we can say that he is deprived of his 'civil rights'.

Too often, military authorities treat the civil authorities with arrogance and contempt. In this context, the instructions given by President George Washington for the governance of the troops on 20 October 1794 at Bedford are meaningful: "You are to exert yourselves by all possible means to preserve discipline amongst troops, particularly a scrupulous regard to the rights of person and property, and a respect for the authority of the civil magistrates, taking care to inculcate and cause to be observed this principle, that the duties of the army are confined to attacking and subduing armed opponents of the laws, and to supporting and aiding the civil officers in the execution of their functions."[28]

Future of martial law in India

Martial law is the gravest form of emergency power to deal with insurrection or a national emergency. In a few modern Constitutions, the power to proclaim martial law lies with the Parliament or chief executive. The parliaments in these States have passed legislation specifying restrictions and the powers available to the military during the proclamation of martial law. Unlike times when the armed forces are used to restore law and order during riots, where the military is subject to the direction of the civil authorities and to the control of the courts, if excessive force is used, under martial law, the military authorities remain the sole judges of the steps that should be taken. These steps might involve taking drastic measures

---

in the border area of Machil in Jammu and Kashmir. They were held guilty by the SGCM, which sentenced them to life imprisonment in November 2015. The convicts have appealed against the verdict to the Principal Bench of the AFT in New Delhi. The Tribunal, under the power vested in it by Section 15 of the AFT Act, has suspended the sentence awarded to the military personnel and granted them bail.

28 Quoted in, Winthrop Henry, Qualified Martial Law, a Legislative Proposal, Part II, *Michigan Law Review*, Vol. 14, No. 3, January 1916, pp. 197-218.

against civilians, for example, taking away life, liberty or property without due process of law. After the termination of the state of martial law, the courts have the jurisdiction to review the legality of the acts committed under martial law. In order to protect the armed forces and other persons who were administering martial law, Parliament may pass an Indemnity Act. However, the Act will not be intended to indemnify a defendant for wanton or cruel acts that were unjustified by the circumstances.

The International Covenant on Civil and Political Rights (ICCPR) has a provision that permits derogation from Convention rights in the event of a public emergency threatening the life of the nation. However, the circumstances giving rise to the need to proclaim martial law must fall within the scope of this provision and a number of Convention rights cannot be compromised, even in such an extreme public emergency. After martial law has been lifted, those responsible would thus be liable for any violations of core Convention rights.[29] In case the domestic courts fail to enforce these rights in the aftermath of martial law, the possibility of prosecution at an international forum cannot be totally ruled out.[30]

Martial law in a democratic State cannot be a "legal black hole",[31] as thought earlier. A response to an exceptional threat has to be governed

29 Article 4(1) of the International Covenant on Civil and Political Rights provides, "In time of public emergency which threatens the life of the nation and the existence of which is officially proclaimed, the States Parties to the present Covenant may take measures derogating from their obligations under the present Covenant to the extent strictly required by the exigencies of the situation, provided that such measures are not inconsistent with their other obligations under international law and do not involve discrimination solely on the ground of race, colour, sex, language, religion or social origin." Article 4(2) of the Covenant stipulates that no derogation may be made from articles 6, 7, 8 (paragraphs 1 and 2), 11, 15, 16 and 18 under this provision. This provision protects the following rights: the right to life (Article 6); the right to freedom from torture, cruel, inhuman and degrading treatment or punishment (Article 7); the right to freedom from slavery, the slave trade and servitude (Article 8); the right not to be imprisoned on the ground of inability to fulfill a contractual obligation (Article 11); the right not to be subjected to retroactive legislation (Article 15); the right to recognition as a person before the law (Article 16); and the right to freedom of thought, conscience and religion (Article 18).

30 See: Basic Principles and Guidelines on the Right to a Remedy and Reparation for Victims of Gross Violations of International Human Rights Law and Serious Violations of International Humanitarian Law, adopted and proclaimed by General Assembly Resolution 60/147 of 16 December 2005; Tomuschat Christian, 2014, *Human Rights: Between Idealism and Realism*, Oxford University Press, pp. 520; Bradley, A.W., Ewing, K.D. and Knight, C.J.S., 2015, *Constitutional and Administrative Law*, UK: Pearson Education Limited, pp. 561–565.

31 The term "legal black holes" in contemporary law has been examined by a few

by the rule of law. The need to impose martial law in the territory of a State has to be based on exceptional necessity and intended only to meet a pressing public emergency. It has been held by the European Commission of Human Rights that a public emergency must have the following characteristics: (i) it must be actual or imminent; (ii) its effects must involve the whole nation; (iii) the continuance of the organized life of the community must be threatened; and (iv) the crisis or danger must be exceptional, in that the normal measures or restrictions, permitted by the ICCPR for the maintenance of public safety, health and order, are plainly inadequate.[32] The rights and privileges of citizens may be temporarily curtailed in a democratic State, which must always remain subject to its international obligations relating to civil and political rights and future judicial investigations. A martial law regulation cannot award punishments prohibited under international human rights law. Procedural guarantees must be provided when an individual is being tried in a military court or special tribunal established under martial law. The Constitutional pardon to a martial law regime may be available only for those acts which were necessary for bringing back normalcy. Those responsible for illegal and unjustified acts and excesses can always be questioned and punished after the restoration of normalcy. Since martial law contains the word 'law', it cannot be used to signify unequivocal and unlawful authority of a military commander. In modern times, martial law cannot be entirely unconstitutional and arbitrary.

---

scholars. David Dyzenhaus, in advocating that a robust, substantive version of the rule of law should prevail even when the government is responding to contemporary security emergencies, decries legal black holes as "lawless voids" where the executive can act without legal constraint, either because the substantive law does not cover the situation or judicial review is unavailable. International law was also a realm of categorical distinctions and legal black holes where no protection was available. David Dyzenhaus, 2006, *The Constitution of Law: Legality in a Time of Emergency*, UK: Cambridge University Press, pp. 1–3.

32 European Commission of Human Rights, *The Greek Case: Report of the Commission*, Application Nos. 3321/67, 3322/67, 3323/67, 3344/67 of 1970.

Appendices

Appendix 'A'

THE BENGAL STATE OFFENCES REGULATION, 1804[1]

A Regulation for declaring the powers of the Governor General in Council to provide for the immediate punishment of certain offences against the State, by the sentence of courts-martial.[2]

---

1 Regulation X of 1804 appears to have been based on a general recognition and acceptance of the doctrine of immediate necessity regarding martial law. The preamble recites the expediency during the existence of any war or open rebellion of dealing and establishing martial law for the safety of the British provinces and the security of the lives and property of the inhabitants thereof, by the immediate punishment of persons owing allegiance to the British Government who may be taken in arms in open hostility to the Government or in the commission of any overt act of open rebellion or in the act of openly aiding or abetting the enemies of the British Government, and in conformity to these recitals the enacting part empowers the Governor-General in Council, to establish martial law in any part of the British territories for any period of time while the Government shall be engaged in war as well as during the existence of open rebellion and to direct the immediate trial by courts-martial of people, taken *flagrante delicto* in the commission of the acts mentioned in the preamble. Regulation X prescribed the punishment of immediate death and forfeiture of all property as the only punishment to be awarded on conviction. The legislature thus carefully limited the jurisdiction of the courts-martial to cases clearly and indisputably of the highest criminality and of easiest proof. Report of the Committee Appointed by the Government of India to Investigate the Disturbances in Punjab, etc, London, His Majesty's Stationery Officer, 1920, p. 98

2 This Regulation as declared was to apply to the whole of the Lower Provinces of Bengal and of the North-Western Provinces, except as regards the Scheduled Districts, by the Laws Local Extent Act, 1874 (XV of 1874), s. 6. It was also been declared in force by the Santhal Parganas' Settlement Regulation (III of 1872), s. 3 as amended by the Santhal Parganas Laws Regulation, 1886 (III of 1886), s. 2, in the Santhal Parganas, and, by notification under s. 3 of the Scheduled Districts Act, 1874 (XIV of 1874), in West Jalpaiguri, Western Dooars, Hazaribagh, Lohardugga, Manbhoom, Pergunnah Dhalbhoom, Assam (except the North Lushai Hills), the scheduled portion of the Mirzapur District and Jaunsar Bawar. It was extended, under s. 5 of the same Act, to Kumaon and Garhwal and to the North-Western Provinces Tarai. It was in force in Oudh by virtue of s. 3 (e) of the Oudh Laws Act 1876 (XVIII of 1876). It was in force in the Punjab vide the Punjab Laws Act 1872 (IV of 1872), s. 3, and Sch. I.) It was extended to Arakan, see Regulation IX of 1874, schedule.

Preamble

WHEREAS, during wars in which the British Government has been engaged against certain of the Native Powers of India, certain persons owing allegiance to the British Government have borne arms, in open hostility to the authority of the same, and have abetted and aided the enemy, and have committed acts of violence and outrage against the lives and properties of the subjects of the said Government;

AND WHEREAS, it may be expedient that, during the existence of any war in which the British Government in India may be engaged with any power whatever, as well as during the existence of open rebellion against the authority of the Government, in any part of the British territories, subject to the Government of the Presidency of Fort William, the Governor General in Council should declare and establish martial law, within any part of the territories aforesaid, for the safety of the British possessions, and for the security of the lives and property of the inhabitants thereof, by the immediate punishment of persons owing allegiance to the British Government, who may be taken in arms, in open hostility to the said Government, or in the actual commission of any overt act of rebellion against the authority of the same, or in the act of openly aiding and abetting the enemies of the British Government, within any part of the territories above specified;

THE following Regulation has been enacted by the Governor General in Council, to be in force throughout the British territories immediately subject to the Government of the Presidency of Fort William, from the date of its promulgation.

Power in time of war to suspend functions of ordinary criminal courts, and establish Martial Law

2. The Governor General in Council is hereby declared to be empowered to suspend, or to direct any public authority, or officer, to order the suspension of, wholly or partially, the functions of the ordinary criminal courts of judicature, within any zilla, district, city or other place, within any part of the British territories, subject to the Government of the Presidency of Fort William, and to establish martial law therein, for any period of time, while the British Government in India shall be engaged in war with any Native or other power; as well as during the existence of open rebellion against the authority of the Government in any part of the territories aforesaid:

and also to direct the immediate trial, by courts-martial, of all persons owing allegiance to the British Government, either in of their having been born, or of their being resident, within its territories, and under its protection, who shall be taken in arms, in open hostility to the British Government, or in the act of opposing by force of arms the authority of the same, or in the actual commission of any overt act of rebellion against the State, or in the act of openly aiding and abetting the enemies of the British Government, within any part of the said territories.

Lieges convicted by court-martial of crime specified in section 2 liable to immediate punishment of death; and to forfeit property

3. Any person born or residing under the protection of the British Government within the territories aforesaid and consequently owing allegiance to the said Government, who, in violation of the obligations of such allegiance, shall be guilty of any of the crimes specified in the preceding section, and who shall be convicted thereof by the sentence of a court-martial during the suspension of the functions of the ordinary criminal courts of judicature ......,[3] and the establishment of the martial-law, shall be liable to the immediate punishment of death, and shall suffer the same accordingly by being hung by the neck till he is dead.

All persons who shall, in such cases, be adjudged by a court-martial to be guilty of any of the crimes specified in this Regulation, shall also forfeit to the British Government all property and effects, real and personal, which they shall have possessed within its territories at the time when the crime of which they may be convicted shall have been committed.

Governor General not precluded from causing persons charged with offences to be tried by ordinary courts

4. The Governor General in Council shall not be precluded by this Regulation from causing persons charged with any of the offences described in the present Regulation to be brought to trial, at any time, before the ordinary courts of judicature instead of causing such persons to be tried by court-martial, in any cases wherein mode of trial shall not appear to be indispensably necessary.

3 The words and figures "or before any special court appointed for the trial of such offences, under Regulation IV of 1799 and Regulation XX of 1803," which were repealed by the Repealing Act, 1874 (XVI of 1874), have been omitted.

MADRAS REGULATION VII OF 1808

A Regulation for declaring the powers of the Governor General in Council to provide for the immediate punishment of certain offences against the State by the sentence of court-martial.[4]

Whereas, during wars in which the British Government has been engaged against certain of the Native Powers of India, certain persons owing allegiance to the British Government have borne arms in open hostility to the authority of the same, and have abetted and aided the enemy, and have committed acts of violence and outrage against the lives and properties of the subjects of the said Government ; and whereas it may be expedient that, during the existence of any war in which the British Government in India may be engaged with any Power whatever, as well as during the existence of open rebellion against the authority of the Government in any part of the British territories subject to the Government of the Presidency of Fort St. George, the Governor General in Council shall declare and establish martial-law within any part of the territories aforesaid, for the safety of the British possessions, and for the security of the lives and property of the inhabitants thereof, by the immediate punishment of persons owing allegiance to the British Government who may be taken in arms in open hostility to the said Government, or in the actual commission of any overt act of rebellion against the authority of the same, or in the act of openly aiding and abetting the enemies of the British Government within any part of the territories above specified,—the following Regulation has been enacted by the Governor in Council to be in force throughout the British territories immediately subject to the Government of the Presidency of Fort St. George.

Governor General in Council to establish martial-law; and to direct trial by courts-martial, of lieges offending against Regulation

2. The Governor General in Council [5] is hereby declared to be empowered to establish martial-law within the territories subject to the Government of the Presidency of Fort St. George for any period of time while the British Government in India shall be engaged in war with any Native or

4 This Regulation corresponds with the Bengal State Offences Regulation, 1804 (X of 1804). It was declared to be in force in the whole of the Madras Presidency, except as regards the Scheduled Districts, by the Laws Local Extent Act, 1874 (XV of 1874), s. 4.

5 These words were substituted for the words "Governor in Council" by the Repealing and Amending (Army) Act, 1894 (XIII of 1894), Sch. II.

other Power, as well as during the existence of open rebellion against the authority of the Government in any part of the territories aforesaid; and also to direct the immediate trial by courts-martial of all persons owing allegiance to the British Government, either in consequence of their having been born, of their having served under it in any capacity, or of their being resident within its territories and under its protection, who shall be taken in arms in open hostility to the British Government, or in the act of opposing by force of arms the authority of the same, or in the actual commission of any overt act of rebellion against the State, or in the act of conspiring with, or of openly aiding and abetting, the enemies of the British Government within any part of the said territories.

Punishment of lieges convicted by court-martial of crime specified in section 2; Forfeiture of property

3. It is hereby further declared that any person born or residing under the protection of the British Government within the territories aforesaid and consequently owing allegiance to the said Government, who, in violation of the obligation of such allegiance, shall be guilty of any of the crimes specified in the preceding section, and who shall be convicted thereof by the sentence of a Court-martial during the establishment of martial-law, shall be liable to immediate punishment of death, and shall suffer the same accordingly by being hanged by the neck until he is dead.

All persons who shall in such cases be adjudged by a Court-martial to be guilty of any of the crimes specified in this Regulation, shall also forfeit to the British Government all property and effects, real and personal, which they shall have possessed within its territories at the time when the crime of which they may be convicted shall have been committed.

Power to cause trial before ordinary courts

4. The Governor General in Council shall not be precluded by this Regulation from causing persons charged with any of the offences described in the present Regulation to be brought to trial at any time before the ordinary courts of judicature..... .[6]

6 The words "or before any special court, instead of causing such persons to be tried by courts-martial, in any case wherein the latter mode of trial shall not appear to be indispensably necessary," which were repealed by the Repealing Act, 1876 (XII of 1876), have been omitted.

Appendix 'B'

THE MARTIAL LAW ORDINANCE NO. II OF 1921

[26 August 1921]

An Ordinance to provide for the proclamation of Martial Law, to empower military authorities to make regulations for administering it, and to provide for other matters connected therewith

[Published in the Gazette of India Extraordinary of the 26th August, 1921]

Whereas an emergency has arisen which makes it necessary to provide for the proclamation of Martial Law, to empower military authorities to make regulations and issue orders to provide for the public safety and the maintenance and restoration of order, to authorize the trial of certain offences by Special Courts constituted under this Ordinance, and to provide for other matters connected with the administration of Martial Law;

Now therefore, the Governor General, in exercise of the power conferred by section 72 of the Government of India Act, 1915 [5&6 of Geo. V, c. 61], is pleased to make and promulgate the following Ordinance:-

Short title

1. This Ordinance may be called the Martial Law Ordinance, 1921.

Proclamation of Martial Law

2. Martial Law shall be in force and the provisions of this Ordinance shall apply in the area which is specified in the Schedule and in such other areas as the Governor General in Council, may by notification in the Gazette of India direct, and in all such areas Martial Law shall be proclaimed by such means and in such manner as the Local Government may direct and shall remain in force in any such area until withdrawn by the Governor General in Council by notification in the Gazette of India, whereupon the provisions of the Ordinance shall cease to apply in such areas;

Provided that no failure to comply with any directions of the Local Government as to the manner of proclamation in any area shall invalidate anything done in the administration of Martial Law in pursuance of this Ordinance in that area;

Provided further that the validity of any sentences passed, or of anything already done or suffered, or any liability incurred or indemnity granted in accordance with the provisions of this Ordinance shall not be affected by reasons only of the fact that this Ordinance has ceased to be in force.

Administration of Martial Law

3. In any area in which Martial Law is for the time being in force, the Commander-in-Chief in India or an officer not below the rank of major general empowered by him in this behalf, shall appoint one or more military officer, not being lower in rank than a Lieutenant-Colonel, to be Military Commander to administer Martial Law (any such officer being hereinafter referred to in this Ordinance as "the Military Commander"), and the Military Commander shall exercise his powers in respect of such area or such parts thereof (hereinafter referred to as an "administration area") as appointing authority mat direct.

Regulations

4. (1) Subject to the provisions of this Ordinance, the Military Commander shall have the power to make Regulations to provide for the public safety and the maintenance and restoration of order and as to the powers and duties of military officers and others in furtherance of that purposes.

(2) Such Regulations may provide that any contravention thereof, or any order issued thereunder or supplementary thereto, shall be punishable with any punishment authorized, by any law in force in any part of British India, and any such contravention shall, for the purposes of this Ordinance, be deemed to be an offence against a regulation or an order, as the case may be.

(3) The power to make regulations shall be subject to the following conditions, namely:-

(i) In making any regulation the Military Commander shall interfere with the ordinary avocations of life as little as may be consonant with the exigencies of the measures which he deems to be required to be taken for the purposes of Martial Law;

(ii) Before making any regulation the Military Commander shall, if possible, consult the senior civil officer in direct charge of the administration area in which he exercises power, but shall not be bound to follow his advice;

(iii) The penalty, if any, for the contravention of a regulation shall be specified therein.

(4) The Military Commander shall cause any regulation made by him to be published in such manner as he thinks best fitted to bring it to the notice of those affected, and shall transmit through the normal channel a copy of every regulation to the Commander-in Chief- in India.

Martial Law Orders

5. (1) The Military Commander may, by order in writing, empower any Magistrate or any military officer of seven years' service not below the rank of a Captain to make Martial Law Orders in any part of the administration area for the purpose of supplementing the regulations in that area, and the punishment for the contravention of any such Order shall be that specified in the regulations for the contravention of a Martial Law Order:

Provided that no Order shall be made which is inconsistent with the regulations.

(2) Every Magistrate or officer making a Martial Law Order under sub-section (1) shall cause the same to be published in such manner as he thinks best fitted to bring it to the notice of those affected.

(3) A copy of every such Order shall, as soon as may be, be submitted to the Military Commander, who shall have power to add to, modify or rescind any such Order in such way as he thinks fit.

(4) Where a Military Commander has under subsection (3) added to, modified or rescinded any such Order, he shall forthwith communicate the fact to the Magistrate or officer who made the Order, and such Magistrate or officer shall thereupon cause to be published in the manner hereinbefore mentioned the Order as so added to or modified, or the fact that the Order has been rescinded, as the case may be.

Courts under the Ordinance

6. (1) Summary Courts of criminal jurisdiction may be constituted for the purposes of this Ordinance in any administration area in the manner hereinafter provided.

(2) The Military Commander may, by general or special order in writing, empower any Magistrate appointed under the provisions of the Code of Criminal Procedure, 1898, to exercise the powers of a Summary Court

Limitation of jurisdiction of Summary Courts

7. No Summary Court shall try an offence unless such offence was committed:

(a) In the administration area in which such Court was constituted, and

(b) After such date (whether before or after the date of the proclamation of Martial Law in the area) as the Governor General in Council may, in respect of such area, by notification in the Gazette of India, direct in this behalf.

Trial of Offences against Regulations or Martial Law Orders

8. (1) Every offence against a regulation or a Martial Law Order which is triable by a Summary Court shall be tried by such Court, unless the Military Commander directs that it be tried by ordinary Criminal Courts.

(2) The ordinary Criminal Courts are hereby empowered to try any offence in respect of which a Military Commander has made a direction under sub-section (1) and any offence against a regulation or Martial Law Order which is not triable by a Summary Court.

(3) Contraventions of any regulations or order made or issued in any area, after the date notified in respect of that area by the Governor General in Council under clause (b) of section 7 and prior to the enforcement of Martial Law by or under this Ordinance in that area, by any officer acting in the exercise of military control for the purpose of providing for the public safety or the maintenance or restoration of order shall be deemed to be offences against a regulation or a Martial Law Order in force in that area under this

Ordinance, and shall be triable and punishable as if any sentence authorised by any such aforesaid regulation or order were a sentence authorized by a regulation under this Ordinance.

Trial of Offences connected with events necessitating Martial Law

9. (1) Subject to the provisions of section 7, offences, other than offences of the kind referred to in section 8, connected with the events which have necessitated the enforcement or continuance of Martial Law, or any class of such offences, may, if the Military Commander by general or special order so directs, be tried by Summary Courts.

(2) If any question arises whether or not an offence is an offence of the nature described in subsection (1), the decision of the Summary Court shall be conclusive on the point, and such decision shall not be questioned in any Court.

(3) The Military Commander or any authority empowered by him in this behalf may, by a general or special order, give directions as to the distribution among the Summary Courts of cases to be tried by them under section 8 or this section.

Trial of other offences

10. Save as otherwise provided in this Ordinance, all offences shall be dealt with by the ordinary Criminal Courts exercising jurisdiction in the administration area in the ordinary course of law.

Jurisdiction of Ordinary Civil Courts

11. The ordinary Civil Courts shall continue to exercise civil jurisdiction in the areas in which Martial Law is in force by or under this Ordinance, provided that no Civil Court shall exercise any jurisdiction by way of interference with any regulation nor Martial Law Order made under this Ordinance.

Procedure of Summary Courts

12. In the trial of any case a Summary Court shall, as far as possible, follow the procedure laid down in the Code of Criminal Procedure, 1898 [V of 1898], for the trial of warrant-cases, and shall have all the powers conferred by the said Code on a Magistrate in regard to the issue of processes to

compel appearance and to compel the production of documents and other moveable property.

Provided that the Court shall not be required to record more than a memorandum of the evidence or to frame a formal charge;

Provided further that, in the trial of any offence punishable with imprisonment for a term not exceeding one year, the Court may follow the procedure for the summary trial of cases in which an appeal lies laid clown in Chapter XXII of the said Code.

Sentences by Summary Courts

13. Summary Courts may pass any sentence authorized by law or by regulations under this Ordinance provided that such Courts shall not pass a sentence of imprisonment for a term exceeding two years, or of fine exceeding one thousand rupees.

Jurisdiction of Summary Court

14. (1) No person shall be tried by a Summary Court for an offence which is punishable with imprisonment for a term exceeding five years.

(2) If a Summary Court is of opinion that the offence disclosed is one which it is not empowered to try, it shall send it for trial to an ordinary Criminal Court having jurisdiction.

(3) If a Summary Court is of opinion that an offence which it is empowered to try should be tried by an ordinary Criminal Court, or that it requires a punishment in excess of that which it is empowered to inflict, it shall stay proceedings and report the case for the orders of the Military Commander, who may direct that the case shall be tried by a Summary Court, or may send it to an ordinary Criminal Court having jurisdiction.

Legal practitioners

15. Every person accused of an offence before a Summary Court shall be entitled to be defended by a legal practitioner:

Provided that the Court shall not be required to grant an adjournment for the purpose of securing the attendance of a legal practitioner if, in the opinion of the Court, such adjournment would cause unreasonable delay in the disposal of the case.

Exclusion of interference of other Courts

16. (1) Notwithstanding the provisions of the Code of Criminal Procedure 1898, or of any other for the time being in force, or of anything having the force of law by whatsoever authority made or done, there shall be no appeal from any order or sentence of a Summary Court, and no Court shall have authority to revise such order or sentence, or to transfer any case from a Summary Court, or to make any order under section 491 of the Code of Criminal Procedure, 1898, or have any jurisdiction of any kind in respect of any proceedings of a Summary Court.

(2) The power of the Governor General in Council or the Local Government to make orders under section 401 or section 402 of the Code of Criminal Procedure, 1898, shall apply in respect of persons sentenced by Summary Courts.

Limitation of power of Summary Court to whip

17. Notwithstanding anything contained in sub-section (2) of section 4, no Summary Court shall pass a sentence of whipping, for any offence against a regulation or Martial Law Order except where the offender has in the commission of the offence used criminal force within the meaning of the India Penal Code [XLV of 1860].

Execution of sentence of whipping

18. In the execution of any sentence of whipping passed by a Summary Court, the provisions of sub-section (2) of section 392 and the provisions of section 393 and 394 of the Code of Criminal Procedure, 1898, shall apply, and every such sentence shall, as far as possible, be carried out in a place to which the public shall not be admitted.

Offence defined

19. Unless there is anything repugnant in the subject or context, the word "offence" shall be deemed for the purposes of this Ordinance and of sections 401 and 402 of the Code of Criminal Procedure, 1898, to include an act which is, or which under the provisions of this Ordinance is deemed to be, an offence against a regulation or a Martial Law Order.

Saving

20. Nothing in this Ordinance shall be construed as in derogation of any power for the maintenance of law and order exercisable by the Governor General in Council or any other authority.

Validation of Martial Law sentences prior to proclamation

21. Any sentence passed in any area, after the date notified in respect of that area by the Governor General in Council under clause (b) of section 7 and prior to the enforcement of Martial Law by or under this Ordinance in that area, in respect of any contravention of a regulation or order made or issued within the same period by any officer acting in the exercise of military control for the purpose of providing for the public safety or the maintenance or restoration of order shall be deemed to be as valid as if it were a sentence passed under this Ordinance in respect of an offence against a regulation or a Martial Law Order in force in that area under this Ordinance.

Proceedings not invalidated by certain irregularities

22. No sentence, finding or order passed by a Summary Court shall be invalid by reasons only of any error, omission or irregularity in any proceedings before or during the trial, unless such error, omission or irregularity has in fact occasioned a failure of justice.

Protection of *bona fide* action

23. No suit, prosecution or other legal proceeding whatsoever shall lie against any person for or on account of or in respect of any act, matter or thing ordered or done, or purporting to have been ordered or done,

(a) Under this Ordinance, or

(b) In the exercise of military control in any area for the purpose of providing for the public safety or the maintenance or restoration of order, after the date modified in respect of that area by the Governor General in Council under clause (b) of section 7 and prior to the enforcement of Martial Law by or under this Ordinance

Provided that such person has acted in good faith and in a reasonable belief that his action was necessary for the said purposes;

Provided further that nothing in this section shall prevent the institution of proceedings by or on behalf of the Government against any person in respect of any matter whatsoever.

THE SCHEDULE

(See section 2)

The area comprised within the following taluks in the Malabar district of the Madras Presidency, namely:-

Walavanad,

Ponnai,

Ernad and

Calicut.

READING,

Viceroy and Governor General

Appendix 'C'

THE MARTIAL LAW (INDEMNITY) ORDINANCE, 1943

Ordinance No XVIII of 1943

An Ordinance to indemnify servants of the Crown and other persons in respect of acts done under martial law, and to provide for certain other matters in connection with the administration of martial law

(Published in the Gazette of India Extraordinary, dated 31 May 1943)

WHEREAS an emergency has arisen which makes it necessary to indemnify servants or the Crown and other persons in respect of acts done under martial law, and to provide for certain other matters in connection with the administration of martial law;

Now, THEREFORE, in exercise of the powers conferred by section 72 of the Government of India Act, as set out in the Ninth Schedule to the Government of India Act, 1935 (26 Geo. 5, c. 2), the Governor-General is pleased to make and promulgate the following Ordinance:—

1. Short title, extent and commencement.

(1) This Ordinance may be called the Martial Law (Indemnity) Ordinance, 1943.

(2) It extends to the whole of British India.

(3) It shall come into force at once.

2. Definitions.

In this Ordinance —

(1) "Martial law area" means —

(a) With reference to the martial law period beginning on the 1st day of June, 1942, and ending on the 31st day of May, 1943, the area bounded—

(i) on the east by the eastern boundary of the Provinces of Sind and of the Khairpur State from the river Indus at Kashmor to the Jodhpur-Bikaner Railway and including that Railway;

(ii) on the south by the Jodhpur-Bikaner Railway and the North-Western Railway, and including those Railways, from the eastern boundary of the Province of Sind to the river Indus at Kotri;

(iii) on the west by the river Indus from Kotri to Kashmor, including that river; and

(b) With reference to the martial law period beginning on the 29th day of July, 1942, and ending on the 31st day of May, 1943 the aforesaid area together with the area bounded —

(i) On the east by the river Indus from Rohri to Kotri;

(ii) On the south by a line running due west from the Indus at Kotri so as to include the municipal area of Kotri, to a point five miles therefrom;

(iii) On the west by a line running from the westernmost point of the aforesaid southern boundary parallel to and five mile distant from the North-Western Railway line passing from Kotri through Larkhana and Sukkur to Ilabibkhot;

(iv) On the north by a line running from Habibkhot to Rohri.

(2) "Martial law period" means with reference to the area described in sub-clause (a) of the foregoing definition the period beginning on the 1st day of June, 1942, and ending on the 31st day of May, 1943, and with reference to the area described in sub-clause (b) of the foregoing definition the period beginning on the 29th day of July, 1942, and ending on the 31st day of May, 1943.

3. **Indemnity of servants of the Crown and other persons for certain acts.**

(1) No suit, prosecution or other legal proceeding shall lie in any court against any servant of the Crown for or on account of or in respect of any act ordered or done by him or purporting to have been ordered or done by him in the martial law area during the martial law period for the purpose of maintaining or restoring order or of carrying into effect any regulation, order or direction issued by any authority responsible for the administration of martial law in the said area to which he was subordinate; and no suit, prosecution or other legal proceeding shall lie in any court against any other person for or on account of or in respect of any act done or purporting to have been

done by him under any order of a servant of the Crown given for any such purpose as aforesaid:

Provided that the act was done in good faith and in a reasonable belief that it was necessary for the purpose intended to be served thereby.

(2) For the purposes of this section it shall be conclusive proof that an act was done under an order of a servant of the Crown given for one of the aforesaid purposes if the Central Government, in the case of an officer employed in connection with the affairs of the Central Government or the Provincial Government, in the ease of an officer employed in connection with the affairs of a Provincial Government, so certifies; and an act shall be deemed to have been done in good faith and in a reasonable belief that it was necessary for the purpose intended to be served thereby unless the contrary is proved.

4. **Sanction necessary for institution of certain legal proceedings**. Without prejudice to the operation of any other provision of law for the time being in force requiring any sanction for the institution of legal proceedings, no suit, prosecution or other legal proceeding such as is referred to in section 3 shall be instituted in any court on an allegation that the act complained of was not done in good faith or was not done in a reasonable belief that it was necessary for the purpose intended to be served thereby except with the previous sanction —

(a) Where the act complained of was ordered or done by a servant of the Crown employed in connection with the affairs of the Central Government, of the Central Government, and

(b) Where the act complained of 'was ordered or done by a servant of the Crown employed in connection with the affairs of the Provincial Government, of the Provincial Government.

5. **Confirmation of orders for seizure or destruction of property**. Where in the course of operations conducted in the martial law area during the martial law period property whether movable or immovable has been seized, confiscated, destroyed or damaged by or under the directions of a servant of the Crown acting under martial law, such seizure, confiscation, destruction or be deemed to have been lawfully ordered and authorised, and no claim shall be maintainable in any court in respect of any such property for the restoration thereof or for compensation for any loss sustained in consequence of the seizure, confiscation, destruction or damage thereof.

6. **Validity of sentences passed by martial law courts.** All sentences passed during the martial law period by a court or other authority constituted or appointed under martial law and acting in a judicial capacity shall be deemed to have been lawfully passed, and all sentences executed according to the tenor thereof shall be deemed to have been lawfully executed.

7. **Confirmation and continuance of martial law sentences of confinement.**

(1) Every person confined under and by virtue of a sentence passed by a court or other authority constituted or appointed under martial law and acting in a Judicial capacity shall continue liable to confinement until the sentence, reduced by remission, if any, earned under the rules applicable to the serving of such sentence, is served, or until he is released by order of the Central Government.

(2) The provisions of Chapter XXIX of the Code of Criminal Procedure, 1898 (V of 1898), shall not apply to any sentence or confinement referred to in this section.

8. **Application of sections 6 and 7 to certain trials under martial law.** The provisions of sections 6 and 7 apply to sentences passed during the martial law period by a court or other authority constituted or appointed under martial law notwithstanding that such court or authority held the whole or a part of its sittings outside the martial law area, or notwithstanding that the offence or a part of the offences for which the accused person was tried and convicted was committed before the beginning of the martial law period.

9. **Saving.** Nothing in this Ordinance shall prevent the institution of proceedings by or on behalf of Government against any person in respect of any matter whatsoever.

Appendix 'D'

The Indemnity Act, 1919

(Act No. XXVII of 1919)

25 September 1919

An Act to indemnify officers of Government and other persons in respect of certain acts done under martial law, and to provide for other matters in connection therewith.

Whereas owing to the recent disorders in certain districts in the Punjab and in other parts of India, martial law has been enforced,

And whereas it is expedient to indemnify officers of government and other persons in respect of acts, matters and things ordered or done or purporting to have been ordered or done for the purpose of maintaining or restoring order, provided that such acts, matters or things were ordered or done in good faith and in a reasonable belief that they were necessary for the said purposes;

And whereas certain persons have been convicted by courts and other authorities constituted an appointed under martial law, and it is expedient to confirm and provide for the continuance of certain sentences passed by such courts or authorities.

It is hereby enacted as follows:-

1. Short title

This Act may be called the Indemnity Act, 1919.[1]

2. Indemnity of Government officers and other persons for certain acts

No suit or other legal proceedings whatsoever, whether civil or criminal, shall lie in any court of law against any officers of government, whether civil or military, or against any other person acting under the orders of any

1 The Indemnity Act No XXVII of 1919 was passed to indemnify military and civil officers of Government and other persons in respect of certain acts done under martial law which was declared end enforced in some districts in the Punjab. Under Article 5 of the Act, provisions were made for allowing reasonable compensation for property taken or used by any officer of Government, whether civil or military. It was to be assessed upon failure of agreement by a person holding judicial office not inferior to that of a District Judge to be appointed by the Government in this behalf.

such officer for or on account of or in respect of any act, matter or thing ordered or done or purporting to have been ordered or done for the purpose of maintaining or restoring order in any part of British India where martial law was enforced, on or after 30 March 1919 and before 26 August 1919 by any such officer or person; provided that such officer or person has acted in good faith and in a reasonable belief that his action was necessary for the said purposes;

And if any such proceeding has been instituted before the passing of this Act it is hereby discharged.

3. Certificate of the Secretary to the Government

For the purposes of Section 2 a certificate of a Secretary to Government that any act was done under the orders of an officer of Government shall be conclusive proof thereof, and all action taken for the aforesaid purposes shall be deemed to have been taken in good faith and in a reasonable belief that it was necessary therefor unless the contrary is proved.

4. Confirmation continuance of martial law sentences

Every person confined under and by virtue of any sentence passed by a court or other authority constituted or appointed under martial law and acting in a judicial capacity shall be deemed to have been lawfully confined and shall continue liable to confinement until the expiration of such sentence or until released by the Governor-General in Council as otherwise discharged by lawful authority.

5. Compensation in respect of loss attributable to certain acts

When under martial law the property of any person has been taken or used by any officer of Government, whether civil or military, the Governor-General in Council shall pay to such person reasonable compensation for any loss immediately attributable to such taking or using, to be assessed upon failure of agreement by a person holding judicial office not inferior to that of a District Judge to be appointed by the Government in this behalf.

6. Savings

Nothing in the Act shall –

(a) Apply to any sentence passed or punishment inflicted by or under the orders of any commission appointed under the Martial Law Ordinance, 1919.

(b) Be deemed to bar a full and unqualified exercise of His Majesty's pleasure in receiving or rejecting appeals to His Majesty in or to affect any question or matter to be decided therein, or

(c) Prevent the institution of proceedings by or on behalf of the government against any person in respect of any matter whatsoever.

Appendix 'E'

Constituent Assembly Debates on the Revised Draft Constitution[1]

(Debated on 14 November and 16 November 1949, Article 34)

Prof. Shibban Lal Saksena: Yes, Sir, this article 34 is a new article. It says that when martial law is declared, then Parliament will have the power to indemnify the officers. I think that this new article should be ruled out of order. It was never passed by the Assembly before. Secondly, I think the provision of this article will encourage officers working in the martial law area to commit excesses and hope for indemnification by an Act of Parliament. Therefore, I say it is not proper. Martial law whenever proclaimed should be proclaimed according to the law about it. It should not be permitted to go beyond the law. So I think this article is not necessary and it should be removed from the Constitution, and also as I said, it is out of order. I move:

> "That article 34 be deleted."

Shri H. V. Kamath: Mr. President, Sir, I move amendments Nos. 122, 123 and 124.

> "That in article 34, the words 'or any other person' be deleted."
>
> "That in article 34, for the word 'order' the words 'public order' be substituted."
>
> "That in article 34, for the words 'done under martial law' the words 'done by such person under martial law' be substituted."

Sir, at the very outset, let me make it clear that I would welcome the deletion of any reference to martial law in the Constitution, as suggested by my Friend Prof. Shibban Lal Saksena. There are sufficient provisions in the Constitution for the maintenance of public order and peace and tranquility in the country. We have also adopted Chapter I dealing with emergency provisions in the Constitution. But once we accept, or assume that a situation may arise when martial law will have to be proclaimed, then certain consequences follow. There are certain acts done during the administration of martial law. We are. all very well aware of the operation

1 Constituent Assembly Debates, Vol. XI, pp. 468-470 and 577-578; Debated on 14 November and 16 November 1949.

of marital law, and there are acts done by persons in charge, or in authority which strictly under the law of the Constitution may be illegal, and so those persons may have to be indemnified later on so as to safeguard their position against any undue penalty or punishment for acts done by them. It is with a view to this that I submit these amendments to the House.

Article 34, as moved by the Drafting Committee, seeks to indemnify any person in the service of the Union or of a State, and any other person also. I do not desire that we should go so far as to indemnify any person, whoever he may be. We may make an exception of persons who arc in the service of the Union or of a State. But the change proposed is to insert a provision with regard to all persons. Such a change is far too sweeping, and must not be allowed to find a place in the Constitution. Therefore, I have moved this amendment, that the words "or any other person" be deleted. If we indemnify at all, we should indemnify only those persons who are in the service of the Union or of a State during the administration of martial law in any area.

The other two amendments are, more or less, formal ones. The first one seeks to bring article 34 in conformity with the phraseology of article 33, where the words used are "public order" and therefore, I have suggested that this article also may be on the same lines as article 33 and the word "order" be replaced by the words "public order".

The last amendment follows from the wording of the first part of article 34. When we refer to acts done by any person in the service of the Union or of a State, it is necessary to make it specifically clear in the latter part of the article as well, when we refer to the acts of such persons. Therefore, the word "such" in my judgment, is necessary so as to avoid any confusion with regard to acts done by any person other than the public servants referred to in the first part of the article.

Sir I move amendments Nos. 122, 123 and 124 and I commend them to the House for its earnest consideration.

Dr B.R. Ambedkar: As this is a new article altogether, the question arises whether I should allow it to be moved by way of an amendment. I think in all Constitutions, either written or unwritten, I do not know, but my idea is that all Constitutions allow such indemnity Acts to be passed after martial law has been in force; and difficulty might arise if there was no specific provision in our Constitution for indemnifying acts done during the period of martial law, if we do not have a specific provision here. And therefore, I allow this amendment of the Drafting Committee.

As regards the other amendments which have been moved, they are now for discussion. Members, if they wish, can speak now on this article as well as on the amendments which have been moved.

Shri Brajeshwar Prasad: Mr. President, Sir, I rise to support this new article will not traverse the ground already covered, or repeat the arguments in favour of it, as you have, Sir, already admitted this article. The Drafting Committee had the power to suggest the necessary amendments. Therefore, I think that they have not gone out of the scope of their jurisdiction. I think, that when a revolutionary situation has arisen in the country, then the Government may be forced to resort to martial law. And extraordinary situations cannot be tackled by the ordinary law of the land. It is only when a revolutionary situation has arisen that martial law is enforced. Revolutionary situations can only be tackled by revolutionary methods. The danger that all officers will escape scot-free is not a real danger or a serious danger at all. I say this because Parliament has got the power to review such cases. If an officer has acted without jurisdiction, if he has exceeded the requirements of the martial law, then Parliament will not indemnify those officers. Parliament has got the full right to review the conduct of these officers who have acted in an arbitrary manner. But it is only in an arbitrary manner that you can tackle the situation which has arisen in the country when martial law has been enforced. I support this provision not merely on the ground that similar provisions exist in other Constitutions of the world but also because it is a necessary and desirable, provision. Having due regard to the facts of our political life, I heartily support this article.

Dr B. R. Ambedkar: Now, Sir, I come to article 34 which relates to martial law. This article, too, has been subjected to some strong criticism. I am sorry to say that Members who spoke against article 34 did not quite realize what article 20, clause (1) and article 21 of the Constitution propose to do. Sir, I would like to read article 20, clause (a) and also article 21, because without a proper realization of the provisions contained in these two articles it would not be possible for any Member to realize the desirability of---I would even go further and say the necessity for---article 34. Article 20, clause (1) says:

> "No person shall be convicted of any except offence for violation of a law in force at the time of the commission of the act charged as an offence."

Article 21 says:

> "No person shall be deprived of his life or personal liberty except according to procedure established by law."

Now, it is obvious that when there is a riot, insurrection or rebellion, or the overthrow of the authority of the State in any particular territory martial law is introduced. The officer in charge of martial law does two things. He declares by his order that certain acts shall be offences against his authority, and, secondly, he prescribes his own procedure for the trial of persons who offend against the acts notified by him as offence, is quite clear that any act notified by the military commander in charge of the disturbed area is not an offence enacted by law in force, because the Commander of the area is not a law-making person. He has no authority to declare that a certain act is an offence, and secondly the violation of any order made by him would not a be an offence within the meaning of the phrase "law in force", because "law in force" can only mean law made by a law-making authority. Moreover, the procedure that the Commander-in-Chief or the military commander prescribes is also not procedure according to law, because he is not entitled to make a law. These are orders which he has made for the purpose of carrying out his functions, namely, of restoring law and order. Obviously, if article 20 clause (1) and article 21 remain as they are, without any such qualification as is mentioned in article 34, martial law would be impossible in the country, and it would be impossible for the State to restore order quickly in an area which has become rebellious.

It is therefore necessary to make a positive statement or positive provisions to permit that notwithstanding anything contained in article 20 or article 21, any act proclaimed by the Commander-in-Chief as an offence against his order shall be an offence. Similarly, the procedure prescribed by him shall be procedure deemed to be established by law. I hope it will be clear that if article 34 was not in our Constitution, the administration of martial law would be quite impossible and the restoration of peace may become one of the impossibilities of the situation. I therefore submit, Sir, that article 34 is a very necessary article in order to mitigate the severity of articles 20(1) and 21.

Shri H. V. Kamath: May I ask why the indemnification of persons other than public servants is visualized in this article?

Dr. B. R. Ambedkar: .... that when martial law is there it is not merely the duty of the Commander-in-Chief to punish people, it is the duty of every individual citizen of the State to take the responsibility on his own shoulder and come to the help of the Commander-in-Chief. Consequently if it was found that any person who was an ordinary citizen and did not belong to the Commander-in-Chief's entourage, so to say, does any act it is absolutely essential that he also ought to be indemnified because whatever act he does he does it in the maintenance of the peace of the State and there is a no reason why a distinction should be made for a military officer and a civilian who comes to the rescue of the State to establish peace.

Shri H. V. Kamath: I withdraw Nos. 122 and 123, but not 124.

Amendments 122 and 123 were, by leave of the Assembly, withdrawn.

Mr President: The question is:

> That in Article 34, for the words, 'done under martial law' the words 'done by such person under martial law' be substituted.

The amendment was negativated and Draft Article 34 was adopted without any amendment.

Appendix 'F'

Martial Law of the People's Republic of China

(Adopted at the 18th Meeting of the Standing Committee of the Eighth National People's Congress, promulgated by Order No. 61 of the President of the People's Republic of China on March 1, 1996)

Contents

Chapter I: General Provisions

Article 1: Pursuant to the Constitution of the People's Republic of China, the present Law is formulated.

Article 2: In case of occurrence of turmoil, tumult or serious riot that imperils the unity, safety or social public order of the state to such an extent that the social order would not be maintained and the people's personal and property safety not protected if extraordinary measure should not be adopted, the state may decide to enforce the martial law.

Article 3: The enforcement of martial law over the whole state or in particular province, autonomous region or municipality directly under the central government shall be proposed by the State Council and submitted to the Standing Committee of the National People's Congress for decision; the President of the People's Republic of China shall proclaim the order of martial law according to the decision of the Standing Committee of the National People's Congress. The enforcement of martial law in certain district of a province, autonomous region or municipality directly under the central government shall be decided by the State Council and the order of the martial law be proclaimed by the Premier of the State Council.

Article 4: During the period of the enforcement of the martial law, with a view to ensuring the enforcement of the martial law, maintaining the social public order, the state may formulate according to the present Law special provisions of the district under martial law regarding the exercise of citizens' rights and freedom provided for by the Constitution and the law.

Article 5: The people's governments of the district under martial law shall according to the present Law adopt necessary measures to restore normal social order as soon as possible, safeguard the personal and property safety of the people and ensure the supply of life necessities.

Article 6: All organizations and individuals of the district under martial law shall rigorously abide by the order of the martial law and the prescriptions for the enforcement of the martial law and actively assist the people's government in restoring normal social order.

Article 7: The state shall adopt effective measures to protect from infringement the legitimate rights and interests of the organizations or individuals who abide by or implement the prescriptions of the order of the martial law.

Article 8: The tasks for the enforcement of the martial law shall be fulfilled by the people's police and armed people's police and, where necessary, the State Council may propose to the Central Military Commission for decision that the people's liberation army be dispatched for assisting to enforce the martial law.

Chapter II: Enforcement of the Martial Law

Article 9: The enforcement of the martial law over the whole country or in particular province, autonomous region or municipality directly under the central government shall be organized by the State Council. The enforcement of the martial law in certain district of a province, autonomous region or municipality directly under the central government shall be organized by the people's government of the province, autonomous region or municipality directly under the central government, or, when necessary, directly by the State Council. The agency organizing the enforcement of the martial law is referred to as the martial law enforcement organ.

Article 10: The martial law enforcement organ shall establish a martial law commanding body, which shall command and coordinate concerned departments to fulfill tasks for enforcement of the martial law, uniformly make arrangements and adopt measures for the enforcement of the martial law. The people's liberation army undertaking the martial law tasks shall, subject to the uniform arrangements of the martial law commanding body, be commanded by the military organ designated by the Central Military Commission.

Article 11: The order of the martial law shall specify the area scope under the martial law, the starting and ending time and the enforcement organ, etc.

Article 12: Upon the removal of urgent situation for which the martial law was enforced according to provisions of Article 2 of the present Law, the martial law shall be lifted in time. The procedures regarding lifting of the martial law are the same with that governing the decision for the introduction of the martial law.

Chapter III: Measures for Enforcement of the Martial Law

Article 13: During the period of the enforcement of the martial law, the martial law enforcement organ may decide to adopt the following measures in the district under martial law and formulate more detailed procedures for implementation thereof:

(1) Prohibiting or imposing restrictions on assembly, procession, demonstration, speech on street or other gathering activities;

(2) Prohibiting strike of employees, students and shopkeepers;

(3) Practicing press censorship;

(4) Putting under control correspondence, post and telecommunications;

(5) Putting under control the exit from or entry into the border;

(6) Prohibiting any resisting activities against the enforcement of the martial law.

Article 14: During the period of enforcement of the martial law, the martial law enforcement organ may decide to adopt measures in the district under martial law to control the traffic, impose restrictions on passengers' entry into and exit from the district under traffic control and inspect certificates of passengers, vehicles and commodities when they exit from or enter the district under traffic control.

Article 15: During the period of enforcement of the martial law, the martial law enforcement organ may decide to impose a curfew on the district under the martial law. During the period of curfew, passengers when going through the street or other public places of the district under curfew shall hold identity card of their own and the special pass issued by the martial law enforcement organ.

Article 16: During the period of enforcement of the martial law, the martial law enforcement organ or the martial law commanding body shall adopt special measures in the district under martial law for management of the following commodities and articles:

(1) Weapons and ammunitions;

(2) Cutting tools subject to control;

(3) Inflammables and explosives;

(4) Dangerous chemicals, radioactive substances and highly poisonous substances.

Article 17: In light of the necessity for implementing the tasks of enforcement of the martial law, the people's government at and above the county level in the district under martial law may temporarily requisition the state organs, enterprises, institutions, social organizations or individual citizens for their houses, premises, facilities, conveyances or project machines. In most urgent cases the on-the-spot commanding officials of the people's police, the armed people's police or the people's liberation army undertaking martial law enforcement tasks may directly decide to make temporary requisitions and the local people's government shall provide assistance therefor. Requisition receipts shall be made out when the requisition is made.

The aforesaid materials for temporary requisition shall be timely returned after their use have been finished or the martial law is lifted. In case of any damage because of the requisition the people's government at and above the county level shall make compensations according to relevant state provisions.

Article 18: During the period of enforcement of the martial law, measures shall be adopted to strengthen guarding of the following units and premises of the district under martial law:

(1) Headquarters;

(2) Military agencies and important military facilities;

(3) Foreign consulates and embassies instituted in China, representative offices of international organizations in China and residing places of state guests;

(4) Import news units such as broadcasting stations, television stations, the state news agency and the important facilities thereof;

(5) Public enterprises or public facilities that have important significance to the national economy and the people's livelihood;

(6) Airports, railway stations and harbours;

(7) Prisons, labour reformatories and detention houses;

(8) Other units or premises that need to be guarded.

Article 19: To safeguard the supply of life necessities for residents of the district under the martial law, the martial law enforcement organ may adopt special measures for the management of the production, transportation, supply and price of those life necessities.

Article 20: The measures and procedures for the enforcement of the martial law adopted by the martial law enforcement organ according to the present Law shall be publicized if they require the observation of the public. During the period of enforcement those measures and procedures that are not necessary for continuous implementation shall in light of the situation be timely proclaimed for termination of their implementation.

Chapter IV Duties of the Martial Law Enforcers

Article 21: The people's police, the armed people's police and the People's liberation army undertaking tasks of martial law enforcement are the enforcers of the martial law. Martial law enforcers undertaking martial law enforcement tasks shall bear the badge uniformly specified by the martial law enforcement organ.

Article 22: Martial law enforcers shall according to prescriptions of the martial law enforcement organ have the power to make inspection on certificates, vehicles and commodities of passengers on the public roads or other public places of the district under the martial law.

Article 23: Martial law enforcers shall according to prescriptions of the martial law enforcement organ have the power to detain persons who violate prescriptions regarding the curfew until the early morning when the curfew is lifted for that day, to make body search of the detained persons and to inspect the materials and commodities brought along with them.

Article 24: Martial law enforcers shall according to prescriptions of the martial law enforcement organ have the power to put under detention the following persons:

(1) Persons who are found or highly suspect of committing crimes of imperiling the state safety or sabotaging the social order;

(2) Persons who obstruct or resist the enforcers' implementation of tasks for enforcement of the martial law;

(3) Persons who resist traffic control or defy the prescriptions for the curfew;

(4) Persons who resist the enforcement of the martial law in other forms.

Article 25: Martial law enforcers shall according to prescriptions of the martial law enforcement organ have the power to make body inspection of the detained persons, to inspect the residence of criminal suspects, or places suspected of hiding criminals, criminal suspects or weapons, ammunitions or other dangerous articles.

Article 26: In any of the following cases of gathering in the district under martial law, the martial law enforcers, when failing to stop the gathering by persuasion, may, according to relevant prescriptions, use police apparatus to stop or disperse the gathering by force, bring by force the organizers and resisters away from the gathering place and/or put them under detention immediately:

(1) Illegal assembly, procession, demonstration or other gathering activities;

(2) Illegally occupying public places or provoking sabotaging activities in public places;

(3) Assaulting state organs or other important units or places;

(4) Disturbing the traffic order or intentionally obstructing the traffic;

(5) Gathering to plunder or sabotage the properties of government organs, associations, enterprises, institutions or individual citizens.

Article 27: Martial law enforcers shall timely register and interrogate the persons detained in accordance with the present Law and shall set free those persons immediately after finding it unnecessary to put them under custody. The procedures and length in respect to detention and arrest during the period of martial law enforcement may not be subject to restrictions provided for by relevant stipulations of the Criminal Procedure Law of the People's Republic of China; but the act of arrest shall subject to the approval or decision of the people's procuratorate.

Article 28: In any of the following cases of extraordinary emergency in the district under martial law, the military law enforcers, when failing to put an end by using police apparatus, may use firearms or other weapons:

(1) The safety of the life of citizen or martial law enforcer being endangered by violence;

(2) The offender resisting by violence, committing murder or escaping when it is attempted to detain or arrest them or send them away under escort;

(3) The offender seizing weapons or ammunitions by force;

(4) The important body or target guarded being assaulted by violence or in the severe danger of being assaulted by violence;

(5) The operation of fire fighting, dealing with emergency, rescue or implementation of other important urgent tasks being obstructed by serious violence;

(6) Other cases in which firearms and other weapons may be used according to law or administrative regulations. Martial law enforcer shall strictly observe the prescriptions regarding using of firearms or other weapons.

Article 29: Martial law enforcers shall strictly observe the law, regulations and enforcement rules, obey the orders, perform the duties, respect the customs and traditions of local nationals and must not infringe upon or damage the legitimate rights and interests of the citizens.

Article 30: The actions conducted by martial law enforcers for fulfillment of tasks according to law shall be protected by law. In case of violation of the present Law, abuse of power, violation or damage of the legitimate rights and interests of citizens by martial law enforcers, the legal liabilities shall be investigated into according to law.

Chapter V: Supplementary Provisions

Article 31: In case the state does not decide to enforce a martial law when serious riot arises in partial district of a particular county or city that severely endangers the state safety, social public security and the people's lives and property, the local people's government of the respective province may, subject to approval of the State Council, decide to organize the people's police and the armed people's police to put under control the traffic and the site, make restrictions on entry into and exit from the controlled area, inspect certificates, vehicles, materials and commodities of passengers entering or exiting from the controlled area, disperse, search or bring away from the site by force the participants in the riot and immediately put under detention the organizers and resisters. In case the people's police and the armed people's police are not adequate to maintain the social order, the State Council may be requested to propose to the Central Military Commission for decision that the people's liberation army be dispatched to assist the local people's government in restoring and maintaining the normal social order.

Article 32: The present Law comes into force as of the date of promulgation.

Bibliography

A. M. P., Constitutional Law--Court-Martial--Jurisdiction Over Civilian Dependents and Employees, *West Virginia Law Review*, Vol. 62, Issue 4, 1960, pp. 380-384.

A Collection of the Ordinances made by the Governor General of India, 1861 to 1930, Calcutta: Government of India Press, 1931.

Andreu-Guzman Federico, 2004, *Military Court and Gross Human Rights Violations*, Vol. I, Geneva: International Commission of Jurists, pp. 394.

Anthony Garner, Martial Law, Military Government and the Writ of Habeas Corpus in Hawaii, *California Law Review*, Vol. XXXI, No. 5, December 1943, pp. 477-514.

Banks William C., Providing "Supplemental Security"–The Insurrection Act and the Military Role in Responding to Domestic Crises, *Journal of National Security Law and Policy*, Vol. 3, 2009, pp. 39-94.

Barber Charles F., Trial of Unlawful Enemy Belligerents, *Cornell Law Review*, Vol. 29, Issue I, September 1943, pp. 53-85.

Bari M. Ershadul, The Imposition of Martial Law in Bangladesh, 1975: A Legal Study, *The Dhaka University Studies*, Part –F, Vol. 1(1), p. 73.

Baty T. and Morgan J.H., 1915, *War: Its Conduct and Legal Results*, New York: E.P. Dutton and Company, pp. 578.

Bhatia H.S., 1979, *Martial Law: Theory and Practice*, New Delhi: Deep & Deep, pp. 240.

Birkhimer Willaim, 1914, *Military Government and Martial Law*, USA: Franklin Hudson Publishing Company, pp. 672.

Bowman Harold M., Martial Law and the English Constitution, *Michigan Law Review*, Vol. XV, No. 2, December 1916, pp. 93-126.

Capua J.V., The Early History of Martial Law in England from the Fourteenth Century to the Petition of Right, *Cambridge Law Journal*, Vol. 36 (1), April 1977, pp. 152-173.

Chavez Francisco I., Martial Law: Scope, Problems and Proposal, *Philippines Law Journal*, Vol. 45, 1970, pp. 325-343.

Chopra Surabhi, National Security Laws in India: The Unraveling of Constitutional Constraints, *Oregon Review of International Law*, Vol. 17, 2015, pp. 1-69.

Clode Charles M., 1874, *The Administration of Justice under Military and Martial Law: As Applicable to the Army, Navy, Marines and Auxiliary Forces*, London: John Murray, Albemarle Street, pp. 411.

Clode Charles M., 1872, *The Administration of Justice under Military and Martial Law*, London: John Murray, Albemarle Street, pp. 370.

Clode Charles M., 1869, *Military Forces of the Crown: Their Administration and Government*, Vol. I, London: John Murray, pp. 596.

Clode Charles M., 1869, *Military Forces of the Crown: Their Administration and Government*, Vol. II, London: John Murray, pp. 596.

Collin, John M., 2016, *Martial Law and English Laws, c. 1500-1700*, UK: Cambridge University Press.

Conscientious Objection to Military Service, 2012, United Nations Human Rights: Office of the High Commissioner, Geneva, pp. 90.

Criddle Evan J. and Evan Fox-Decent, Human Rights, Emergencies, and the Rule of Law, *Human Rights Quarterly*, Vol. 34, 2012, pp. 39-87.

Dyzenhaus David, The Puzzle of Martial Law, *University of Toronto Law Journal*, Vol. 59, 2009, pp. 1-64.

Davies Major Kirk L., The Imposition of Martial Law in the United States, *The Air Force Law Review*, Vol. 49, 2000, pp. 67-112.

Dicey, A. V., 1885, *Introduction to the study of the law of the constitution*, London, pp. 435.

Ekeland Tor, Suspending Habeas Corpus: Article I, Section 9, Clause 2, or the United States Constitution and the War on Terror, *Fordham L. Rev.*, Vol. 74, 2005, pp. 1475-1519.

Engdahl, David E., Foundations for Military Intervention in the United States, *University of Puget Sound Law Review*, Vol. 7, 1983, pp. 1-79.

Engdahl David E., The Legal Background and Aftermath of the Kent State Tragedy, *Cleveland State Law Review,* Vol. 22, No. 3, 1973, pp. 3-25.

Engdahl David E., Soldiers, Riots, and Revolution: The Law and History of Military Troops in Civil Disorders, *Iowa Law Review*, Vol. 57 (1), 1971, pp. 1-74.

Evelegh Robin, 1978, *Peacekeeping in a Democratic Society: Lessons of Northern Ireland*, London: C. Hurst & Company, pp. 174. ISIL Lib.341.1 EVE.

Everett, Robinson O., Persons Who Can Be Tried by Court-Martial, *Journal of Public Law*, Vol. 5, 1956, pp. 148-173.

Everett Robinson O., Criminal Investigation Under Military Law, *J. Crim. L. Criminology & Police Sci.*, Vol. 46, 1956, pp. 707-721.

Fairman Charles, The Law of Martial Rule and the National Emergency, *Harvard Law Review*, Vol. LV, No. 8, June 1942, pp. 1253-1302.

Fairman Charles, 1930, *The Law of Martial Rule*, Chicago: Callaghan and Company, pp. 263.

Fairman Charles, The Supreme Court on Military Jurisdiction: Martial Rule in Hawaii and the Yamashita Case, *Harvard Law Review*, Vol. LIX, No. 6, 1946, pp. 833-882.

Farrell Brian R., 2018, *Habeas Corpus in International Law*, Cambridge: Cambridge University Press, pp. 257.

Farrell Brian, From Westminster to the World: The Right to Habeas Corpus in International Constitutional Law, *Mich. St. U. Coll. L. J. Int'l L.*, Vol. 17, No. 3, 2009, p. 551-565.

Farrell Brian, Habeas Corpus in Times of Emergency: A Historical and Comparative View, *Pace Int'l L. Rev.*, Vol. 1, No. 9, April 2010, pp. 74-95.

Fein Helen, 1977, *Imperial Crime and Punishment: The Massacre at Jallianwala Bagh and British Judgment*, 1919-1920, Honolulu: The University Press of Hawaii, pp. 250.

Feldman Herbert, 1967, *Revolution in Pakistan: A Study of Martial Law Administration*, Oxford: Oxford University Press.

Feldman, William, Theories of Emergency Powers: A Comparative Analysis of American Martial Law and the French State of Siege, *Cornell International Law Journal,* Vol. 38: Issue 3, 2005, pp. 1021-1048.

Ferejohn John and Pasquale Pasquino, The Law of Exception: A Typology of Emergency Powers, *New York University of Law*, Volume 2, Number 2, 2004, pp. 210–239.

Finalson W.F., 1868, *A Review of the Authorities as to the Riot or Rebellion, with special reference to Criminal and Civil Liability*, London: Steven & Sons, pp. 224.

Flood Gerald F., Martial Law and Its Effect Upon the Soldier's Liability to the Civilian, *University of Pennsylvania Law Review*, Vol. 73, 1925, pp. 381-401.

Gautam Khagesh, Martial Law in India: The Deployment of Military under the Armed Forces Special Powers Act, 1958, *Southwestern Jour of International law*, Vol. 24, 2018, pp. 117-146.

Ghose Akshaya K., 1921, *Laws Affecting the Rights and Liberties of the Indian People: From Early British Rule,* Calcutta: Mohun Brothers, pp. 275.

Gross Oren and Fionnuala Ni Aolain, 2006, *Law in Times of Crisis: Emergency Powers in Theory and Practice,* Cambridge University Press, pp. 481.

Gutierrez Juan Carols and Cantu Silvano, The Restriction of Military Jurisdiction in International Human Rights Protection Systems, *SUR-International Journal on Human Rights*, Vol. 7, No. 13, December 2010, pp. 75-97.

Gwynn Charles W, Major General, 1939, *Imperial Policing*, London: Macmillan and Co. Limited, pp. 429.

Halchin L. Elaine, National Emergency Powers, Congressional Research Service, 5 December 2019.

Hale Sir Matthew, 1739, *The History of the Common Law of England*, Savoy: E. and R. Nutt, pp. pp. 479.

Hamilton Rebecca J., *State-Enabled Crimes*, *Yale Journal of International Law*, Vol. 41, 2016, pp. 302-346.

Hartman John, Derogation from Human Rights Treaties in Public Emergencies, *Harvard International Law Journal*, Vol. 22, No. 1, 1981, pp. 1-52.

Head Michael and Scott Mann, 2009, *Domestic Deployment of the Armed Forces: Military Powers, Law and Human Rights*, England: Ashgate, pp. 203.

Head Michael, Another Expansion of Military Call Out Powers in Australia: Some Critical Legal, Constitutional and Political Questions, *UNSW Law Journal Forum*, No. 5, 2019, pp. 1-14.

Henry Winthrop Ballantine, Unconstitutional Claims of Military Authority, *J. Am. Inst. Crim. L. & Criminology*, Vol. 5, Issue 5, 1915, pp. 718-743.

Hessbrugge Jan Arno, 2017, *Human Rights and Personal Self-Defence in International Law*, Oxford: Oxford University Press, pp. 388.

Holdsworth W. W., Martial law historically considered, *Law Quarterly Review*, Vol. 18(2), 1902, pp. 117-132.

Huges Geraint, 2011, *The Military's Role in Counterterrorism: Examples and Implications for Liberal Democracies*, US Army War College: Strategic Studies Institute, pp. 228.

Hussain Nasser, 2003, *The Jurisprudence of Emergency: Colonialism and the Rule of Law*, The University of Michigan Press, pp. 193.

Idrees Muhammad and N. Khan, A Survey of the Role of Judiciary in Validating Military and Authoritarian Regimes in Pakistan, *Social Criminology*, Vol. 6, No. 1, 2018, pp. 1-3.

Ignatius Yordan Nugraha, Human rights derogation during coup situations, *The International Journal of Human Rights*, Vol. 22, No. 2, 2018, pp.194-206.

Ilahi, Shereen Fatima, The Empire of Violence: Strategies of British Rule in India and Ireland in the Aftermath of the Great War, Unpublished Ph D dissertation, The University of Texas at Austin, 2008, pp. 402.

International Legal Protection of Human Rights in Armed Conflict, UN Human Rights, Office of the High Commissioner, New York and Geneva, 2011, pp. 124.

Jackson Tatlow, 1862, *Martial Law: What it is? Who can declare it?* Philadelphia, John Campbell, pp. 19.

Jacobus tenBroek, Wartime Power of the Military over Citizen Civilians within the Country, *Cal. L. Rev.* Vol. 41, Issue 2, 1953, pp. 167-208.

Jacques deLisle, Security First? Patterns and Lessons from China's Use of Law to Address National Security Threats, *Journal of National Security Law & Policy*, Vol. 4, 2010, p. 397-436.

Jawale, Sopan S., Marshal Law & Four Martyrs in Solapur, *Golden Research Thoughts*, Volume 2, Issue 12, June. 2013, pp. 1-3.

Jones Jared J., You've Come a Long Way Baby: The Model State Code of Military Justice and its Implications for the National Guard and Private Joe Snuffy, *West Virginia Univ Law Review*, Vol. 114, Issue 2, 2012, pp. 787-823.

Kalhan Anil, et.al., Colonial Continuities: Human Rights, Terrorism, and Security Laws in India, *Columbia Law Journal*, Vol. 20, No. 1, 2007, pp. 93-234.

Kikon Dolly, The predicament of justice: fifty years of Armed Forces Special Powers Act in India, *Contemporary South Asia*, Vol. 17:3, pp. 271-282.

Kodalkar A.V., Solapur Martial Law: 1930, *Journal of Art and Culture*, Volume 3, Issue 1, 2012, pp.-102-104.

Leary Virginia, Ellis A.A. and Madlener Kurt, 1984, *The Philippines: Human Rights After Martial Law*, Geneva: International Commission of Jurists, pp. 127.

Lieber G. Norman, 1898, *The Use of the Army in Aid to Civil Power*, Washington: Government Printing Office, pp. 86.

Lieber G. Norman, The Justification of Martial Law? *The North American Review*, Vol. 163, No. 480, 1896, pp. 549-563.

Lubell Naom, Pejic Jelena and Simmons Claire, *Guidelines on Investigating Violations of International Humanitarian Law: Law, Policy, and Good Governance*, The Geneva Academy of International Humanitarian Law and Human Rights, September 2019, pp. 70.

Mallick P.K., Role of the Armed Forces in Internal Security: Time for Review, *CLAW Journal*, Winter 2007, pp. 68-90.

Martial Law in Burma, *Legal Issues on Burma Journal*, No.2, June 1998, pp. 51-64.

Meyler Bernadette, Originalism and Forgotten Conflict Over Martial Law, *North Western University Law Review*, Vol. 113, 2019, pp. 1335-1370.

McGiverin Brian, In the face of Danger: A Comparative Analysis of the Use of Emergency Powers in the United States and the United Kingdom in the 20th Century, *Ind. Int'l & Comp Law Rev*, Vol. 18, No. 1, 2008, pp. 233-275.

McLaughlin Rob, The Use of Lethal Force by Military Forces on Law Enforcement Operations – Is There a "Lawful Authority"? *Federal Law Review*, Vol. 37 (3), 2009, pp. 441-469.

Michael F. Noone, Legal Liability of the Armed Forces When Dealing With Internal Disturbances: The Unsatisfactory Anglo-American Approach, CUA Law Scholarship Repository, 1991, pp. 9.

Minattur Joseph, 1962, *Martial Law in India, Pakistan and Ceylon*, The Hague: Martinus Nijhoff, pp. 99.

Minattur Joseph, Emergency Power in the States of Southern Asia, Unpublished Ph D Thesis, University of London, July 1959, pp. 521.

Moore Cameron, 2017, *Crown and Sword: Executive power and the use of force by the Australian Defence Force*, ANU Press, pp. 364.

Muller Sam, Stavros Zouridis Morly Frishman and Laura Kistemaker (ed), 2012, *The Law of the Future and the Future of Law*, Vol. II, The Hague: Torkel Opsahl Academic EPublisher, pp. 528.

Munim F.K. Md. Abdul, Martial Law in the Indo-Pakistan Sub-Continent, Ph D Thesis, 1960, ProQuest LLC (2017), pp. 534.

Nair C. Gopalan, 1923, *The Moplah Rebellion, 1921*, Calicut: Norman Printing Bureau, pp. 240.

Nair Vikraman K., Right to Personal Liberty under the Indian Constitution—With Special reference to Judicial Process, Unpublished Thesis, Cochin University: Department of Law, 1992, pp. 620.

Neocleous Mark, From Martial Law to the War on Terror, *New Criminal Law Review*, Vol. 10, Number 4, 2007, pp. 489-513.

Neocleous Mark, Whatever happened to martial law? Detainees and the logic of emergency, *Radical Philosophy*, Vol. 143, 2007, pp. 13-22.

Noorani A.G., Habeas corpus law: A sorry decline, *Frontline*, 25 October 2019

Omar Imtiaz, 2002, *Emergency Powers and the Courts in India and Pakistan*, The Netherlands: Kluwer Law International, pp. 217.

Parker Joel, 1861, *Habeas Corpus and Martial Law: A Review*, Cambridge: Welch, Bigelow, and Company, pp. 58.

Petern Gustaf, Cull Helen, McBride Jeremy and Ravindran D., 1987, *Pakistan: Human Rights After Martial Law*, Geneva: International Commission of Jurists, pp. 159.

Pollock F., What is Martial Law, *Law Quarterly Review*, Vol. 18(2), 1902, pp. 152-158.

Poole Thomas, Reason of State: Whose Reason? Which Reason? LSE Law, Society and Economy Working Papers 1/2013, pp. 22.

Poole Thomas, The Law of Emergency and Reason of State, LSE Law, Society and Economy Working Papers 18/2016, pp. 24.

Pye A. Kenneth and Cym H Lowell, The Criminal Process During Civil Disorder (Part I), *Duke Law Journal*, Vol. 1975, No. 3, August, pp. 581-690.

Pye A. Kenneth and Cym H Lowell, The Criminal Process During Civil Disorder: Permissible Powers in Serious Civil Disorder (Part II), *Duke Law Journal*, Vol. 1975, No. 5, August, pp. 1021-1101.

Radin Max, Martial Law and the State of Siege, *Cal. L. Rev.*, Vol. 30, Issue 6, 1942, pp. 634-747.

Rajput Parvesh Kumar, Undeclared Martial Law in India: An Analysis of Article 34 vis-à-vis Armed Forces (Special Powers) Act, 1958, *IRJMSH*, Vol. 7, No. 10, 2016, pp. 33-42.

Ramnathan P., 2005, Riots and Martial Law in Ceylon, 1915, New Delhi: Asian Education Services, pp. 314.

Randall James G., The Indemnity Act of 1863: A Study in the War-Time Immunity of Governmental Officers, *Michigan Law Review*, Vol. 20, No. 6, 1922, pp. 589-613.

Rankin, R., Constitutional Basis of Martial Law, *Constitutional Review*, Vol. 13(2), 1929, pp. 75-84.

Rankin Rober S., 1935, *When Civil Law Fails: Martial Law and its Legal Basis in the United States*, Duke University Press, pp. 224.

Relyea Harold C., Martial Law and National Emergency, CSR Report for Congress, 7 January 2005.

Report of the Committee Appointed by the Government of India to Investigate the Disturbances in the Punjab, etc., London: His Majesty's Stationery Office, 1920, pp. 183.

Resource book on the use of force and firearms in law enforcement, UN High Commissioner for Human Rights, New York, 2017, pp. 198.

Reynolds John, The Long Shadow of Colonialism: The Origin of the Doctrine of Emergency in International Human Rights Law, *CLPE Research Paper*, 19/2010, Vol. 06, No. 5, pp. 51.

Reza sadiq, Endless Emergency: The Case of Egypt, *New Criminal Law Review*, Vol. 10, 2007, p. 532-553.

Richards H. Erle., Martial Law, *Law Quarterly Review*, Vol. 18(2), 1902, pp. 133-142.

Riley, Marguerite Maude, Army rule in Pakistan: a case study of a military regime, Unpublished Master's Thesis, 1978, pp. 166.

Roark James E., Constitutional Law--Martial Law--Preserving Order in the State: A Traditional Reappraisal, *West Virginia Law Review*, Vol. 75, Issue 2, 1972, pp. 143-165.

Roberts, Christopher N.J., From the State of Emergency to the Rule of Law: The Evolution of Repressive Legality in the Nineteenth Century British Empire, *Chicago Journal of International Law*, Vol. 20: No. 1, 2019, pp. 1-61.

Roht-Arriaza Naomi, State Responsibility to Investigate and Prosecute Grave Human Rights Violations in International Law, *California Law Review*, Vol. 78, 1990, pp. 449-513

Rule by Martial Law in Indiana: The Scope of Executive Power, *Indiana Law Journal*: Vol. 31: Issue 4, Article 2, 1956, pp. 456-473.

Sassoli Marco, State Responsibility for Violations of International Humanitarian Law, *International Review of the Red Cross*, Vol. 84, No. 846, 2002, pp. 401-433.

Scott P. Sheeran, Reconceptualizing States of Emergency under International Human Rights Law: Theory, Legal Doctrine, and Politics, *Mich. J. Int'l L.*, Vol. 34, No. 3, 2013, pp. 491-557.

Scharf Michael, The Letter of the Law: The Scope of the International Obligation to Prosecute Human Rights Crimes, *Law and Contemporary Problems*, Vol. 59, No. 4, Autumn 1996, pp. 41-61.

Scheppele Kim Lane, North American emergencies: The use of emergency powers in Canada and the United States, *Int'l J Con Law*, Vol. 4, No. 2, Apr 2006, pp. 213-243.

Scheppele Kim Lane, Law in Time of Emergency: State of Exception and the Temptations of 9/11, *Journal of Constitutional Law*, Vol. 6, No. 5, May 2004, pp. 1001-1083.

Scott P. Sheeran, Reconceptualizing States of Emergency under International Human Rights Law: Theory, Legal Doctrine, and Politics, *MICH. J. INT'L L.*, Vol. 34, 2013, pp. 491-557.

Sebastian V.D., Martial Law and Defence of Constitutional Order in India, *Kerala University Law Review*, Vol. 1(2), 1971, pp. 172-195.

Shah Sayed Wiqar Ali, The 1930 Civil Disobedience Movement in Peshawar Valley from the Pashtoon Perspective, *Studies in History*, Vol. 29(1), 2013, pp. 87–118.

Sherman Edward F., The Civilianization of Military Law, *Maine Law Review*, Vol. 22, 1970, pp. 1-103.

Sherman Edward F., Military Justice without Military Control, *The Yale Law Journal*, Vol. 82, 1973, pp. 1398-1425.

Shoul Simeon, Soldiers, Riot Control and Aid to the Civil Power in India, Egypt and Palestine, 1919-39, *Journal of the Society for Army Historical Research*, Vol. 86, 2008, pp. 120-139.

Siddique Osama, The Jurisprudence of Dissolutions: Presidential Power to Dissolve Assemblies under the Pakistani Constitution and Its Discontent, *Arizona Journal of International & Comparative Law*, Vol. 23, No. 3, 2006, pp. 615-716.

Tewari R B, Martial Law in England, Vol. II, *Journal of Indian Law Institute*, Vol. 2, No. 1, 1959, pp. 71-100.

Svensson-McCarthy Anna-Lena, 1998, *The International Law of Human Rights and States of Exception*, The Hague: Martinus Nijhoff Publishers, pp. 780.

Tovey Lieut. Colonel, 1886, *Martial Law and the Custom of War Or Military Force and jurisdiction in Troublous Times*, London: Chapman and Hall, pp. 386.

Tripathi, P.K., Martial Law in India, *AIR*, Jour Section, July 1963, pp. 66-67.

Tytler Alexander Fraser, 1806, *An essay on Military Law and the Practice of Court Martial*, London: T. Egreton, pp. 423.

Ullah Aman and Uzair Samee, Derogation of Human Rights under the Covenant and their Suspension during Emergency and Civil Martial Law, in India and Pakistan, *Research Journal of South Asian Studies,* Vol. 26, No. 1, January-June 2011, pp. 181-189.

Victor V. Ramraj, Michael Hor and Kent Roach, 2012, *Global Anti-Terrorism Law and Policy*, Second Edition, Cambridge University Press, pp. 691.

Vladeck Stephen I., The Laws of War as a Constitutional Limit on Military Jurisdiction, *Journal of National Security Law & Policy*, Vol. 4, 2010, pp. 295-342.

Vladeck Stephen I., Emergency Power and the Militia Acts, *Yale Law Journal*, Vol. 114, No. 3, 2004, pp. 149-194.

Vladeck Stephen I., The *Field* Theory: Martial Law, The Suspension Power, and the Insurrection Act, *Temple Law Review*, Vol. 80, No. 2, Summer 2007, pp. 391-439.

Wallace George S., Need the Propriety and Basis of Martial Law with a Review of the Authorities, *J. Am. Inst. Crim. L. & Criminology*, Vol. 8, Issue 2, 1917, p. 167-189.

War Powers and Military Jurisdiction, JAGS Text No. 4, The Judge Advocate General's School, Ann Arbor, Michigan, 1943, pp. 189.

Waseem Mohammad, 1987, *Pakistan under Martial Law: 1977-1985*, Lahore: Vanguard, pp. 246.

Weida Jason Collins, A Republic of Emergencies: Martial Law in American Jurisprudence, *Connecticut Law Review*, Vol. 36, 2004, pp. 1397-1438.

Whisker James B., The Citizen-Soldier under Federal and State Law, *West Virginia Law Review*, Vol. 94, 1992, pp. 947-988.

Winthrop William, 1920, *Military Law and Precedents*, Washington: Government Printing Office, pp. 1111.

Wolters Jacob F., 1929, *Martial Law and Its Administration*, Texas Ranger Hall of Fame E-Book, pp. 234.

Index

T

U

W

www.ingramcontent.com/pod-product-compliance
Lightning Source LLC
Chambersburg PA
CBHW031338230920
51848CB00002B/297
9789389620696